English Literature

Close Reading and Analytical Writing

Barbara Bloy, Ph.D.

Publisher: Tom Maksym

Executive Editor: Steven Jay Griffel

Editor: Carol Alexander, Ph.D.

Vice President, Production and Manufacturing: Doreen Smith

Art Director: Eric Dawson

Production Manager: Jason Grasso

Project Manager: Steven Genzano

Production Editor: Carol Deckert

Design: Carol Deckert, Steven Genzano

Cover Design: Shani Hawkins

Copy Editor: Dee Josephson

Proofreader: Pat Smith

Permissions Manager: Kristine Liebman

About the Author

Barbara Bloy, Ph.D.

Barbara Bloy has 30 years of teaching experience that includes high school AP English Literature and college teaching. A former reader of the AP English Literature exam for the College Board, Dr. Bloy leads summer workshops for AP English teachers at the Taft Educational Center, Watertown CT. She has also conducted workshops at the AP Annual Conference and NCTE meetings. Dr. Bloy is the co-author of the Peoples Education Shakespeare Skillbook series, which includes student guides for comprehension and analysis of the plays *Macbeth*, *King Lear*, *Hamlet*, and *Othello*. She has also published numerous articles about helping students develop their skills in close reading and analytic writing.

Copyright © 2006
Peoples Education, Inc.
299 Market Street
Saddle Brook, New Jersey 07663

ISBN 978-1-4138-1346-3
ISBN 1-4138-1346-1

Printed in the United States of America.

10 9 8 7

Table of Contents

FICTION

DRAMA

POETRY

Preface

This hands-on skillbook is designed to complement an Honors or Advanced Placement literature course that includes fiction, drama, and poetry spanning five centuries of literature in English. The Table of Contents mirrors the balance of genre found in the AP exam each year: there is more fiction than drama, the drama section includes two excerpts from Shakespeare's plays and other poetic drama, and the poetry section comprises nearly half of the total. The skillbook is designed to develop skills tested by the AP English Literature and Composition Exam, as well as by college courses in literature and composition. We have selected passages and poems that are not usually featured in anthologies, so there should be little overlap with literature texts. Every lesson is a fresh opportunity to practice reading and writing skills.

ABOUT THE A.P. EXAM

Whereas the English Language exam emphasizes prose and its rhetorical effect and intent, so that students must focus on a study of style (tone, diction, syntactical and rhetorical devices), the English Literature exam is inclusive and emphasizes the techniques of poetry, as well as those of fiction and drama. The focus is not only on the elements that comprise style, but also on literary dimensions such as figurative language, sound devices, prosody, form, and structure. As you work through this skillbook, you will master the techniques of reading and then writing an analytical essay about a literary text and will be able to apply these techniques to the selections presented in the exam.

Effective preparation for the exam, as well as for college courses in literature and composition, requires practice in close reading and explication. It involves asking the right questions of texts, and writing cogent, analytical essays about them. The first part of the exam asks multiple-choice questions about four or five texts, two of which will be poems. Close reading skills and a working knowledge of literary terminology are stringently tested. The second part of the AP exam calls for the writing of three essays within two hours. One responds to a prompt about a poem or a pair of poems, another about a prose selection, and the third, "open" question, asks for an essay that applies the prompt to a novel or full-length play of the student's choice.

(Visit the College Board's Web site, apcentral.collegeboard.com, for course descriptions, sample syllabi, and related information. Their store offers "released exams" with multiple-choice questions, essay prompts, sample student essays, as well as scoring guidelines and commentary for essays.)

SCOPE AND DISTRIBUTION OF LITERATURE

This skillbook teaches students to hone their skills on texts taken from the genres and periods covered by the AP exam. The exam's poetry prompt often calls for a comparison of two poems with a similar subject or theme; a recent poem may be paired with an older one. Accordingly, several lessons in the skillbook provide practice with paired texts. Selections are gender balanced and represent a multicultural perspective. The scope of this skillbook reflects the welcome new diversity of authorial voices without slighting the acknowledged giants of our literary heritage.

PRACTICE FOR MULTIPLE CHOICE

The best preparation for the multiple-choice section of the exam is to learn how to ask the right questions about a text. Once you have at your command the full array of useful questions, you will be better able to anticipate what the testers might ask. Also, you will more confidently identify the correct answers among multiple choices. Through intensive practice in using literary terminology, you will learn how to eliminate wrong answers and avoid distractors, those tempting but incorrect answers. The experience of classroom teachers over the years indicates that practicing sets of multiple-choice questions, even if they are taken from exams released by the College Board, does little to improve a student's performance on the actual exam. The difficulty of the questions may in fact have the negative effect of discouraging students who have not had extensive experience in working with literary terminology.

Among the most essential skills is the ability to read a text with attention to linguistic nuance, with sensitivity to figurative language and syntactical and rhetorical devices. The richest literature tends to favor the figurative over the literal, indirect over direct expression of meaning, deep over surface meaning, and form over content. Fine fiction typically favors symbolism and psychology over plot; poetry tends to favor the lyrical over the narrative.

USING THIS SKILLBOOK

Unlike the standard commercial test-prep book, this skillbook is designed as an instructional supplement to the AP curriculum. As a tool for exploring literature, the book will help you to develop the critical thinking and writing skills needed to achieve success in your coursework and on the AP Literature and Composition exam.

LESSON FORMAT

Background and Purpose begins each lesson. This feature provides a historical and cultural context to the passage, so that the author of the story, drama, or poem is not forgotten. It highlights literary elements and stylistic qualities of the passage and explains its context within the larger work. Read this section carefully before you begin reading the passage and answering the questions.

The lessons are divided into three units, by genre. The most familiar genre, fiction, appears first. The drama and poetry sections build on and add to the terminology and skills. Within each unit the passages vary in length as well as in complexity, and are increasingly challenging. Each lesson is self-contained. The literature chosen is rich in artistry and meaning and is of recognized literary importance. Nearly every selection of fiction or drama is a passage from a longer work. All but two of the poetry passages are complete poems. As noted above, many of the poetry lessons present poems in pairs, as does the AP exam, and call for comparison and contrast.

The AP exam uses multiple choice as the only practical way to assess your skill in close reading. This skillbook allows for practice without regard to timing. Each lesson offers the full experience of reading, responding, explicating, and analyzing. During a first reading of the passage or poem, you should be actively responding by noting issues, making inferences, and forming judgments. Becoming aware of how you feel about a passage or poem makes you a more sensitive reader as you move on to discover, through close reading and analysis, how your feelings were formed: why you respond to the situation as you do, why you dislike or are sympathetic to a fictional character, how you feel about the outcome of the dramatic action in a play, or the precise mood the language of a poem conveys. Close reading goes far beyond interpretation of the content to questions of how various literary elements and devices form that content and influence the reader's response.

Using Skills to Understand the Passage is a series of questions that accompanies each reading selection. These questions are at the heart of a close reading. The answers take shape as you review relevant literary terms and carefully reread the passage. You will practice answering questions about many aspects of literature, such as the style of a work, its narrative voice, the author's manipulation of language, and the conventions of genre. The multiple-choice sections of many standardized tests, including the Advanced Placement English Literature exam, test your skill in responding to thoughtful questions about a passage. As you work with the skill questions in this book, you will sharpen your knowledge of the vocabulary of literary study and your ability to find the answers within a selected text. Practice the useful art of succinctness in your answers—don't bother to repeat the question, and avoid a series of simple sentences. Always cite specific evidence from the passage, but only in the service of analysis.

An **Essay Question** concludes each lesson. Your response to the Essay Question provides practice in analyzing and synthesizing the results of your close reading. The primary advantage to answering the skills questions first, fully and in writing, is that you will be well prepared to answer the essay question. You can and should borrow liberally from your answers as you frame your fully-developed analysis. Although the essay questions on the AP exam will require you to frame relevant questions and answers on your own, they often provide a hint of what sort of evidence to include.

Passages/Poems for Independent Analysis follows the last lesson in each of the three units. Here, as in the lessons, there is a "Background and Purpose" section to orient you, a literature passage, and an essay question. Your job is to ask and answer relevant questions before you plan and write the essay. You are on your own! Practice assessing the passage or poem quickly and accurately. Your essay need not be fully comprehensive nor must it provide a full exegesis, but it should focus on the essay question. After you have tried your hand at several untimed essays, practice writing them in the same time allotted by the AP exam (typically 40 minutes for reading the passage and writing the essay). This practice in fluency will also be a great help to you when you are actually taking the test.

ANALYSES AND GUIDELINES

Appearing at the end of each unit, this section provides you with fully-reasoned responses to each lesson's skill questions and with guidelines for crafting your essay.

Analyses of Skill Questions provides full responses to each question asked in a lesson. Note that these responses do not repeat the question, and that they always cite specific examples from the passage as the basis of analysis. It is fruitless (and boring) to read these answers before you have worked through the questions on your own. These sample answers are useful only as a measure of how your skills are improving. Carefully note anything in the model responses that did not appear in your own—such elements may reappear in other lessons and on the exam. Your goal, after all, is to develop the skills necessary for answering questions about a variety of literary texts, not just about the selections in this book.

Guidelines for Responding to the Essay Question supply suggestions to help you generate a clear thesis that responds directly and appropriately to the essay question. This section suggests ways to organize your argument by using strong and pertinent evidence in support of the thesis. It points to a conclusion that will pull together the argument and make a broader statement about the thesis. Use these guidelines only as needed. As your skill increases, state your own thesis, organize your argument, posit a conclusion, and only then compare your work with the guidelines. Your goal is to wean yourself from them as you work through the skillbook.

Certain conventions should be followed in all of your writing about literature. The literary present tense is to be used for all but antecedent action. When you are analyzing a passage it is always better (and far more specific) to cite exact words from the passage, tailoring such quotations with care and incorporating them into your own sentences smoothly. This type of direct quotation always appears within quotation marks ["…"] unless the quoted material is lengthy; in that rare case, it may be single-spaced and indented.

When you paraphrase or summarize a passage, you should do so only in the service of analysis, not as a substitute for it. You will choose your own language, staying true to the content of the work. A paraphrase should provide a sentence for each sentence in the original (ignoring lines in poetry). It should change figurative to literal language, and preserve the point of view of the speaker rather than changing to third person.

Keep in mind that all literary critics aim to write clearly and with appropriate diction. This diction will be fairly formal yet not pretentious. It is often better to choose concrete language over abstract or florid diction. If you need to use an abstraction, try to support it with a solid example. It is *always* appropriate to use specialized literary terms.

SPECIAL FEATURES

This skillbook contains several other important features to help you discover the terminology for many literary elements and techniques and the relationships among them. It also supplies lists for further reading and study.

- **Literary Terms Arranged by Category** — This chart supplies an outline of all the terms in the Glossary, grouping them within larger units, such as "Rhetorical Devices" or "Prosody." The chart serves as a study aid, illustrating the relationships and hierarchies among the groups of terms.

- **Literary Terms for Study and Review** — This chart tracks, by lesson, the use of each literary term that appears in the Glossary. The user can thus group all the satirical works for study, or all the works that use dramatic irony, or all examples of indirect characterization across genres.

- **Norton Editions** — This chart lists the passages or poems in this skillbook that can be found in their entirety in W.W. Norton Critical Editions or Norton Anthologies.

- **Further Reading** — This list includes the fiction and drama authors and titles that regularly appear on AP exams as possible choices for the "open" question, the last of the three essays, as well as those that have been or may be excerpted for the essay on prose. Also listed are poets whose work has appeared on the exam or is of the quality that may be used for the essay on poetry.

- **Glossary** — This alphabetical listing provides clear definitions of each literary term to be found in the skillbook, comprising a sophisticated vocabulary that goes well beyond the basic requirements of most college literature courses. Consult the Glossary when you encounter unfamiliar literary terms. Your goal is to become a more self-reliant, flexible, and productive reader and writer.

ON THE ROAD TO SUCCESS

The skills you acquire as you work through this book will serve you well in an Honors or AP Literature course and on the AP Literature and Composition exam. The lessons provided offer intensive practice in close reading and analytical writing that builds skills applicable to any academic discipline. Your increased independence and self-confidence as a thinker will be invaluable in college and far beyond. You will have the tools you need to be a lifelong reader of fine literature, and a writer of practical and perhaps even imaginative works of your own.

Literary Terms Arranged by Category

The following arrangement of literary terms by category can be used as an effective study aid for preparing for the English Literature and Composition Exam. It clarifies the relationships among the groups of terms and the hierarchies of terms within each group. For example, if an essay question directed you to discuss the *diction* of a passage from a novel, you would want to know what *diction* means and all the important literary terms related to *diction*. The Glossary at the back of this skillbook would remind you of the term's meaning, and a perusal of this chart would show you that *ambiguity, connotation*, etc., all defined in the Glossary, are important terms related to *diction*.

CHARACTER
Antagonist
Caricature
Characterization
 – Direct
 – Indirect
Dynamic/Round character
Foil
Motivation
Narrator/Persona/Speaker
Protagonist
Static/Flat character
Stereotype
Stock character

CONTEXT
Atmosphere
Frame
Mood
Occasion
Setting
Speaker/Persona
Stream of consciousness

DICTION
Abstract language
Ambiguity
Cliché
Concrete language
Connotation
Denotation
DialectEpithet
Euphemism

Literal language
Usage

DRAMA
Aside
Dialogue
Soliloquy
Stage directions
Subtext

FIGURATIVE LANGUAGE
Apostrophe
Conceit
Metaphor
 – Grounds
 – Tenor
 – Vehicle
Metonymy
Personification
Simile
Symbol
Synecdoche
Synesthesia

FIXED FORMS OF POETRY
Ballad
Cinquain
Epic
Sestina
Sonnet
 – Elizabethan (Shakespearean)
   • Couplet
   • Quatrain

- Italian (Petrarchan)
  - Octave
  - Sestet
  - Turn
Villanelle

IMAGERY
Auditory
Gustatory
Olfactory
Tactile
Visual

LITERARY CRITICISM, TERMS
Analysis
Explication
Inference
Literary present tense
Paraphrase
Summary
Thesis

LITERARY DEVICES
Archetype
Epiphany
Motif
Poetic justice
Theme
Title

LITERARY MODES
Carpe diem
Comedy/Comedy of manners
Complaint
Dramatic monologue
Elegy, elegiac verse
Epic/Mock epic/Mock heroic
Lyric verse
Ode
Parody
Romance
Satire
- Horatian satire
- Juvenalian satire
Tragedy

METER/PROSODY/ VERSIFICATION
Duple meters
- Iambic (rising)
- Trochaic (falling)
Falling meter
Foot, feet

Line length (note prefixes)
- Monometer (one foot)
- Dimeter (two feet)
- Trimeter (three feet), etc.
- Tetrameter
- Pentameter
- Hexameter
- Septameter
- Octameter
Metrical substitutions
- Pyrrhic
- Rest
- Spondee
- Trochee
Rising meter
Scansion/Scanning
Stress/Accent
Triple meters
- Anapestic (rising)
- Dactylic (falling)

PLOT
Antecedent action
Climax
Conflict
Denouement
Exposition
Falling action
Flashback
Foreshadowing
Frame/frame story
Resolution
Rising action
Subplot

POETIC FORMS
Blank verse
Common meter/Hymn meter/ Ballad stanza
Continuous form
Couplet
- Closed couplet
- Heroic couplet
- Open couplet
Epigram
Free verse
Nonce form
Verse paragraph

POETIC LINE
Caesura
End-stopped line
Enjambed line/Enjambment

POINT OF VIEW
Interior monologue
Narrator
- First person
- Limited omniscient
- Naïve
- Objective
- Omniscient
- Second person
- Unreliable

Stream of consciousness

RHETORICAL DEVICES
Allusion
Analogy
Anaphora
Anticlimax
Antithesis
Caesura/Rhetorical pause
Catalog
Incongruity
Incremental repetition
Oxymoron
Paradox
Parallelism
Pun
Repetition
Rhetorical accent/Stress
Rhetorical question
Structure
Turn

RHYME
Couplet
Double rhyme
End rhyme
Full/Perfect/True rhyme
Internal rhyme
Rhyme scheme
Slant/Near/Partial/Imperfect/Half rhyme
Triple rhyme

SOUND DEVICES
Alliteration
Assonance
Cacophony
Consonance
Euphony

Onomatopoeia
Sibilance

STANZA FORMS
Ballad stanza/Hymn stanza
Cinquain (five lines)
Couplet (two lines)
Envoy
Nonce form
Ottava rima (eight lines)
Quatrain (four lines)
Refrain
Rime royal (seven lines)
Septet (seven lines)
Sestet (six lines)
Spenserian stanza (nine lines)
Tercet (three lines)

SYNTAX
Emphasis
Inversion of word order (grammatical inversion)
Juxtaposition
Level of discourse (Usage)
Order
- Emphatic position
- Subordinate position

Sentence length, complexity, variety, pattern
Sentence type
- Loose sentence
- Periodic sentence

Usage/Level of discourse
Voice
- Active
- Passive

TONE
Authorial voice
Humor
Hyperbole (overstatement)
Irony
- Dramatic irony
- Irony of Situation
- Verbal irony

Sarcasm
Sentimentalism
Understatement
Wit

Literary Terms for Study and Review

Before you begin working through the lessons in this skillbook, it may be helpful to scan the left column of the chart below. These terms are all defined in the Glossary at the end of the book. The other three columns in the chart set out, by genre, the numbers of the lessons in which the term appears. These numbers also refer to the "Analyses and Guidelines" section at the end of each genre unit. Lessons 1–13 cover fiction; lessons 14–22 cover drama; lessons 23–42 cover poetry. This scheme makes it easy to cross-reference literary terms and to note which appear across genres. An asterisk (*) after a term indicates that the term is not mentioned in a lesson or in the "Analyses and Guidelines" sections but is included in a genre introduction and may be part of the "Background and Purpose" of the passages for independent analysis that end each genre unit.

Literary Term	Fiction	Drama	Poetry
Alliteration		16	23–25, 29, 33, 40, 42
Allusion		22	31, 42
Ambiguity*			
Analogy		21	
Analysis	1–4, 6–8, 11, 13	14, 17, 19-22	23–25, 28, 29, 31, 33, 37–40, 42
Anaphora			26, 42
Antagonist	2, 4, 6		25
Antecedent action			40
Anticlimax	13		
Antithesis	16		
Apostrophe			26, 30, 37, 42
Archetype*			
Aside		20, 22	
Assonance			24, 25, 29, 33
Atmosphere	12	14	27
Authorial voice*			
Ballad*			
Blank verse*			
Cacophony			25, 29
Caesura			25, 42

Literary Term	Fiction	Drama	Poetry
Caricature		18	
Carpe Diem poetry			36
Catalog			27, 40, 42
Character	4–7, 11–13	15, 16, 18, 21, 22	25, 29, 37, 40
Characterization	1, 2, 4, 5, 7–13	14, 15, 17, 19, 22	25, 27, 29, 37, 39
Cliché	9	14, 20	23, 28
Climax	13	20	35
Comedy			25
Common meter	7, 9, 11	18, 20, 22	37
Complaint			27, 34
Conceit			30
Conflict	2, 4, 6, 10, 12, 13	14, 15, 21	25, 31
Connotation	3, 5, 9	18	23, 24, 31–33, 35, 39, 42
Consonance			24, 25, 29, 33
Continuous form			26, 37
Couplet			29, 30, 33, 38, 40–42
Denotation	3	18	
Denouement		21	35
Dialect	13		34
Dialogue	13	14, 17, 18, 20	
Diction	2, 4–7, 9–11, 13	16, 18, 20, 22	23–25, 27–29, 33, 34, 37, 39, 40, 42
Direct characterization	4, 13		25
Double rhyme		20	40, 41
Dramatic irony	3, 7, 9, 13	21	
Dramatic monologue	11		
Elegy			39
Emphasis			25, 28, 29, 32, 36, 39, 41
End-stopped line*			
Enjambment			25, 26, 29, 39, 41
Envoy (envoi)			31, 34, 36
Epic			25, 31, 40, 42
Epigram		16	
Epiphany	12		
Epithet		22	34
Euphemism	2, 3		
Euphony			25, 29
Explication	1	17, 20, 21	35

Literary Term	Fiction	Drama	Poetry
Exposition		15	
Figurative language	3, 9, 10		23–30, 33, 36–39, 42
Flashback	6		
Foil	2	17	
Foreshadowing	2	14, 19	23, 32
Form			26, 28, 30–32, 36, 39, 42
Frame story	13		
Free verse*			
Grounds*			
Heroic couplets		20	30, 40
Horatian satire		16	40
Humor	7, 9	15, 20	25, 34, 39, 40
Hyperbole	6, 7, 11	18	25, 34, 35, 40
Iamb (iambic)		20	25, 26, 28, 33, 42
Imagery	6, 8, 9, 11, 13	19	24, 27, 28, 30–32, 34, 35, 38, 39, 40, 42
Incongruity	7, 8, 11	15, 16, 20	40
Indirect characterization	2, 5, 7, 13		25
Inference	1, 2, 10–12	16, 18, 19	
Interior monologue	10	17	
Irony	1, 3, 5, 7, 8, 11, 13	15–18, 21	23, 25, 28, 29, 32, 35, 40, 42
Irony of situation	1, 5		
Italian sonnet			33, 38
Juvenalian satire		16	40
Juxtaposition			29, 40, 42
Line length		20	26, 29, 33, 34, 36–39
Literal language	3	20	23, 24, 27, 30, 35, 37, 39, 42
Literary present tense*			
Lyric verse			33, 34, 38
Metaphor	3–5	19, 22	24–26, 28, 31, 33–38, 41
Meter		20	25, 26, 29, 30, 33, 34, 36, 38, 42
Metonomy*			
Metrical substitutions			25, 26, 36
Mock heroic (mock epic)			25, 40
Mood	12	14	24, 27, 29, 31–33, 39
Motif			33
Motivation	2, 4, 5, 10, 11, 13	14, 19–22	25, 26
Narrator	1–5, 7–11, 13	14	

Literary Term	Fiction	Drama	Poetry
Nonce form			33
Occasion			25, 28, 36
Ode			37
Onomatopoeia			24, 29, 42
Oxymoron			27
Paradox		17	23, 28, 30, 38, 41
Parallelism		16	26–29, 36, 38, 42
Paraphrase	4, 11	18, 21	30, 33, 36–38, 41
Parody			34, 39, 42
Perfect rhyme		20	25, 33
Persona*			
Personification		19	30, 31, 36, 37, 42
Plot	2, 4, 13	15, 22	25, 35, 37, 40
Poetic justice	4	21, 22	
Point of view	1, 10, 11, 13		24
Prosody		20	26, 28, 31, 34, 36–38, 40-42
Protagonist	1–4, 6, 7, 13		25
Pun	11	16, 22	23, 40
Quatrain			30, 32, 38, 41
Refrain			32, 34
Repetition		17	26–29, 31–36, 38, 39, 42
Resolution	2, 13	14	33
Rest*			
Rhetorical accent/stress*			
Rhetorical devices		16	27, 37, 38, 40, 42
Rhetorical question	4	14	
Rhyme		20	24, 25, 28–30, 32, 33, 36, 37
Rhyme scheme			25, 29–34, 36, 38
Rime royal			34
Rising action	4		
Romance	9	20	
Sarcasm	3	17, 20	
Satire	7, 9, 11	15, 16, 18, 20	40
Scansion*			
Sentimentality	1, 5, 9, 11	15	37, 39
Sestina			31
Setting	1, 6, 8, 10–13	14	24, 25, 27, 29, 35, 37, 40

Literary Term	Fiction	Drama	Poetry
Sibilance			29
Simile	9	16	25
Slant rhyme		20	25, 40, 42
Soliloquy		21	
Sonnet			30, 33, 38, 41
Speaker			23, 25, 27, 31, 36, 38, 41
Spondee			25, 36
Stage directions		14, 15, 19, 22	
Stanza forms			25, 26, 28, 29, 31, 32, 34, 36, 37, 39, 42
Stereotype	6, 11		31
Stream of consciousness	10		
Structure	13		24, 26–28, 30, 31, 33, 34, 36–42
Subtext		17, 22	
Symbol	8, 12, 13	17, 21	33
Synecdoche*			
Synesthesia			24, 35
Syntax	4, 7, 11, 13	18, 22	26, 28, 30, 41
Tenor*			
Tercet			32
Theme	1, 6, 13	17	29, 31–33, 35–37, 39, 41, 42
Thesis	1, 4, 6, 9, 11–13	15–22	23, 24, 26, 28, 30–42
Title			23, 28, 31, 39
Tone	1, 4, 6, 9, 11–13	15, 18, 20, 22	23, 25, 29, 30, 32–34, 37–41
Tragedy		19–21	
Trochee			25, 26, 36, 41
Turn			30, 33, 36, 38, 39, 42
Understatement	8, 10, 12		35, 39, 40
Unreliable narrator	9, 10		
Usage*			
Vehicle	9		25
Verbal irony	3	16, 18, 20	
Verse paragraph			40
Versification*			
Villanelle			32
Wit	7	15, 16, 18, 20, 22	25, 30

Fiction

This skillbook begins with fiction because most students are familiar with novels and short stories. Even very young children are exposed to fiction in the form of fairy tales and picture books. A review of common literary terms will remind you of what you already know about stories, and what you must consciously ask of each new one you encounter. Many terms used in the lessons are defined in the glossary at the end of this book. For additional information, you can turn to a dictionary or a book of literary terms.

Setting and Mood — The best way to get oriented to a work of fiction is to discover the setting and the situation in which events unfold. Every story has a setting, the time and place of the action. The time may be approximate–a season or a century–or specific–a date, the hour of the day. The place may be a continent, a city, or a room. The setting of the work often evokes a special mood or atmosphere. Mood produces an emotional response in the reader and colors how we view the situation and the characters.

Characterization — We call the main character the protagonist, and there may be an oppositional figure, the antagonist. Character traits are revealed in various ways. Direct characterization may be offered through a narrator's description of himself or another character. Indirect characterization is revealed by what the character says and how she says it; what the character does, in initiating or responding to action; and what others reveal about the character through verbal and non-verbal responses. The reader should look for evidence of motivation to explain why the characters behave as they do.

Narrative Voice and Point of View — We must be aware of who is telling the story, and whether the same person narrates the entire story. The author's choice of point of view is a device for conveying the meaning and theme of the fictional work. The author is never the storyteller; at the very least, a thin veil separates the creator from the work. A first-person narrative may be told by the protagonist or by a minor character, a bystander. A third-person narrator, who is outside the story, may be unreliable, not perceiving or interpreting as the reader is expected to, and thus creating dramatic irony. A third-person narrator may be limited—unable to read the minds of the characters or able to get inside the heads of only certain characters. An omniscient narrator is not only outside the story, but is all-knowing and holds the threads of the plot and characters together. A third-person narrator who does not speculate about character motivation or action is called objective. Such a narrator is "a fly on the wall," merely listening, observing, and reporting. A technique called "stream of consciousness" gives us the flood of unordered thoughts in a person's mind.

Plot — Elements of the plot include rising action, which introduces the conflict and may foreshadow its resolution. Conflicts can take the form of simple external struggles, such as a human being pitted against another person, an institution, or a force of nature, or may involve complex internal choices, in which a character must make a critical decision. The climax, or the turning point of the action, produces the resolution, in which the issue is decided. Many stories include falling action, whatever remains to be told after the resolution.

Diction and Tone — The tone of a story is determined partly by a careful use of diction, or word choice. The narrator's tone (attitude) toward characters and events is also revealed through diction. We characterize people by their level of diction: colloquial (informal, conversational), formal, abstract, slangy, etc. So do writers of fiction.

Tone may also be produced by irony. Irony can be detected if the speaker means the opposite of what he says (verbal irony). In situational irony, the circumstances are the opposite of what we would expect. In dramatic irony, the reader knows more than the narrator or the character does. We should be able to recognize sarcasm when we come across it, and to be careful not to confuse it with verbal irony: sarcasm is nasty, intended to ridicule or hurt. Verbal irony is witty and restrained, intended to express the opposite of what is meant.

Other figures of speech that contribute to tone are hyperbole (exaggeration or overstatement of what one means) and understatement (making far less of something than one actually means to.)

Imagery and Figurative Language — Fiction writers frequently employ imagery, literal description that conjures up sights, sounds, tastes, smells, and tactile sensations. They may use figurative language, such as various kinds of metaphor and symbolism, to suggest comparisons or deeper meanings. Such literary devices will be more fully explored in the Poetry section of this book.

If this sounds like far too much to keep in mind, remember that as an experienced reader, you are accustomed to figuring out many conventions of narrative and plot. You will find that using literary terms is a help rather than a hindrance in getting inside a story, and there is plenty of practice ahead.

1
lesson

from The Things They Carried
Tim O'Brien

Background and Purpose

The Things They Carried, Tim O'Brien's 1990 collection of linked stories about an infantry company in Vietnam, is an enormously popular and critically acclaimed contribution to the literature of modern war. In this story, "The Dentist," the emphasis is on characterization, which is achieved largely through the narrator's perspective of the protagonist. The immediate setting, and the inferences we are meant to make about the larger setting, are also important. O'Brien's selection of detail is key to the theme.

When Curt Lemon was killed, I found it hard to mourn. I knew him only slightly, and what I did know was not impressive. He had a tendency to play the tough soldier role, always posturing, always puffing *Line* himself up, and on occasion he took it way too far. It's true that he 5 pulled off some dangerous stunts, even a few that seemed plain crazy, like the time he painted up his body and put on a ghost mask and went out trick-or-treating on Halloween. But afterward he couldn't stop bragging. He kept replaying his own exploits, tacking on little flourishes that never happened. He had an opinion of himself, I think, that 10 was too high for his own good. Or maybe it was the reverse. Maybe it was a low opinion that he kept trying to erase.

In any case, it's easy to get sentimental about the dead, and to guard against that I want to tell a quick Curt Lemon story.

In February we were working an area of operations called the Rocket 15 Pocket, which got its name from the fact that the enemy sometimes used the place to launch rocket attacks on the airfield at Chu Lai. But for us it was like a two-week vacation. The AO lay along the South China Sea, where things had the feel of a resort, with white beaches and palm trees and friendly little villages. It was a quiet time. No casu-20 alties, no contact at all. As usual, though, the higher-ups couldn't leave well enough alone, and one afternoon an Army dentist was choppered in to check our teeth and do minor repair work. He was a tall, skinny young captain with bad breath. For a half hour he lectured us on oral hygiene, demonstrating the proper flossing and brushing techniques, 25 then afterward he opened up shop in a small field tent and we all took turns going in for personal exams. At best it was a very primitive setup. There was a battery-powered drill, a canvas cot, a bucket of sea water for rinsing, a metal suitcase full of the various instruments. It amounted to assembly-line dentistry, quick and impersonal, and the young cap-30 tain's main concern seemed to be the clock.

As we sat waiting, Curt Lemon began to tense up. He kept fidgeting, playing with his dog tags. Finally somebody asked what the problem

Using Skills to Understand the Passage

1. The immediate setting, the Rocket Pocket, is described in such a way that we are invited to make inferences about the ordinary lives of these soldiers in the larger setting, the theater of war. What are conditions like in more typical areas of military operation? Which details of the setting help you to picture these conditions?

2. What is ironic about what happens to Curt Lemon at the Rocket Pocket? What kind of irony is this?

3. How does the narrator feel about Curt Lemon, the protagonist? What evidence does he provide as the basis of his attitude? Explain why the narrator chooses to tell this particular story about Curt and the dentist, keeping in mind the definition of sentimentalism. Then describe the overall tone of the story, and refer to specific details that contribute to this tone.

was, and Lemon looked down at his hands and said that back in high school he'd had a couple of bad experiences with dentists. Real sadism, he said. Torture chamber stuff. He didn't mind blood or pain—he actually enjoyed combat—but there was something about a dentist that just gave him the creeps. He glanced over at the field tent and said, "No way. Count me out. Nobody messes with *these* teeth."

But a few minutes later, when the dentist called his name, Lemon stood up and walked into the tent.

It was over fast. He fainted even before the man touched him.

Four of us had to hoist him up and lay him on the cot. When he came to, there was a funny new look on his face, almost sheepish, as if he'd been caught committing some terrible crime. He wouldn't talk to anyone. For the rest of the day he stayed off by himself, sitting alone under a tree, just staring down at the field tent. He seemed a little dazed. Now and then we could hear him cussing, bawling himself out. Anyone else would've laughed it off, but for Curt Lemon it was too much. The embarrassment must've turned a screw in his head. Late that night he crept down to the dental tent. He switched on a flashlight, woke up the young captain, and told him he had a monster toothache. A killer, he said—like a nail in his jaw. The dentist couldn't find any problem, but Lemon kept insisting, so the man finally shrugged and shot in the Novocain and yanked out a perfectly good tooth. There was some pain, no doubt, but in the morning Curt Lemon was all smiles.

Using Skills to Understand the Passage

4. What is the purpose of the details about the dentist and his field tent? What is ironic about Curt Lemon's response to him?

5. What is the theme of this story, and how did you arrive at an understanding of it?

Essay Question

Write an explication of the story's last paragraph, taking into account both objective information about Lemon and the narrator's interpretations.

2 from Sula
Toni Morrison
lesson

Background and Purpose

Toni Morrison's fiction has won her the Nobel Prize in Literature and her work often adorns the best-seller lists. This passage from *Sula*, published in 1973, is an example of Morrison's skill with indirect characterization. We must make inferences about Helene, based largely on diction, but also on more subtle means, such as the viewpoints of the narrator, the other woman on the train, and the men at the station. How the experience changes Helene is also indirectly revealed.

In the passage, Helene and her young daughter are traveling by train from Ohio to New Orleans to visit her dying grandmother. The setting is the early 1940s, a generation before the Civil Rights Act enforced integration in the American South.

For two days they rode; two days of watching sleet turn to rain, turn to purple sunsets, and one night knotted on the wooden seats (their heads on folded coats), trying not to hear the snoring soldiers. When they changed trains in Birmingham for the last leg of the trip, they discovered what luxury they had been in through Kentucky and Tennessee, where the rest stops had all had colored toilets. After Birmingham there were none. Helene's face was drawn with the need to relieve herself, and so intense was her distress she finally brought herself to speak about her problem to a black woman with four children who had got on in Tuscaloosa.

"Is there somewhere we can go to use the restroom?"

The woman looked up at her and seemed not to understand. "Ma'am?" Her eyes fastened on the thick velvet collar, the fair skin, the high-tone voice.

"The restroom," Helene repeated. Then, in a whisper, "The toilet."

The woman pointed out the window and said, "Yes, ma'am. Yonder."

Helene looked out of the window halfway expecting to see a comfort station in the distance; instead she saw gray-green trees leaning over tangled grass. "Where?"

"Yonder," the woman said. "Meridian. We be pullin' in direc'lin." Then she smiled sympathetically and asked, "Kin you make it?"

Helene nodded and went back to her seat trying to think of other things—for the surest way to have an accident would be to remember her full bladder.

At Meridian the women got out with their children. While Helene looked about the tiny stationhouse for a door that said COLORED WOMEN, the other woman stalked off to a field of high grass on the far side of the track. Some white men were leaning on a railing in front of the stationhouse. It was not only their tongues curling around tooth-

Line
5

10

15

20

25

Using Skills to Understand the Passage

1. What do we discover about Helene from her surprise about the realities of the segregated South, from her behavior on the train, from her confusion at the station, and from her diction?

2. What does the woman with four children add to the characterization of Helene? Consider what she sees when she looks at Helene, what she says, and what she does.

3. The woman can be considered a foil to Helene. What details create this role?

4. What does the narrator add to the characterization of Helene? Consider the selection of details as well as the diction of the narrative voice.

30 picks that kept Helene from asking information of them. She looked around for the other woman and, seeing the top of her head rag in the grass, slowly realized where "yonder" was. All of them, the fat woman and her four children, three boys and a girl, Helene and her daughter, squatted there in the four o'clock Meridian sun. They did it again in

35 Ellisville, again in Hattiesburg, and by the time they reached Slidell, not too far from Lake Pontchartrain, Helene could not only fold leaves as well as the fat woman, she never felt a stir as she passed the muddy eyes of the men who stood like wrecked Dorics under the station roofs of those towns.

Essay Question

Analyze devices of plot and characterization within this short scene: identify the protagonist, antagonist, and foil, and consider the motivations of the characters. Then explain the conflict(s) and resolution.

3 lesson

from The Curious Incident of the Dog in the Night-Time
Mark Haddon

Background and Purpose

The Curious Incident of the Dog in the Night-Time (2003) is the first novel of British writer Mark Haddon. His first-person narrator is an autistic teenager, a savant in math and physics, but an innocent in every other respect. At fifteen, the protagonist must learn by rote how to understand and navigate the frightening world of emotions, including his own. Some critics have hailed Christopher as a new kind of postmodern hero, but his voice is as distinctive as that of Huck Finn, Holden Caulfield, or David Copperfield. In the passages below ("chapters" are numbered using only prime numbers), we encounter Siobhan, Christopher's main teacher and counselor at his school for children with "Special Needs."

Chapter 29.

I find people confusing.

This is for two main reasons.

The first main reason is that people do a lot of talking without using
Line any words. Siobhan says that if you raise one eyebrow it can mean lots
5 of different things. It can mean "I want to do sex with you" or it can
also mean "I think that what you just said is very stupid."

Siobhan also says that if you close your mouth and breathe out loudly through your nose, it can mean that you are relaxed, or that you are
bored, or that you are angry, and it all depends on how much air comes
10 out of your nose and how fast and what shape your mouth is when you
do it and how you are sitting and what you said just before and hun-
dreds of other things which are too complicated to work out in a few
seconds.

The second main reason is that people often talk using metaphors.
15 These are examples of metaphors

I laughed my socks off.
He was the apple of her eye.
They had a skeleton in the cupboard.
We had a real pig of a day.
20 **The dog was stone dead.**

The word *metaphor* means carrying something from one place to
another, and it comes from the Greek words μετα (which means *from
one place to another*) and φερειν (which means *to carry*), and it is when
you describe something by using a word for something that it isn't.
25 This means that the word *metaphor* is a metaphor.

I think it should be called a lie because a pig is not like a day and
people do not have skeletons in their cupboards. And when I try and

Using Skills to Understand the Passage

1. What is the basis of Christopher's confusion about people? What skills does he lack that most children learn effortlessly in their earliest years? What do we discover in the first thirteen lines about the limitation of verbal communication?

2. What do we learn throughout the passage from Chapter 29 about the limitation of literal thinking? What kind of meaning do metaphors "carry"? What is the value of connotations? Why does Christopher want his name to signify only himself?

make a picture of the phrase in my head it just confuses me because imagining an apple in someone's eye doesn't have anything to do with

30   liking someone a lot and it makes you forget what the person was talking about.

My name is a metaphor. It means *carrying Christ* and it comes from the Greek words χριστος (which means *Jesus Christ*) and φερειν and it was the name given to St. Christopher because he carried Jesus Christ

35   across a river.

This makes you wonder what he was called before he carried Christ across the river. But he wasn't called anything because this is an apocryphal story, which means that it is a lie, too.

My mother used to say that it meant Christopher was a nice name

40   because it was a story about being kind and helpful, but I do not want my name to mean a story about being kind and helpful. I want my name to mean me.

Chapter 71.

All the other children at my school are stupid. Except I'm not meant to call them stupid, even though this is what they are. I'm meant to say

45   that they have learning difficulties or that they have special needs. But this is stupid because everyone has learning difficulties because learning to speak French or understanding relativity is difficult and also everyone has special needs, like Father, who has to carry a little packet of artificial sweetening around with him to put in his coffee to

50   stop him from getting fat, or Mrs. Peters, who wears a beige-colored hearing aid, or Siobhan, who has glasses so thick that they give you a headache if you borrow them, and none of these people are Special Needs, even if they have special needs.

But Siobhan said we have to use those words because people used

55   to call children at school *spaz* and *crip* and *mong*, which were nasty words. But that is stupid too because sometimes the children from the school down the road see us in the street when we're getting off the bus and they shout, "Special Needs! Special Needs!" But I don't take any notice because I don't listen to what other people say and

60   only sticks and stones can break my bones and I have my Swiss Army Knife if they hit me and if I kill them it will be self-defense and I won't go to prison.

Using Skills to Understand the Passage

3. The passage from Chapter 71 concerns euphemisms, which Christopher might well have told you is a word that comes from the Greek ευ, meaning *good*, and φημι, meaning *speak*. As he points out, modern British children are taught that words like *spastic*, *cripple*, and *mongoloid* are "nasty," and the label "special needs" is to be substituted. What ironic effect does this change have on connotation? What does Christopher's analysis of this situation tell us about the nature of meaning?

Essay Question

Dramatic irony results when a narrator understands less than the reader. Analyze how dramatic irony works in these passages and discuss its overall effect on the reader.

4 *from* The Scarlet Letter
Nathaniel Hawthorne

lesson

Background and Purpose

Nathaniel Hawthorne wrote his most famous novel, *The Scarlet Letter*, in 1850. Hawthorne sets the novel in Boston between 1642 and 1649 (the pilgrims landed at Plymouth in 1620). Hester Prynne, the protagonist, is a woman who preceded her husband to the colony, has committed adultery, and has borne an illegitimate child. She will not reveal the paternity of the child. Her punishment, besides being imprisoned until three months after the child's birth, is to wear on the bodice of her gown a scarlet A, signifying adultery, so long as she lives among these Puritans. In this passage, taken from the second chapter, Hester Prynne, child in arms, is to be released from jail. Many of her neighbors are waiting by the door to witness her disgrace.

The diction and syntax of a novel written at the height of the Romantic movement require some effort for modern readers, but Hawthorne's use of direct characterization should be familiar.

It was a circumstance to be noted, on the summer morning when our story begins its course, that the women, of whom there were several in the crowd, appeared to take a peculiar interest in whatever penal inflic-
Line
5   tion might be expected to ensue. The age had not so much refinement, that any sense of impropriety restrained the wearers of petticoat and farthingale from stepping forth into the public ways, and wedging their not unsubstantial persons, if occasion were, into the throng nearest to the scaffold at an execution. Morally, as well as materially, there was a coarser fibre in those wives and maidens of old English birth and breed-
10 ing, than in their fair descendants, separated from them by a series of six or seven generations; for, throughout that chain of ancestry, every successive mother has transmitted to her child a fainter bloom, a more delicate and briefer beauty, and a slighter physical frame, if not a character of less force and solidity, than her own. The women who were now
15 standing about the prison-door stood within less than half a century of the period when the man-like Elizabeth had been the not altogether unsuitable representative of the sex. They were her country-women; and the beef and ale of their native land, with a moral diet not a whit more refined, entered largely into their composition. The bright morning sun,
20 therefore, shone on broad shoulders and well-developed busts, and on round and ruddy cheeks, that had ripened in the far-off island, and had hardly yet grown paler or thinner in the atmosphere of New England. There was, moreover, a boldness and rotundity of speech among these matrons, as most of them seemed to be, that would startle us at the pres-
25 ent day, whether in respect to its purport or its volume of tone.

Using Skills to Understand the Passage

1. How are the women in the crowd characterized by the narrator's comparison of them to American women of the nineteenth century, contemporaries of Hawthorne?

2. What is predictable about the various opinions of the four speakers who are each briefly described? Cite the descriptions of them and paraphrase each of their opinions before you analyze their motivations.

---

16 **Elizabeth:** Elizabeth I, Queen of England

"Goodwives," said a hard-featured dame of fifty, "I'll tell ye a piece of my mind. It would be greatly for the public behoof, if we women, being of mature age and church-members in good repute, should have the handling of such malefactresses as this Hester Prynne. What think ye, gossips? If the hussy stood up for judgment before us five, that are now here in a knot together, would she come off with such a sentence as the worshipful magistrates have awarded? Marry, I trow not!"

"People say," said another, "that the Reverend Master Dimmesdale, her godly pastor, takes it very grievously to heart that such a scandal should have come upon his congregation."

"The magistrates are God-fearing gentlemen, but merciful over-much,—that is a truth," added a third autumnal matron. "At the very least, they should have put the brand of a hot iron on Hester Prynne's forehead. Madam Hester would have winced at that, I warrant me. But she,—the naughty baggage,—little will she care what they put upon the bodice of her gown! Why, look you, she may cover it with a brooch, or such like heathenish adornment, and so walk the streets as brave as ever!"

"Ah, but," interposed, more softly, a young wife, holding a child by the hand, "let her cover the mark as she will, the pang of it will be always in her heart."

"What do we talk of marks and brands, whether on the bodice of her gown, or the flesh of her forehead?" cried another female, the ugliest as well as the most pitiless of these self-constituted judges. "This woman has brought shame upon us all, and ought to die. Is there not law for it? Truly, there is, both in the Scripture and the statute-book. Then let the magistrates, who have made it of no effect, thank themselves if their own wives and daughters go astray!"

"Mercy on us, goodwife," exclaimed a man in the crowd, "is there no virtue in women, save what springs from a wholesome fear of the gallows? That is the hardest word yet! Hush, now, gossips! For the lock is turning in the prison-door, and here comes Mistress Prynne herself."

Using Skills to Understand the Passage

3. Consider the effect of the man's speech at the end of the passage on our understanding of the author's viewpoint and the unfolding of the plot. Why does the man ask these questions of the angry woman? How does this speech prepare for the subsequent action in the novel?

Essay Question

What clues do we have about the narrator's attitude toward this community and its views? Consider that Hawthorne's contemporary reader inhabits a community that is a democracy under a constitution, rather than the theocracy (a state governed by divine guidance) in which the action of *The Scarlet Letter* is set. In your analysis, include the narrator's description of the demeanor of the spectators, and the words of the women, paying close attention to how the diction of the narration reveals the tone.

5 lesson

from **Jane Eyre**
Charlotte Brontë

Background and Purpose

This passage from Charlotte Brontë's novel *Jane Eyre* (1847) is a fictionalized version of the author's early experiences at a charity school. Three of Brontë's sisters also attended this grim institution, two of them dying during their first year. The author attributed their deaths to the bad management of the school, which neglected the physical and emotional health of its students. Written at a time when sentimental novels were all the rage, *Jane Eyre* provided psychological realism and a pointed modern sensibility that transcended mere melodrama and sentiment. The novel has won a huge readership in every generation since it was first published.

The following scene comes from Chapter Seven in which the orphaned Jane is new to the charity school, having been shipped off by an aunt who dislikes her. Brontë could assume that her original audience understood the cultural context, but many modern readers need help with the scriptural references. (See the notes that follow the passage). Observant Jane notices the inscription over the door of a new building: 'Lowood Institution—This portion was rebuilt AD__, by Naomi Brocklehurst, of Brocklehurst Hall, in this county.' 'Let your light so shine before men that they may see your good works, and glorify your Father which is in heaven.' —St. Matt. V. 16. She is puzzled by the word "Institution," and cannot connect it to the verse of scripture. Jane has learned that Lowood is a charity school for orphans, and that the headmistress, Miss Temple, must answer to Mr. Brocklehurst, a clergyman and the son of the woman named in the inscription. As treasurer and manager of the school, Brocklehurst doles out meager amounts of food, clothing, and heat, and directs every aspect of life at the school. He zealously preaches his gospel of self-denial, "saving" the girls from luxury and indulgence.

Meantime, Mr Brocklehurst, standing on the hearth with his hands behind his back, majestically surveyed the whole school. Suddenly his eye gave a blink, as if it had met something that either dazzled or shocked its pupil; turning, he said in more rapid accents than he had hitherto used:—

'Miss Temple, Miss Temple, what—*what* is that girl with curled red hair? Red hair, ma'am, curled—curled all over?' And extending his cane he pointed to the awful object, his hand shaking as he did so.

'It is Julia Severn,' replied Miss Temple, very quietly.

'Julia Severn, ma'am! And why has she, or any other, curled hair? Why, in defiance of every precept and principle of this house, does she conform to the world so openly—here in an evangelical, charitable establishment—as to wear her hair one mass of curls?'

Line 5 ... *10* ...

Using Skills to Understand the Passage

1. Characterize Mr. Brocklehurst by citing only his words and actions. Consider especially his diction.

2. How do Miss Temple and the older girls respond to Brocklehurst? Use examples of indirect characterization to support your interpretation of Brocklehurst's personality and behavior.

---

12 **evangelical:** Mr. Brocklehurst's attitude here is that of a fundamentalist preacher. Brocklehurst is complacent in his belief that his religion is the only true one. The evangelical tries to convert others to a particular faith and assumes that those who don't share this belief and its moral certainties will burn in hell for eternity.

'Julia's hair curls naturally,' returned Miss Temple, still more quietly.

15 'Naturally! Yes, but we are not to conform to nature: I wish these girls to be the children of Grace: and why that abundance? I have again and again intimated that I desire the hair to be arranged close-ly, modestly, plainly. Miss Temple, that girl's hair must be cut off entirely; I will send a barber to-morrow: and I see others who have far

20 too much of the excrescence—that tall girl, tell her to turn round. Tell all the first form to rise up and direct their faces to the wall.'

Miss Temple passed her handkerchief over her lips, as if to smooth away the involuntary smile that curled them; she gave the order, how-ever, and when the first class could take in what was required of them,

25 they obeyed. Leaning a little back on my bench, I could see the looks and grimaces with which they commented on this manoeuvre: it was a pity Mr Brocklehurst could not see them too; he would perhaps have felt that, whatever he might do with the outside of the cup and platter, the inside was further beyond his interference than he imagined.

30 He scrutinized the reverse of these living medals some five minutes, then pronounced sentence. These words fell like the knell of doom:—

'All those top-knots must be cut off.'

Miss Temple seemed to remonstrate.

'Madam,' he pursued, 'I have a Master to serve whose kingdom is

35 not of this world: my mission is to mortify in these girls the lusts of the flesh; to teach them to clothe themselves with shamefacedness and sobriety, not with braided hair and costly apparel; and each of the young persons before us has a string of hair twisted in plaits which vanity itself might have woven: these, I repeat, must be cut off; think

40 of the time wasted, of—'

Mr Brocklehurst was here interrupted: three other visitors, ladies, now entered the room. They ought to have come a little sooner to have heard his lecture on dress, for they were splendidly attired in velvet, silk, and furs. The two younger of the trio (fine girls of sixteen and seventeen) had

45 grey beaver hats, then in fashion, shaded with ostrich plumes, and from under the brim of this graceful head-dress fell a profusion of light tresses, elaborately curled; the elder lady was enveloped in a costly velvet shawl, trimmed with ermine, and she wore a false front of French curls.

These ladies were deferentially received by Miss Temple, as Mrs

50 and the Misses Brocklehurst, and conducted to seats of honour at the top of the room. It seems they had come in the carriage with their rev-erend relative. . . .

Using Skills to Understand the Passage

3. What are the implications of the "cup and platter" scriptural reference which the first-person narrator uses? Why is this reference ironic? Analyze how the metaphor works to illuminate Brocklehurst's poor judgment.

4. On what does the scene turn? What kind of irony does the author employ? Which details from the scene support your response?

Essay Question

In exploring the cultural context of the passage, consider what motivates Brocklehurst to apply one standard to himself and his family, and another to the charity students.

---

16 **Grace:** John Calvin's distinction between 'nature' and 'Grace' puts an emphasis on the redemption of certain individuals, through God's special favor, from the fallen condition of ordinary people.

28 **cup and platter:** Jesus' warning in Matt 23:25–6: "Woe unto you, scribes and Pharisees, hypocrites! For ye make clean the outside of the cup and of the platter, but within they are full of extortion and excess. Thou blind Pharisee, cleanse first that which is within the cup and platter, that the outside of them may be clean also."

34–35 **kingdom is not of this world:** John 18:36: "My kingdom is not of this world."

48 **false front:** hairpiece over forehead

6 *from* **The Toughest Indian in the World**
Sherman Alexie

lesson

Background and Purpose

This passage is from a story by Sherman Alexie called "Saint Junior," in his short fiction collection, *The Toughest Indian in the World* (2000). Like the author, Roman Gabriel Fury is a Spokane/Coeur d'Alene Indian. He has just received two letters: one congratulates him on his exceptional performance on the CAT test (the thinly veiled SAT) while the other requests a meeting with the test administrator, a white man named Williams. The young man travels once more from the reservation to Spokane, Washington, not knowing whether he is to be congratulated or confronted by the bureaucrat. The passage records the gist of the meeting; the tone of Roman's parting shots should be easy to surmise.

"Hmmm," said Mr. Williams, as if the guttural were an important part of his vocabulary.

"Yes," said Roman, because he wanted to be the first one to use a
Line   word actually found in *Webster's Dictionary*, Ninth Edition.

5   "Well," said Mr. Williams. "Let me see here. It says here in your file that you're eighteen years old, a member of the Spokane Tribe of Indians, valedictorian of Wellpinit High School on said reservation, captain of the chess, math, history, and basketball teams, accepted on full academic scholarship to St. Jerome the Second University here in Spokane."

10   "Yes," said Roman, with the same inflection as before.

"That's quite an all-American resume, Mr. Fury."

"No, I think it's more of an all-Native American resume."

Mr. Williams smiled. His teeth, skin, and pinstriped suit were all the same shade of gray. Roman couldn't tell where the three-season wool

15   ended and where the man began.

"Roman Gabriel Fury," said Williams. "Quite an interesting name."

"Normally, I'd say thank you, sir, but I don't think that that was a sincere compliment, was it?"

"Just an observation, young Mr. Fury. I am very good with observa-

20   tions. In fact, at this very moment, I am observing the fact that your parents are absent. A very distressing observation, to be sure, considering our specific request that your mother and father attend this meeting with you."

"Sir, my parents are dead. If you'd read my file in its entirety, you

25   might have observed that."

Mr. Williams' eyes flashed with anger, the first display of any color. He flipped through the file, searching for the two words that would confirm the truth: *deceased, deceased.*

At that moment, if Roman had closed his eyes, he could have seen

30   the yellow headlights of the red truck that smashed head-on into his

Using Skills to Understand the Passage

1. What do we learn about Roman's character from the passage? What social and personal factors have influenced his development?

2. What is the source of the conflict between Roman Fury and Mr. Williams?

3. What is the significance of the details that describe the private school and the reservation? What contrast is implied through the choice of details?

4. Consider the role of diction and tone in the story. Examine both the language of the narrator and the characters' use of words as weapons. What effect does this highly deliberate use of language have in establishing the tone of the passage?

5. How is color imagery used in the story? What qualities do the presence or absence of color suggest?

father's blue Chevy out on Reservation Road. He could have remembered that his father was buried in a brown suit. At that moment, if Roman had closed his eyes, he could have seen his mother's red blood coughed into the folds of a white handkerchief. Roman was three
35 years old when his mother was buried in a purple dress. He barely remembered her.

"Yes," said Mr. Williams. "I see now. Your grandmother has been your guardian for the last three years. Why didn't she come?"

"She doesn't speak much English, sir."

40 "And yet, you speak English so well, speak it well enough to score in the ninety-ninth percentile in the verbal section of our little test. Quite an amazing feat for someone from, well, let's call it a modest background."

"I've never been accused of modesty."

45 "No, I would guess not," said Williams, setting the file down on his desk. He picked up a Mont Blanc pen as if it were a weapon.

"But I guess you've been called arrogant," added Williams. "And, perhaps, calculating?"

"Calculating enough for a ninety-nine on the math section of your
50 little test," Roman said. He really hated wooden chairs.

"Yes, indeed," said Williams. "A nearly perfect score. In fact, the second-highest score ever for a Native American. Congratulations."

"Normally, I'd say thank you, sir, but I don't think that was a sincere compliment, was it?"

55 Mr. Williams leaned across his desk, straightened his back, placed his hands flat on either side of his desk, took a deep breath, exhaled, and made himself larger. He owned all ten volumes of Harris Brubaker's *How to Use Body Language to Destroy Your Enemies*.

"Son," said Williams, using what Brubaker considered to be the sec-
60 ond-most effective diminutive. "We've been informed there were certain irregularities in your test-taking process."

"Could you be more specific, sir?"

"You were twenty minutes late for the test."

"Yes, I was."

65 "I also understand that your test-taking apparel was, to say the least, quite distracting."

Roman smiled. He'd worn his red, yellow, white, and blue grass-dance outfit while taking the test—highly unusual, to say the least—but he had used two standard number two pencils, as specified in the
70 rule book.

"There's nothing in the rule book about a dress code," said Roman.

"No, no, there's not. But I certainly would enjoy an explanation."

"My grandmother told me your little test was culturally biased," said Roman. "And that I might need a little extra power to do my best.
75 I was going to bring my favorite drum group and let them sing a few honor songs, but I thought the non-Indians in the room might get a little, as you say, distracted."

"Power?" asked Williams, using Harris Brubaker's favorite word.

Roman stood and leaned across the desk. He'd read Brubaker's first
80 volume, had found it derivative and ambiguous, and never bothered to read any of the others.

"Well, you see, sir," said Roman. "The thing is, I was exhausted from having to walk seventy-five miles to get from my reservation to Spokane for the test, because my grandmother and I are too poor to
85 afford a dependable car."

"You hitchhiked?" asked Williams.

"Oh, no, hitchhiking would mean that I actually got a ride. But people don't pick up Indians much, you know?"

"Do you expect me to believe you walked seventy-five miles?"

90   "Well, that's the way it is," said Roman. "Anyway, I get to the city, but then I have to run thirty blocks to get to the private high school where they're giving the test, because I had enough money for lunch or a bus, but not both, and sometimes you have to make hard choices.

    "And then, once I got to the private high school, I had to convince the
95 security guard, who looked suspiciously like a member of the Seventh Cavalry, that I was there to take the test, and not to vandalize the place. And hey, thank God I wasn't wearing my grass-dance outfit yet because he might have shot me down on the spot.

    "Anyway, once I got past him, I was, as you observed, twenty min-
100 utes late. So I ran into a bathroom, changed into my grass-dance outfit, then sat down with your little test, realizing belatedly that I was definitely the only Injun in the room, and aside from the black kid in the front row and the ambiguously ethnic chick in the back, the only so-called minority in the room, and that frightened me more than you
105 will ever know."

Essay Question

Analyze the conflicted character of Roman Gabriel Fury, considering the cultural factors that influence his attitudes. In your analysis, consider the way in which the protagonist's language reveals his complex feelings about growing up Indian in a predominantly white world.

7 *from* **Pride and Prejudice**
Jane Austen

lesson

Background and Purpose

Jane Austen's novels have many of the characteristics of an earlier dramatic form called comedy of manners. Her enduring works, which concern the manners and conventions of early nineteenth-century England's artificial, highly sophisticated gentry, continue to charm readers with their psychologically astute characterizations and wry wit. Austen's Horatian satire is mainly directed against the follies and deficiencies of typical characters: the snob, the coquette, the cad, the domestic tyrant, and not least, the social climber. Austen's didactic intent is to provoke the reform of manners, and to do so she often strips away the social veneer to expose the shoddy goods that lie beneath.

In this passage from *Pride and Prejudice* (1813) Austen employs a stock character, a young clergyman named Collins, to ridicule stylized fashions and manners. Collins is proposing marriage to a young woman whom he has known for all of three days. Here the satire is indirect: Mr. Collins is ridiculed entirely by what he himself says. He has at first decided on Jane, the eldest of his five female cousins, because she is the most beautiful, but also because it is improper to pass over the eldest. Upon a hint from her mother that Jane may shortly be engaged, he instantly switches to Elizabeth, the second daughter and the witty and lively protagonist of the novel. Marrying was a serious matter in an age in which genteel folks lived on inherited money or owed their positions (as Collins does) to an aristocrat. Thus marriage, with or without romantic love, had profound social and financial ramifications. The passage opens as Collins begins his proposal.

"Believe me, my dear Miss Elizabeth, that your modesty, so far from doing you any disservice, rather adds to your other perfections. You would have been less amiable in my eyes had there *not* been this little
Line unwillingness; but allow me to assure you that I have your respected
5 mother's permission for this address. You can hardly doubt the purport of my discourse, however your natural delicacy may lead you to dissemble; my attentions have been too marked to be mistaken. Almost as soon as I entered the house I singled you out as the companion of my future life. But before I am run away with by my feelings on this sub-
10 ject, perhaps it will be advisable for me to state my reasons for marrying—and moreover for coming into Hertfordshire with the design of selecting a wife, as I certainly did."

The idea of Mr. Collins, with all his solemn composure, being run away with by his feelings, made Elizabeth so near laughing that she
15 could not use the short pause he allowed in any attempt to stop him farther, and he continued,

"My reasons for marrying are, first, that I think it a right thing for every clergyman in easy circumstances (like myself) to set the exam-

Using Skills to Understand the Passage

1. Characterize Mr. Collins based on the narrator's words and Elizabeth's reaction.

2. Characterize Lady Catherine based on what Collins reveals about her (indirect characterization).

3. List the reasons Collins presents for wanting to marry Elizabeth. Then consider the order in which he presents them, and what this order reveals about his priorities.

ple of matrimony in his parish. Secondly, that I am convinced that it
20 will add very greatly to my happiness; and thirdly, which perhaps I
ought to have mentioned earlier, that it is the particular advice and
recommendation of the very noble lady whom I have the honour of calling patroness. Twice has she condescended to give me her opinion
(unasked too!) on this subject; and it was but the very Saturday night
25 before I left Hunsford—between our pools at quadrille, while Mrs.
Jenkinson was arranging Miss de Bourgh's footstool, that she said, 'Mr.
Collins, you must marry. A clergyman like you must marry. Choose
properly, choose a gentlewoman for *my* sake, and for your *own*, let her
be an active, useful sort of person, not brought up high, but able to
30 make a small income go a good way. This is my advice. Find such a
woman as soon as you can, bring her to Hunsford, and I will visit her.'
Allow me, by the way, to observe, my fair cousin, that I do not reckon
the notice and kindness of Lady Catherine de Bourgh as among the
least of the advantages in my power to offer. You will find her manners
35 beyond anything I can describe; and your wit and vivacity I think must
be acceptable to her, especially when tempered with the silence and
respect which her rank will inevitably excite. Thus much for my general intentions in favour of matrimony; it remains to be told why my
views were directed to Longbourn instead of my own neighbourhood,
40 where I assure you there are many amiable young women. But the fact
is that being, as I am, to inherit this estate after the death of your hon-
oured father (who, however, may live many years longer), I could not
satisfy myself without resolving to choose a wife from among his
daughters, that the loss to them might be as little as possible, when the
45 melancholy event takes place—which, however, as I have already said,
may not be for several years. This has been my motive, my fair cousin,
and I flatter myself it will not sink me in your esteem. And now nothing remains but to assure you in the most animated language of the
violence of my affection. To fortune I am perfectly indifferent, and shall
50 make no demand of that nature on your father, since I am well aware
that it could not be complied with; and that one thousand pounds in
the 4 per cents, which will not be yours till after your mother's decease,
is all that you may ever be entitled to. On that head, therefore, I shall
be uniformly silent; and you may assure yourself that no ungenerous
55 reproach shall ever pass my lips when we are married."

Using Skills to Understand the Passage

4. What values of her society is Austen satirizing in this proposal?

Essay Question

Analyze Collins' use of language, including diction, hyperbole, and syntax, and explain how his language largely produces dramatic irony.

8 from When the Emperor Was Divine
Julie Otsuka

lesson

Background and Purpose

Julie Otsuka's novel, *When the Emperor Was Divine*, was published in 2002. It is narrated in the third person and tells the story of a Japanese-American family. Shortly after Pearl Harbor, the father is taken away by FBI agents and imprisoned as an enemy alien for the duration of World War II. In the spring of 1942, the mother and children are taken to a concentration camp in the Utah desert, where they await the end of the war. These four passages are drawn from the narrative of the boy, age 7 in 1941, and are presented in the order in which they appear in the novel. His love, loss, and fears are symbolized by articles of clothing, those present and those absent.

The shoes were black Oxfords. Men's size eight and a half, extra narrow. He took them out of his suitcase and slipped them over his hands and pressed his fingers into the smooth oval depressions left *Line* behind by his father's toes and then he closed his eyes and sniffed 5 the tips of his fingers.

Tonight they smelled like nothing.

The week before they had still smelled of his father but tonight the smell of his father was gone.

. . .

They had come for him just after midnight. Three men in suits 10 and ties and black fedoras with FBI badges under their coats. "Grab your toothbrush," they'd said. This was back in December, right after Pearl Harbor, when they were still living in the white house on the wide street in Berkeley not far from the sea. The Christmas tree was up, and the whole house smelled of pine, and 15 from his window the boy had watched as they led his father out across the lawn in his bathrobe and slippers to the black car that was parked at the curb.

He had never seen his father leave the house without his hat on before. That was what had troubled him most. No hat. And those slip- 20 pers: battered and faded, with the rubber soles curling up at the edges. If only they had let him put on his shoes then it all might have turned out differently. But there had been no time for shoes.

> *Grab your toothbrush.*
> *Come on. Come on. You're coming with us.*
25 > *We just need to ask your husband a few questions.*
> *Into the car, Papa-san.*

. . .

Using Skills to Understand the Passage

1. What is the emotional content of the first passage? How is it conveyed?

2. Analyze the imagery of the second passage. What contrasts and incongruities do you find between the setting and the events described? Consider the details that describe the boy's home, as well as his concern about his father's appearance as he is taken away.

3. What is the boy's reaction to the words of the FBI agents? Why does he retain an exact memory of these words?

For four days after his arrest they had not known where he was. The phone had not rung—the FBI had cut the wires—and they could not withdraw any money from the bank. "You account's been frozen," the
30 boy's mother had been told. At dinner she set the table for four, and every night before they went to bed she walked out to the front porch and slipped her house key beneath the potted chrysanthemum. "He'll know where to look," she said. On the fifth day she received a short note in the mail from the immigration detention center in San
35 Francisco. *Still awaiting my loyalty hearing. Do not know when my case will be heard, or how much longer I will be here. Eighty-three Japanese have already been sent away on a train. Please come see me as soon as possible.* She packed a small suitcase full of her husband's things—clothes, towels, a shaving kit, a spare pair of eyeglasses, nose
40 drops, a bar of Yardley soap, a first-aid book—and took the next train across the bay.

"Was he still wearing his slippers?" the boy asked her when she returned.

She said that he was. And his bathrobe, too. She said that he had not
45 showered or shaved for days. Then she smiled. "He looked like a hobo," she said.

That night she had set the table for three.

In the morning she had sent all of the boy's father's suits to the cleaners except for one: the blue pin-striped suit he had worn on his
50 last Sunday at home. The blue suit was to remain on the hanger in the closet. "He asked me to leave it there, for you to remember him by."

But whenever the boy thought of his father on his last Sunday at home he did not remember the blue suit. He remembered the white flannel robe. The slippers. His father's hatless silhouette framed in
55 the back window of the car. The head stiff and unmoving. Staring straight ahead. Straight ahead and into the night as the car drove off slowly into the darkness. Not looking back. Not even once. Just to see if he was there.

. . .

[*In his family's cell in the desert camp, the boy is fantasizing about his father's return*]:

Or maybe the boy would be lying in bed one night and he'd hear a
60 knock, a soft tap. "Who is it?" he'd say. "It's me." He'd open the door and see his father standing there in his white flannel bathrobe all covered with dust. "It's a long walk from Lordsburg" [the prison in New Mexico], his father would say. Then they would shake hands, or maybe they'd even hug.
65 "Did you get my letters?" he'd ask his father.

"You bet I did. I read every single one of them. I got that leaf, too. I thought of you all the time."

"I thought of you too," the boy would say.

He'd bring his father a glass of water and they would sit down side
70 by side on the cot. Outside the window the moon would be bright and round. The wind would be blowing. He'd rest his head on his father's shoulder and smell the dust and the sweat and the faint smell of Burma Shave and everything would be very nice. Then, out of the corner of his eye, he'd notice his father's big toe sticking out through a
75 hole in his slipper. "Papa," he'd say.

"What is it?"

"You forgot to put on your shoes."

Using Skills to Understand the Passage

4. In the third passage, what is the significance of the change in the number of place settings at the dinner table?

5. What effect is achieved by the list of ordinary objects that the mother packs to take to her husband in the detention center? What does she leave out of her care package? In spite of her anxiety, why does she smile as she reports that her husband looked like a hobo?

6. In the third passage, why does the father want to be remembered by his blue pin-striped suit? Why does the boy remember instead the white flannel robe and the slippers? What is added to the father's characterization by the details of the boy's last sight of him?

His father would look down at his feet and he'd shake his head with surprise. "Son of a gun," he'd say. "Would you look at that." Then he'd just shrug. He'd lean back on the cot and make himself comfortable. He'd pull out his pipe. A box of matches. He'd smile. "Now tell me what I missed," he'd say. "Tell me everything."

80

Essay Question

Analyze the imagery, symbolism, and emotional content of the fourth passage, drawing on your observations of the first three passages in the selection.

9 lesson

from The Adventures of Huckleberry Finn
Mark Twain

Background and Purpose

Samuel Clemens, whose pen name was Mark Twain, published *The Adventures of Huckleberry Finn* in 1884. In this satiric passage from the book many acknowledge as the "Great American Novel," Huck, the first person narrator, has been taken in by the Grangerfords, who live in a "big old-fashioned double log house" with a "new rag carpet" in the "big parlor." The lady of the house smokes a corn cob pipe, but the front door has "a brass knob to turn, the same as houses in town." These are classy folks: "There warn't no bed in the parlor. . . . Col. Grangerford was a gentleman, you see." After many more words of admiration for the "beautiful oilcloth" tablecloth and the plaster fruit in the basket, chipped, to be sure, yet "much redder and yellower and prettier than real ones is," the young narrator begins to study the pictures on the walls. In this passage, the author uses Huck's ingenuous voice to indirectly satirize these "aristocrats," mocking their pretensions and sentimentality. Emmeline Grangerford is characterized only by her "crayon" drawings and her "very good poetry," for she is dead. Huck is, of course, an unreliable narrator, naïve enough to be impressed and yet occasionally honest about his feelings.

They had pictures hung on the walls—mainly Washingtons and Lafayettes, and battles, and Highland Marys, and one called "Signing the Declaration." There was some that they called crayons, which one *Line* of the daughters which was dead made her own self when she was only 5 fifteen years old. They was different from any pictures I ever see before—blacker, mostly, than is common. One was a woman in a slim black dress, belted small under the armpits, with bulges like a cabbage in the middle of the sleeves, and a large black scoop-shovel bonnet with a black veil, and white slim ankles crossed about with black tape, and 10 very wee black slippers, like a chisel, and she was leaning pensive on a tombstone on her right elbow, under a weeping willow, and her other hand hanging down her side holding a white handkerchief and a reticule, and underneath the picture it said "Shall I Never See Thee More Alas." Another one was a young lady with her hair all combed up 15 straight to the top of her head, and knotted there in front of a comb like a chair-back, and she was crying into a handkerchief and had a dead bird laying on its back in her other hand with its heels up, and underneath the picture it said "I Shall Never Hear Thy Sweet Chirrup More Alas." There was one where a young lady was at a window look- 20 ing up at the moon, and tears running down her cheeks; and she had an open letter in one hand with black sealing-wax showing on one edge of it, and she was mashing a locket with a chain to it against her mouth, and underneath the picture it said "And Art Thou Gone Yes Thou Art Gone Alas." These was all nice pictures, I reckon, but I didn't

Using Skills to Understand the Passage

1. What is being satirized in this passage? How do Huck's understatements about the pictures serve to deliver Twain's satiric point?

2. Consider the diction in Huck's description of the first two pictures. Is Huck aware of the connotations of his metaphorical vehicles? Are they appropriate to the tone of the pictures? How do the similes contribute to Twain's satire?

3. Is Huck aware that many of the details in the drawings are clichés? What do the clichés contribute to the humor of the passage?

25 somehow seem to take to them, because if ever I was down a little they always gave me the fan-tods. Everybody was sorry she died, because she had laid out a lot more of these pictures to do, and a body could see by what she had done what they had lost. But I reckoned that with her disposition she was having a better time in the graveyard. She was at

30 work on what they said was her greatest picture when she took sick, and every day and every night it was her prayer to be allowed to live till she got it done, but she never got the chance. It was picture of a young woman in a long white gown, standing on the rail of a bridge all ready to jump off, with her hair all down her back, and looking up to

35 the moon, with the tears running down her face, and she had two arms folded across her breast, and two arms stretched out in front, and two more reaching up toward the moon—and the idea was to see which pair would look best, and then scratch out all the other arms; but, as I was saying, she died before she got her mind made up, and now they

40 kept this picture over the head of the bed in her room, and every time her birthday come they hung flowers on it. Other times it was hid with a little curtain. The young woman in the picture had a kind of a nice sweet face, but there was so many arms it made her look too spidery, seemed to me.

Using Skills to Understand the Passage

4. Consider how the Grangerford family has responded to Emmeline's death. How does Huck in his simple honesty undercut the family's opinion of the artist and her pictures?

Essay Question

Romantic novels, poetry, and painting were very much in vogue when Twain was writing. These were often sentimental, overindulging in emotion. The artist's conscious intent was to produce an excess of emotion for the audience to enjoy, arousing, for example, pity or sorrow. In what ways is Emmeline Grangerford a sentimentalist? How does Huck serve as a satirical mouthpiece for Twain's attitude toward the sentimental?

10 lesson

from As I Lay Dying
William Faulkner

Background and Purpose

William Faulkner's novel *As I Lay Dying* was an experiment in narrative technique when it was first published in 1930. Fifteen different narrative voices tell the story of the Bundren family's attempt to cope with the death of the mother and their struggle to bear her coffin many miles to her chosen resting-place. The setting is typical of Faulkner's fiction: an isolated patch of rural Mississippi. The Bundren family consists of Pa and Ma (Addie, the dying woman), and the five children: Darl, Jewel, Cash, Dewey Dell (the only girl), and Vardaman, still a little boy. Vernon and Cora Tull are neighbors. Peabody is the doctor, stranded there by the heavy rain.

The passages below represent two voices from the novel and help to characterize the three older sons. The closest Faulkner comes to omniscient narration is through Darl's voice in the third passage, the other two being interior monologues, also called stream of consciousness. The choice of narrator is always significant, as is the character's bias when telling a part of the story. Faulkner characterizes each speaker through diction and the use of figurative language, simple understatement, and the types of details each includes or omits. When more than one character speaks of the same incident, the details omitted or added, as well as the angle of vision, tell us much.

Darl and Jewel are walking toward the house after a day's work in the fields and come upon their brother Cash.

DARL

When I reach the top he [Cash] has quit sawing. Standing in a litter of chips, he is fitting two of the boards together. Between the shadow spaces they are yellow as gold, like soft gold, bearing on their flanks
Line in smooth undulations the marks of the adze blade: a good carpenter,
5 Cash is. He holds the two planks on the trestle, fitting along the edges in a quarter of the finished box. He kneels and squints along the edge of them, then he lowers them and takes up the adze. A good carpenter. Addie Bundren could not want a better one, a better box to lie in. It will give her confidence and comfort. I go on to the house, followed by the

10   Chuck.   Chuck.   Chuck.
    of the adze.

JEWEL

It's because he [Cash] stays out there, right under the window, hammering and sawing on that goddamn box. Where she's got to see him. Where every breath she draws is full of his knocking and saw-
15 ing where she can see him saying See. See what a good one I am

Using Skills to Understand the Passage

1. What is the immediate situation? Based on the first two sections, make inferences about who is doing what, where, and why. Briefly characterize Cash, taking only the first section (Darl's point of view) into account.

2. What is revealed about Darl in his characterization of Cash?

3. What is revealed about Jewel in the second section? Consider him an unreliable narrator.

making for you. I told him to go somewhere else. I said Good God do you want to see her in it. It's like when he was a little boy and she says if she had some fertilizer she would try to raise some flowers and he taken the bread pan and brought it back from the barn full
20 of dung.

And now them others sitting there, like buzzards. Waiting, fanning themselves. Because I said If you wouldn't keep on sawing and nailing at it until a man cant sleep even and her hands laying on the quilt like two of them roots dug up and tried to wash and you could-
25 n't get them clean. I can see the fan and Dewey Dell's arm. I said if you'd just let her alone. Sawing and knocking, and keeping the air always moving so fast on her face that when you're tired you cant breathe it, and that goddamn adze going One lick less. One lick less. One lick less until everybody that passes in the road will have to
30 stop and see it and say what a fine carpenter he is. If it had just been me . . . it would just be me and her on a high hill and me rolling the rocks down the hill at their faces, picking them up and throwing them down the hill faces and teeth and all by God until she was quiet and not that goddamn adze going One lick less. One lick less
35 and we could be quiet.

DARL

Cash squints at the board. On the long flank of it the rain crashes steadily, myriad, fluctuant. "I'm going to bevel it," he says.

"It'll take more time," Vernon says. Cash sets the plank on edge; a moment longer Vernon watches him, then he hands him the plane.
40 Vernon holds the board steady while Cash bevels the edge of it with the tedious and minute care of a jeweler. Mrs Tull comes to the edge of the porch and calls Vernon. "How near are you to done?" she says.

Vernon does not look up. "Not long. Some, yet."

She watches Cash stooping at the plank, the turgid savage gleam of
45 the lantern slicking on the raincoat as he moves. "You go down and get some planks off the barn and finish it and come in out of the rain," she says. "You'll both catch your death." Vernon does not move. "Vernon," she says.

"We wont be long," he says. "We'll be done after a spell." Mrs Tull
50 watches them a while. Then she reenters the house.

"If we get in a tight, we could take some of them planks," Vernon says. "I'll help you put them back."

Cash ceases the plane and squints along the plank, wiping it with his palm. "Give me the next one," he says.
55 Some time toward dawn the rain ceases. But it is not yet day when Cash drives the last nail and stands stiffly up and looks down at the finished coffin, the others watching him. In the lantern light his face is calm, musing; slowly he strokes his hands on his raincoated thighs in a gesture deliberate, final and composed. Then the four of them—Cash
60 and Pa and Vernon and Peabody—raise the coffin to their shoulders and turn toward the house. It is light, yet they move slowly; empty, yet they carry it carefully; lifeless, yet they move with hushed precautionary words to one another, speaking of it as though, complete, it now slumbered lightly alive, waiting to come awake. On the dark floor their
65 feet clump awkwardly, as though for a long time they have not walked on floors.

They set it down by the bed. Peabody says quietly: "Let's eat a snack. It's almost daylight. Where's Cash?"

Using Skills to Understand the Passage

4. Darl, the omniscient narrator in the third passage, provides a description of the finishing of the coffin. Continue your characterization of Cash based on this new information. Consider what the words and actions of the neighbors reveal about him, as well as the conflict between his plan and everyone else's desire.

70   He has returned to the trestles, stooped again in the lantern's feeble glare as he gathers up his tools and wipes them on a cloth carefully and puts them into the box, with its leather sling to go over the shoulder. Then he takes up box, lantern and raincoat and returns to the house, mounting the steps into faint silhouette against the paling east.

Essay Question

In these passages, how does Faulkner elicit sympathy for his characters and their situation? How do such devices as diction, figurative language, descriptive details, and understatement work to engage us with their sense of loss? Are we equally sympathetic to the three brothers, Darl, Jewel, and Cash?

from Somebody's Luggage
Charles Dickens

lesson

Background and Purpose

No writer in nineteenth-century England was more of a crusader against social ills than Charles Dickens. A reversal of financial fortunes in his family forced the twelve-year-old Dickens to work in a blacking factory for some months, where he suffered hardships that he was never to forget. This dismal experience found expression in some of his most memorable characters, members of London's underclass.

Dickens' enormously popular novels, first serialized in magazines, were read aloud in many a family circle where copious tears were shed over the miseries of his poor and humble characters. Although today's readers may find aspects of Dickens' work sentimental, even maudlin in tone, it should be remembered that his audience, who waited breathlessly for each installment of these novels, greatly admired the melodrama and pathos of his plots. But in fact, Dickens is master of many tones, and often uses his expertise with language to make us laugh as he reveals his attitude toward the social conditions of his time. The following passage is a dramatic monologue first published in a magazine in 1862. The narrator comes from a family of waiters and waitresses. He is describing how his upbringing convinced him to become a waiter in his turn.

You were conveyed, ere yet your dawning powers were otherwise developed than to harbour vacancy in your inside—you were conveyed, by surreptitious means, into a pantry adjoining the Admiral
Line Nelson, Civic and General Dining Rooms, there to receive by stealth
5 that healthful sustenance which is the pride and boast of the British female constitution. Your mother was married to your father (himself a distant Waiter) in the profoundest secrecy; for a Waitress known to be married would ruin the best of businesses—it is the same as on the stage. Hence your being smuggled into the pantry, and that—to
10 add to the infliction—by an unwilling grandmother. Under the combined influence of the smells of roast and boiled, and soup, and gas, and malt liquors, you partook of your earliest nourishment; your unwilling grandmother sitting prepared to catch you when your mother was called and dropped you; your grandmother's shawl ever
15 ready to stifle your natural complainings; your innocent mind surrounded by uncongenial cruets, dirty plates, dish-covers, and cold gravy; your mother calling down the pipe for veals and porks, instead of soothing you with nursery rhymes. Under these untoward circumstances you were early weaned. Your unwilling grandmother, ever
20 growing more unwilling as your food assimilated less, then contracted habits of shaking you till your system curdled, and your food would not assimilate at all. At length she was no longer spared, and

Using Skills to Understand the Passage

1. It is unusual to find the second-person point of view in fiction. What effects are achieved by the narrator referring to himself as "you" as he launches into his story?

2. Briefly paraphrase the long sentence which begins the passage. Describe the syntax, level of diction, and overall effect, then compare the subject and its treatment: do manner and matter match? Does one undercut the other? What can we hypothesize so far about the tone of the passage?

could have been thankfully spared much sooner. When your brothers began to appear in succession, your mother retired, left off her smart dressing (she had previously been a smart dresser), and her dark ringlets (which had previously been flowing), and haunted your father late of nights, lying in wait for him, through all weathers, up the shabby court which led to the back door of the Royal Old Dust-Binn (said to have been so named by George the Fourth), where your father was Head. But the Dust-Binn was going down then, and your father took but little—excepting from a liquid point of view. Your mother's object in those visits was of a housekeeping character, and you were set on to whistle your father out. Sometimes he came out, but generally not. Come or not come, however, all that part of his existence which was unconnected with open Waitering, was kept a close secret, and was acknowledged by your mother to be a close secret, and you and your mother flitted about the court, close secrets both of you, and would scarcely have confessed under torture that you knew your father, or that your father had any name than Dick (which wasn't his name, though he was never known by any other), or that he had kith or kin or chick or child. Perhaps the attraction of this mystery, combined with your father's having a damp compartment to himself, behind a leaky cistern, at the Dust-Binn—a sort of cellar compartment, with a sink in it, and a smell, and a plate-rack and a bottle-rack, and three windows that didn't match each other or anything else, and no daylight—caused your young mind to feel convinced that you must grow up to be a Waiter too; but you did feel convinced of it, and so did all your brothers, down to your sister. Every one of you felt convinced that you were born to the Waitering.

Using Skills to Understand the Passage

3. What details and repetitions contribute to the tone of the grandmother's characterization? How would you describe the tone at this point?

4. What tone is created by the description of the setting, the restaurant's kitchen where the infant is fed? To what effect is the imagery used? Is this imagery consistent with the earlier content of the passage?

5. Make an inference about what motivates the narrator's mother to "haunt" the back door of the restaurant where his father is head waiter. On what evidence do you base your inference? Hint: there's a useful pun involved.

6. Two circumstances attract the children to the job of waitering: the fact that their father's family is a "close secret," and that living quarters are provided by the restaurant. What devices is Dickens using here and to what effect?

Essay Question

How does Dickens wish the reader to feel about the job of waiting tables in restaurants and about the society in which these workers and their families live? How does he achieve his satiric goal?

12

from **The Dubliners**
James Joyce

lesson

Background and Purpose

James Joyce was born in Dublin, Ireland in 1882 and lived there with his family, one of twelve children whose father's drinking took them from the middle class to poverty, until his early twenties. He then went to the continent, and lived abroad for the rest of his life, though writing exclusively about Dublin. In "Eveline," from his collection of stories called *The Dubliners*, published in 1914, he indirectly shows his attitude toward the conventions of family life, morality, and religion with which he grew up. The story is built around Eveline's internal conflict, and the mood of the setting is of great importance in establishing that conflict and Joyce's tone. The conflict is resolved at the end of the story by Eveline's epiphany about herself and her situation. As the story begins Eveline is about to leave home to sail to Buenos Aires and marry her sailor boyfriend. In the second half of the story (not included here), she decides to stay at home.

She sat at the window watching the evening invade the avenue. Her head was leaned against the window curtains and in her nostrils was the odor of dusty cretonne. She was tired.

Line
5 Few people passed. The man out of the last house passed on his way home; she heard his footsteps clacking along the concrete pavement and afterwards crunching on the cinder path before the new red houses. One time there used to be a field there in which they used to play every evening with other people's children. Then a man from Belfast bought the field and built houses in it—not like their little brown hous-
10 es but bright brick houses with shining roofs. The children of the avenue used to play together in that field—the Devines, the Waters, the Dunns, little Keogh the cripple, she and her brothers and sisters. Ernest, however, never played: he was too grown up. Her father used often to hunt them in out of the field with his blackthorn stick; but
15 usually little Keogh used to keep nix and call out when he saw her father coming. Still they seemed to have been rather happy then. Her father was not so bad then; and besides, her mother was alive. That was a long time ago; she and her brothers and sisters were all grown up; her mother was dead. Tizzie Dunn was dead, too, and the Waters
20 had gone back to England. Everything changes. Now she was going to go away like the others, to leave her home.

Home! She looked round the room, reviewing all its familiar objects which she had dusted once a week for so many years, wondering where on earth all the dust came from. Perhaps she would never see again
25 those familiar objects from which she had never dreamed of being divided. And yet during all those years she had never found out the name of the priest whose yellowing photograph hung on the wall above

Using Skills to Understand the Passage

1. The setting is established early in the story. What do the descriptive details in the first three paragraphs tell you about Eveline's home? What objects might be symbolic of the values that rule the home? Does Eveline accept or reject those values? How does she feel about the prospect of leaving?

2. Characterize Eveline's father by citing his actions and the tone with which they are reported. Considering all the details, how would you describe her complex feelings about him?

the broken harmonium beside the colored print of the promises made to Blessed Margaret Mary Alacoque. He had been a school friend of her
30 father. Whenever he showed the photograph to a visitor her father used to pass it with a casual word:

"He is in Melbourne now."

She had consented to go away, to leave her home. Was that wise? She tried to weigh each side of the question. In her home anyway she
35 had shelter and food; she had those whom she had known all her life about her. Of course she had to work hard both in the house and at business. What would they say of her in the Stores when they found out that she had run away with a fellow? Say she was a fool, perhaps; and her place would be filled up by advertisement. Miss Gavan would
40 be glad. She had always had an edge on her, especially whenever there were people listening.

"Miss Hill, don't you see these ladies are waiting?"

"Look lively, Miss Hill, please."

She would not cry many tears at leaving the Stores.
45 But in her new home, in a distant unknown country, it would not be like that. Then she would be married—she, Eveline. People would treat her with respect then. She would not be treated as her mother had been. Even now, though she was over nineteen, she sometimes felt herself in danger of her father's violence. She knew it was that that had
50 given her the palpitations. When they were growing up he had never gone for her, like he used to go for Harry and Ernest, because she was a girl; but latterly he had begun to threaten her and say what he would do to her only for her dead mother's sake. And now she had nobody to protect her. Ernest was dead and Harry, who was in the church deco-
55 rating business, was nearly always down somewhere in the country. Besides, the invariable squabble for money on Saturday nights had begun to weary her unspeakably. She always gave her entire wages— seven shillings—and Harry always sent up what he could but the trouble was to get any money from her father. He said she used to squan-
60 der the money, that she had no head, that he wasn't going to give her his hard-earned money to throw about the streets, and much more, for he was usually fairly bad of a Saturday night. In the end he would give her the money and ask her had she any intention of buying Sunday's dinner. Then she had to rush out as quickly as she could and do her
65 marketing, holding her black leather purse tightly in her hand as she elbowed her way through the crowds and returning home late under her load of provisions. She had hard work to keep the house together and to see that the two young children who had been left to her charge went to school regularly and got their meals regularly. It was hard
70 work—a hard life—but now that she was about to leave it she did not find it a wholly undesirable life.

Using Skills to Understand the Passage

3. What can you infer about Eveline's mother's life? How might the facts of that life contribute to Eveline's conflict?

4. Compare the circumstances of Eveline's work inside and outside the house with what she imagines her status would be in Buenos Aires. How do these differences contribute to her conflict?

Essay Question

What does the first half of the story foreshadow about Eveline's eventual decision? Consider the feelings and attitudes revealed during her internal struggle.

13 *from* The Witness
Katherine Anne Porter

lesson

Background and Purpose

Katherine Anne Porter is an American writer whose stories were published throughout the 1930s and 1940s. She is the winner of a National Book Award and a Pulitzer Prize. The historical and cultural contexts of "The Witness" are important to note, as are the relationship of the characters to each other and the lack of plot structure. The story's theme is not immediately apparent. The dialect of the protagonist looks strange on the page, but reading it phonetically, aloud, will aid comprehension. The last two paragraphs are omitted, but it should be noted that in them Uncle Jimbilly changes the subject, producing an anticlimax.

Uncle Jimbilly was so old and had spent so many years bowed over things, putting them together and taking them apart, making them over and making them do, he was bent almost double. His hands were
Line
5   closed and stiff from gripping objects tightly, while he worked at them, and they could not open altogether even if a child took the thick black fingers and tried to turn them back. He hobbled on a stick; his purplish skull showed through patches in his wool, which had turned greenish gray and looked as if the moths had got in it.

    He mended harness and put half soles on the other Negroes' shoes,
10   he built fences and chicken coops and barn doors; he stretched wires and put in new window panes and fixed sagging hinges and patched up roofs; he repaired carriage tops and cranky plows. Also he had a gift for carving miniature tombstones out of blocks of wood; give him almost any kind of piece of wood and he could turn out a tombstone,
15   shaped very like the real ones, with carving, and a name and date on it if they were needed. They were often needed, for some small beast or bird was always dying and having to be buried with proper ceremonies: the cart draped as a hearse, a shoe-box coffin with a pall over it, a profuse floral outlay, and, of course, a tombstone. As he worked,
20   turning the long blade of his bowie knife deftly in circles to cut a flower, whittling and smoothing the back and sides, stopping now and then to hold it at arm's length and examine it with one eye closed, Uncle Jimbilly would talk in a low, broken, abstracted murmur, as if to himself; but he was really saying something he meant one to hear.
25   Sometimes it would be an incomprehensible ghost story; listen ever so carefully, at the end it was impossible to decide whether Uncle Jimbilly himself had seen the ghost, whether it was a real ghost at all, or only another man dressed like one; and he dwelt much on the horrors of slave times.
30   "Dey used to take 'em out and tie 'em down and whup 'em," he muttered, "wid gret big leather strops inch thick long as yo' ahm, wid

Using Skills to Understand the Passage

1. First, place the story in its historical and cultural context: What details in the first two paragraphs give us the setting?

2. Who are the characters? In what order are they introduced? What is their relationship to each other?

3. What can you infer about the narrator? Given the main purpose of the story, why is this narrative voice appropriate? Consider the kind of irony produced by the choice of narrator.

4. What is the story's tone and the author's viewpoint? How are these revealed? Hint: Consider the imagery, diction, and syntax of the protagonist. Also note the structure of the story.

round holes bored in 'em so's evey time dey hit 'em de hide and de meat done come off dey bones in little round chunks. And wen dey had whupped 'em wid de strop till dey backs was all raw and bloody, dey
35   spread dry cawnshucks on dey backs and set 'em afire and pahched 'em, and den dey poured vinega all ovah 'em . . . Yassuh. And den, the ve'y nex day dey'd got to git back to work in the fiels or dey'd do the same thing right ovah agin. Yassah. Dat was it. If dey didn't git back to work dey got it all right ovah agin."

40   The children—three of them: a serious, prissy older girl of ten, a thoughtful sad looking boy of eight, and a quick flighty little girl of six—sat disposed around Uncle Jimbilly and listened with faint tinglings of embarrassment. They knew, of course, that once upon a time Negroes had been slaves; but they had all been freed long ago and were
45   now only servants. It was hard to realize that Uncle Jimbilly had been born in slavery, as the Negroes were always saying. The children thought that Uncle Jimbilly had got over his slavery very well. Since they had known him, he had never done a single thing that anyone told him to do. He did his work just as he pleased and when he pleased.
50   If you wanted a tombstone, you had to be very careful about the way you asked for it. Nothing could have been more impersonal and faraway than his tone and manner of talking about slavery, but they wriggled a little and felt guilty. Paul would have changed the subject, but Miranda, the little quick one, wanted to know the worst. "Did they act
55   like that to you, Uncle Jimbilly?" she asked.

      "No, mam," said Uncle Jimbilly. "Now whut name you want on dis one? Dey nevah did. Dey done 'em dat way in the rice swamps. I always worked right here close to the house or in town with Miss Sophia. Down in the swamps . . ."

60   "Didn't they ever die, Uncle Jimbilly?" asked Paul.

      "Cose dey died," said Uncle Jimbilly, "cose dey died—dey died," he went on, pursing his mouth gloomily, "by de thousands and tens upon thousands."

      "Can you carve 'Safe in Heaven' on that, Uncle Jimbilly?" asked
65   Maria in her pleasant, mincing voice.

      "To put over a tame jackrabbit, Missy?" asked Uncle Jimbilly indignantly. He was very religious. "A heathen like dat? *No, mam.* In de swamps dey used to stake 'em out all day and all night, and all day and all night and all day wid dey hans and feet tied so dey couldn't stretch
70   and let de muskeeters eat 'em alive. De muskeeters 'ud bite 'em tell dey was all swole up like a balloon all over, and you could heah 'em howlin and prayin all ovah the swamp. Yassuh. Dat was it. And nary a drop of watah noh a moufful of braid . . . Yassuh, dat's it. Lawd, dey done it. Hosanna! Now take dis yere tombstone and don' bother me no
75   more . . . or I'll . . ."

Using Skills to Understand the Passage

5. The narration of the conversations of the children and Uncle Jimbilly does not unfold chronologically. There is no clear conflict, no climax, no resolution. In fact, the last two paragraphs (not included) are anticlimactic. If there is no neat plot to follow, what organizing principle structures and unifies the story? What can you discover about the theme of the story by examining its structure? Consider the story's frame (pet burials) and the order in which Uncle Jimbilly's stories appear. Hint: It is safe to assume that ironies abound of which the children and the narrator are unaware.

6. What elements of "The Witness" might be symbolic? How do these symbols serve to unify the story?

7. Considering the historical and cultural context of the story, what issues are raised? How does the author seem to feel about the issues? Consider the important facts that are left unsaid or merely suggested by Uncle Jimbilly.

Essay Question

Discuss how the author employs both direct and indirect characterization in "The Witness" in order to establish character and motivation and convey the story's theme. In your essay, focus on physical description, dialogue, action, and the interplay of all characters, paying special attention to Uncle Jimbilly and the narrator. Consider also that the protagonist's motivation may be the same as the author's in writing the story. Explore the theme of the story and analyze how the authorial viewpoint develops this theme.

Independent Analysis

from The Book of Small
Emily Carr

Background and Purpose

Emily Carr, a respected Canadian painter, first published her fictionalized memoir, *The Book of Small*, in 1942, and it has been in print ever since. Carr was born in 1871 in Victoria, British Columbia, at the time when the region was slowly losing its provincial character as a Hudson Bay Company fur-trading post. Carr's paintings are now considered a national treasure in Canada and around the world, but during her lifetime galleries rejected her strong presentations of the old growth forests and early cultures of the Pacific as far too bold and revolutionary for current tastes. These qualities were inborn, to judge from her memoir.

As the passage implies, Carr's father defined the cultural context of her childhood. He had been transported into this wilderness on the wild Pacific coast of southwestern Canada along with his sea chest, a sense of British propriety, a Sabbatarian religious tradition, and strict child-rearing practices.

All our Sundays were exactly alike. They began on Saturday night after Bong the Chinaboy had washed up and gone away, after our toys, dolls and books, all but *The Peep of Day* and Bunyan's *Pilgrim's Progress*, had been stored away in drawers and boxes till Monday, and
Line
5 every Bible and prayerbook in the house was puffing itself out, looking more important every minute.

Then the clothes-horse came galloping into the kitchen and straddled round the stove inviting our clean clothes to mount and be aired. The enormous wooden tub that looked half coffin and half baby-bath
10 was set in the middle of the kitchen floor with a rag mat for dripping on laid close beside it. The great iron soup pot, the copper wash-boiler and several kettles covered the top of the stove, and big sister Dede filled them by working the kitchen pump-handle furiously. It was a sad old pump and always groaned several times before it poured. Dede got
15 the brown Windsor soap, heated the towels and put on a thick white apron with a bib. Mother unbuttoned us and by that time the pots and kettles were steaming.

Dede scrubbed hard. If you wriggled, the flat of the long-handled dipper came down spankety on your skin.
20 As soon as each child was bathed Dede took it pick-a-back and rushed it upstairs through the cold house. We were allowed to say our prayers kneeling in bed on Saturday night, steamy, brown-windsory prayers—then we cuddled down and tumbled very comfortably into Sunday.

---

25   At seven o'clock Father stood beside our bed and said, "Rise up! Rise up! It's Sunday, children." He need not have told us; we knew Father's Sunday smell—Wright's coal-tar soap and camphor. Father had a splendid chest of camphor-wood which had come from England round the Horn in a sailing ship with him. His clean clothes lived in it and
30   on Sunday he was very camphory. His chest was high and very heavy. It had brass handles and wooden knobs. The top let down as a writing desk with pigeon-holes; below there were little drawers for handkerchiefs and collars and long drawers for clothes. On top of the chest stood Father's locked desk for papers. The key of it was on his ring with
35   lots of others. This desk had a secret drawer and a brass-plate with R. H. CARR engraved on it.

On top of the top desk stood the little Dutchman, a china figure with a head that took off and a stomach full of little candies like colored hailstones. If we had been very good all week we got hailstones
40   Sunday morning.

Family prayers were uppish with big words on Sunday—reverend awe-ful words that only God and Father understood.

No work was done in the Carr house on Sunday. Everything had been polished frightfully on Saturday and all Sunday's food cooked too.
45   On Sunday morning Bong milked the cow and went away from breakfast until evening milking-time. Beds were made, the dinner-table set, and then we got into our very starchiest and most uncomfortable clothes for church.

Essay Question

How does Carr's account undermine the solemn holiness of Sundays? Consider how her selection of detail, diction, and imagery, as well as her use of figurative language, create the tone of the passage.

from Soldier's Home
Ernest Hemingway

Background and Purpose

Ernest Hemingway volunteered to drive an ambulance in World War I shortly after graduating from high school. His war experience and attempts to resume his life after the war are reflected in the preoccupations of many of the characters in his stories and novels. He is known for his objective narration and the simplicity of his style. "Soldier's Home" was published in 1925.

Independent Analysis

Krebs went to the war from a Methodist college in Kansas. There is a picture which shows him among his fraternity brothers, all of them wearing exactly the same height and style collar. He enlisted in the Marines in 1917 and did not return to the United States until the second division returned from the Rhine in the summer of 1919.

There is a picture which shows him on the Rhine with two German girls and another corporal. Krebs and the corporal look too big for their uniforms. The German girls are not beautiful. The Rhine does not show in the picture.

By the time Krebs returned to his home town in Oklahoma the greeting of heroes was over. He came back much too late. The men from the town who had been drafted had all been welcomed elaborately on their return. There had been a great deal of hysteria. Now the reaction had set in. People seemed to think it was rather ridiculous for Krebs to be getting back so late, years after the war was over.

At first Krebs, who had been at Belleau Wood, Soissons, the Champagne, St. Mihiel, and in the Argonne did not want to talk about the war at all. Later he felt the need to talk but no one wanted to hear about it. His town had heard too many atrocity stories to be thrilled by actualities. Krebs found that to be listened to at all he had to lie, and after he had done this twice he, too, had a reaction against the war and against talking about it. A distaste for everything that had happened to him in the war set in because of the lies he had told. All of the times that had been able to make him feel cool and clear inside himself when he thought of them; the times so long back when he had done the one thing, the only thing for a man to do, easily and naturally, when he might have done something else, now lost their cool, valuable quality and then were lost themselves.

His lies were quite unimportant lies and consisted in attributing to himself things other men had seen, done, or heard of, and stating as facts certain apocryphal incidents familiar to all soldiers. Even his lies were not sensational at the pool room. His acquaintances, who had heard detailed accounts of German women found chained to machine guns in the Argonne forest and who could not comprehend, or were barred by their patriotism from interest in, any German machine gunners who were not chained, were not thrilled by his stories.

Krebs acquired the nausea in regard to experience that is the result of untruth or exaggeration, and when he occasionally met another man who had really been a soldier and they talked a few minutes in the dressing room at a dance he fell into the easy pose of the old soldier among other soldiers: that he had been badly, sickeningly frightened all the time. In this way he lost everything.

Line 5, *10*, *15*, *20*, *25*, *30*, *35*, *40*

Essay Question

How do the stories that Krebs feels compelled to tell damage his sense of integrity and authenticity? What does he lose by telling his war stories to an audience that cannot comprehend what he has been through?

16–17 **Belleau Wood, Soissons, the Champagne, St. Mihiel, and in the Argonne:** sites of horrific battles that ended World War I

from Joseph Andrews
Henry Fielding

Background and Purpose

Henry Fielding, a well-educated eighteenth-century Englishman of aristocratic descent, wrote many comedies and political satires for the stage, and is now best known for his novel *Tom Jones*. *Joseph Andrews*, the novel from which this passage is taken, is a broadly comic romance using Cervantes's mock-heroic Don Quixote as a model for Parson Adams. Like Cervantes's masterpiece, it is a comedy of the road.

Mr *Adams* and *Joseph* were now ready to depart different ways, when an Accident determined the former to return with his Friend. . . . This Accident was, that those Sermons, which the Parson was traveling
Line to *London* to publish, were, O my good Reader, left behind; what he had
5 mistaken for them in the Saddle-Bags being no other than three Shirts, a pair of Shoes, and some other Necessaries, which Mrs. *Adams*, who thought her Husband would want Shirts more than Sermons on his Journey, had carefully provided him.

This Discovery was now luckily owing to the Presence of *Joseph* at
10 the opening of the Saddle-Bags; who having heard his Friend say, he carried with him 9 Volumes of Sermons, and not being of the Sect of Philosophers, who can reduce all the Matter of the World into a Nut-shell, seeing there was no room for them in the Bags, where the Parson had said they were deposited, had the Curiosity to cry out,
15 'Bless me, Sir, where are your Sermons?' The Parson answer'd, 'There, there Child, there they are, under my Shirts.' Now it happened that he had taken forth his last Shirt, and the Vehicle remained visibly empty. 'Sure, Sir,' says *Joseph*, 'there is nothing in the Bags.' Upon which *Adams* starting, and testifying some surprise,
20 cry'd, 'Hey! Fie, fie upon it; they are not here sure enough. Ay, they are certainly left behind.'

Joseph was greatly concerned at the Uneasiness which he apprehended his Friend must feel from his Disappointment: he begged him to pursue his Journey, and promised he would himself return with the
25 Books to him, with the utmost Expedition. 'No, thank you, Child,' answered *Adams*, 'it shall not be so. What would it avail me, to tarry in the Great City, unless I had my Discourses with me, which are, *ut ita dicam*, the sole Cause, the *Aitia monotate* of my Peregrination. No, Child, as this Accident hath happened, I am resolved to return back to
30 my Cure, together with you; which indeed my Inclination sufficiently leads me to. This Disappointment may, perhaps, be intended for my

---

27–28 **ut ita dicam:** Latin for "so to speak"

28 **Aitia monotate:** Greek for "sole cause"

Good.' He concluded with a Verse out of *Theocritus*, which signifies no more than, *that sometimes it rains and sometimes the sun shines*.

35   *Joseph* bowed with Obedience, and Thankfulness for the Inclination which the Parson express'd of returning with him; and now the Bill as called for, which, on Examination, amounted within a Shilling to the Sum Mr *Adams* had in his Pocket. Perhaps the Reader may wonder how he was able to produce a sufficient Sum for so many Days: that he may not be surprized therefore, it cannot be

40 unnecessary to acquaint him, that he had borrowed a Guinea of a Servant belonging to the Coach and Six, who had been formerly one of his Parishioners, and whose Master, the Owner of the Coach, then lived within three Miles of him: for so good was the Credit of Mr *Adams*, that even Mr *Peter* the Lady *Booby's* Steward would have

45 lent him a Guinea with very little security.

Essay Question

Characterize Parson Adams based on his words and actions, the narrator's tone, especially his attitude toward Adams, and the parson's reputation among other people.

---

40 **Guinea:** one pound, one shilling, an enormous sum which would take a servant many months to earn

Fiction

1

from The Things They Carried

Tim O'Brien

Analysis of Skill Questions

1. The Rocket Pocket is "like a two-week vacation" at a resort because it is on the South China Sea, with "white beaches and palm trees and friendly little villages." There are no casualties, no contact with the enemy at all. We can infer that the other areas of operation are the opposite: there is no sea breeze, in fact nothing comfortable or beautiful about the environment; the villages are extremely unfriendly; and there is frequent hostile contact with the enemy, resulting in many casualties. The soldiers can never relax or let down their guard because their lives are always in danger.

2. This safe and comfortable place, where the grunts can relax and do nothing more taxing than have a dental checkup, is for Curt Lemon the battleground which most threatens him and tests his courage. Because his ordeal is the opposite of what we would expect, it represents irony of situation.

3. The narrator makes clear that he "found it hard to mourn" when Curt Lemon was killed. What little he knows of Lemon is "not impressive." Instead of characterizing Lemon as a "tough soldier," he says that he played that role, "posturing" and "puffing himself up." From the narrator's perspective, Lemon played the role all too well, putting himself in danger with "stunts" such as the Halloween escapade, which did not help the war effort. The narrator depicts Lemon as a braggart who exaggerated his own courage, and wonders whether the man suf-

fered from conceit or from low self-esteem; in fact, the narrator's manner of telling of the story of the dentist argues that he considers Lemon ridiculous. He opines that "Anyone else would've laughed it off, but for Curt Lemon it was too much," and "The embarrassment must've turned a screw in his head." The very choice of the anecdote is revealing: The narrator tells the story to prevent himself from becoming "sentimental about the dead." He feels that in the case of a foolish and cowardly braggart, excessive sorrow is unwarranted. The narrator's tone is far from sentimental. He tells the story of Lemon and the dentist in a scornful way, slanted to make the reader see the subject in a ridiculous light. Therefore, the tone of the story is critical.

4. The Army dentist, a "tall, skinny young Captain," could hardly be less threatening. Ironically, the young dentist has bad breath. His mission is far from frightening: he is looking for minor dental problems that he can fix quickly, with little equipment, and this "assembly-line dentistry" is "quick and impersonal." It is ironic that the "tough soldier," who "pulled off some dangerous stunts" in life-threatening situations, would be afraid of this skinny man and his "battery-powered drill." Lemon is not so tough as he waits his turn outside the field tent; though he talks the talk, "Nobody messes with *these* teeth," he meekly enters the tent when it is his turn. It is ironic that the man who "went out trick-or-treating on Halloween," putting himself very much in harm's way just for fun, should faint before the dentist has a chance to touch him.

5. The story's theme is made clear by Lemon's smile the morning after his tooth is pulled. He exemplifies the boy who is unsure of his masculinity, and who goes to elaborate lengths to prove that he has all the requisite qualities to be considered a man. O'Brien's ridicule and his striking presentation of the irony of Lemon's situation suggests that physical courage is not the ultimate test of "manliness," and that facing the dentist's "torture" does not make Lemon more of a man and less of a fool.

Guidelines for Responding to the Essay Question

An explication explores the literary techniques that shape the reader's response to a work of literature. A successful essay will comment on the details which characterize Lemon after he faints. The explication considers the tone of the text and how it is established.

- The explication will cite and analyze the objective descriptions that help characterize Lemon.

- The narrator's conjectures and interpretive remarks must also be taken into account, and analysis will lead to an inference about the tone.

- The analysis will consider the significance of this new information about character and comment on the ironies that surface in the final paragraph.

An appropriate conclusion will consider how the story's ending develops the theme of the story.

2 *from* Sula

Toni Morrison

Analysis of Skill Questions

1. Helene does not discover the reality of segregation until they change trains in Birmingham, Alabama and enter the deep South: there are no "colored toilets" in the trains or at the train stations. Eventually, she is in such distress that she "finally brought herself to speak about her problem" to "a black woman with four children," on a subject she would never speak of to anyone, much less someone that she seems to feel is her social inferior. She does not understand the woman's answer, and looks in vain at the small station for "a door that said COLORED WOMEN." She is prepared to encounter segregation of restaurants, swimming pools, water coolers, and toilet facilities, but it never occurs to her that members of her race would be denied facilities entirely. She would like to ask the white men who are "leaning on the railing," but she reads their "tongues curling around toothpicks" correctly, and does not encourage them to humiliate her. Though she utters very few words in this scene, Helene's diction tells us that she is a respectable member of the African American middle class. She uses the term *restroom*, a euphemism the woman doesn't respond to, and she is forced to change it to *toilet* in order to be understood.

2. The woman's eyes "fastened on the thick velvet collar, the fair skin, the high-tone voice." What we see through her eyes is a prosperous, light-skinned, educated African American woman from the North. She calls her "Ma'am" twice, as though speaking to her social superior. She then points, and vaguely answers, "Yonder," not telling her much more when she is misunderstood. She asserts their common humanity by calling attention to Helene's predicament, smiling "sympathetically" and asking, "Kin you make it?" It may be that Helene's lack of warmth or gratitude is what causes the woman to "stalk" to a field across the tracks without guiding her to "yonder."

3. The woman has four children, suggesting that she is of a lower social class than the fastidious Helene, who has one. She doesn't understand the word *restroom*, having no reason to use euphemisms. She cannot imagine a world larger than her own, one that includes racial integration, so she doesn't understand Helene's ignorance of her world: she sees no need to explain that African Americans must do without plumbing or even an outhouse when they travel. The woman simply accepts these indignities as a natural part of life. She is "black," and "fat," wears a "head rag," and speaks with the telling diction of the uneducated. She is also physically coarser than Helene, being darker, larger, and much more poorly dressed than Helene. If she attracts any attention from the loungers at the station, it is a very different sort of attention than Helene attracts.

4. The details of the first paragraph indicate that Helene and her daughter are not used to the discomfort of making do without beds or privacy. They have never even imagined a lack of modern toilet facilities nor been in the position of having to ask how to solve the problem this lack creates. The adverbs and verbs used throughout the passage are telling: Helene "finally brought herself to speak . . ."; she was "halfway expecting to see a comfort station"; she "nodded" instead of thanking the woman; she "slowly realized where 'yonder' was." The full horror of the situation is voiced in the humiliating word *squatted*.

Guidelines for Responding to the Essay Question

The thesis will indicate that even so brief a scene contains a complete story. Each element of the passage should then be identified, with relevant evidence, and its workings analyzed. The successful essay will explore the following:

- the protagonist and antagonists;
- the role played by the foil;
- the nature of the conflict(s);
- the motivations of the characters.

The conclusion will analyze in detail the last sentence of the passage, which resolves the conflict.

3 | *from* The Curious Incident of the Dog in the Night-Time

Mark Haddon

Analysis of Skill Questions

1. Christopher often can't figure out what people are trying to communicate. He lacks the capacity to read nonverbal signals, such as facial expressions and body language. He understands only the words that are spoken, and these deliver only a small part of the message. At the literal level, words often fail to convey the intended emotional message. Words can even represent the opposite of what the speaker means (as in verbal irony or sarcasm). Typically, people rely heavily on nonverbal communication; the signals are quite complex and subtle. Most of us learned them so early in life that we forget how much we must interpret in order to "read" someone's message.

2. Christopher's mind cannot go beyond the literal. A metaphor points out a similarity between two unlike things, and most human brains can transfer the attributes of one thing to the other and thus derive meaning from the comparison. For example, "a pig of a day" relies on our understanding that a pig has many negative connotations, and we transfer these to what the speaker means about the kind of day he or she had. Christopher thinks that a metaphor is merely a lie. Significantly, he does not produce any fresh metaphors but merely repeats trite expressions he has heard. He does not see the value in the comparison because he cannot make the comparison. For him, words have no connotations, and thus are stripped of their emotional content. Furthermore, he calls the fable of St. Christopher carrying the Christ child a lie because it is not a verifiable piece of history. Being limited to the literal, he is unable to understand the value of myth as a way of understanding reality or teaching ethics. He wants his name to denote himself, not realizing that the "self" others see can be understood only as a complex bundle of emotions, far beyond the literal.

3. People used to use derogatory words such as *moron* or *mongoloid idiot* when referring to "Special Needs." These labels had extremely negative connotations because they denoted people with brain damage whose behavior is not socially normative or acceptable. As society became more sensitive to those with disabilities, we start-

ed to label these individuals differently, calling them "retarded" or saying that they had "Down's syndrome." But then *these* words in turn took on negative connotations, because the unfortunates with brain damage still made us very uncomfortable, and we sought to distance ourselves from them. In some countries, the euphemism "Special Needs" began to be applied to all children with damaged brains, so, in turn, that term also became an insult. It seems to be a law of language that when we try to substitute a pleasant or neutral term for an offensive one, the euphemism soon takes on the connotation of the "nasty" word. It seems impossible to separate what we mean from how we feel. We can tell from Christopher's literal analysis of the situation that certain euphemisms, in this case "special needs," are not useful because they can prove insulting at worst, or at best, they are without meaning. In any case, simply altering the terminology does not alter our perceptions of the people to whom we apply these words.

Guidelines for Responding to the Essay Question

The introduction will address the production of dramatic irony in the text, which grows largely out of Christopher's communication problems. The successful essay will develop the argument that dramatic irony is produced by Christopher's limitations as he reflects on the complexity of language and its social uses. In your essay, consider the following points:

- Christopher's difficulties understanding nonverbal communication in daily social situations;

- The difference between figurative and literal language;

- How myths add to our understanding of the world;

- The richness that connotation gives our language;

- The use of euphemism, including its necessity and its limitations.

The conclusion will reflect on the reader's grasp of language, in comparison with that of Christopher.

from The Scarlet Letter

Nathaniel Hawthorne

Analysis of Skill Questions

1. The Puritan women are very much out in public, while propriety dictated that Victorian women, who were more refined, stayed at home. Certainly it would shock people of Hawthorne's day that wives and mothers would push their way nearer to the scaffold in the event of an execution. The Puritan women whom Hawthorne depicts have characters of "force and solidity." These women, born in England, are characterized as coarser not only in their morality but also in their physical traits, having "broad shoulders and well-developed busts [and] round and ruddy cheeks," unlike the "fainter bloom, a more delicate and briefer beauty, and a slighter phys-

ical frame" of their descendants. These colonizers are compared to "the man-like Elizabeth," England's greatest queen, who reigned only fifty years before Boston was settled. Their morality is no more refined than their English diet of beef and ale. The "paler and thinner" women of Hawthorne's age would be "startled" by the "boldness and rotundity of speech among these matrons," both its content and its volume. The Puritan women are decidedly *not* ladylike in the Victorian sense.

2. We can predict the responses of various characters in the passage by noting details about their age, appearance, and disposition. The "hard-featured dame of fifty" begins by suggesting that mature women like her should be the ones to sentence adulteresses. It is not unusual for women in any age and culture who have lost their youth, good looks, and romantic notions to be envious of the young and beautiful. An "autumnal matron" (notice the metaphor) agrees: they should have branded Hester's forehead with the A, for she would be able to hide a mere token on her dress. Like the first speaker, she secretly envies Hester, and would like to disfigure her beautiful face. She also assumes that Hester would brazenly cover her sign of shame, as perhaps she herself would.

   On the other hand, a "young wife, holding a child by the hand," softly disagrees, saying that Hester's conscience will not be able to shake off her punishment so easily. Here is the only voice of sympathy, from one who is the mother of a child, not yet hardened and embittered by what lies in store for her in middle age.

   Finally, "the ugliest as well as the most pitiless" declares that Hester should die for bringing shame on all women. She cites both Scripture and the law, and assumes that only capital punishment will deter other women from committing adultery. If our analysis so far is correct, then the plainer and older the woman, the more judgmental she is of one who has everything she hasn't. Her opinion is not only without pity, but her morality is oversimplified in the extreme: beautiful young women are so inherently bad that the only way to keep them in line is to threaten them with death. The corollary is that she herself is righteously beyond reproach, backed by religion and law in her stern views.

3. The man's speech turns these judgments back on those who voice them: "Is there no virtue in women?" Will only fear of the gallows keep them honest and faithful? This rhetorical question renders poetic justice, shows us the narrator's attitude, and ushers in the first confrontation of the novel: Mistress Prynne, baby in arms and scarlet letter on bodice, is about to face the women among whom she will be living and rearing that child. The conflict is engaged, and the rising action has begun.

Guidelines for Responding to the Essay Question

A successful essay will provide evidence in support of the thesis: the tone of the narrative is negative toward the community, which is presented as antagonistic. Consider the following points:

- Hawthorne contrasts the Puritan women with the women of his era;

- The diction of the women in the crowd makes all but the young mother seem antagonistic in the extreme.

The concluding remarks of the man in the crowd sum up the tone of the passage.

5

from Jane Eyre

Charlotte Brontë

Analysis of Skill Questions

1. Pride and arrogance, the faults of a rigid character, are displayed in Mr. Brocklehurst's every word and action. He stands surveying the whole school "majestically." When he sees something of which he disapproves, he ostentatiously pretends to be "dazzled or shocked" at the sight and makes a rude comment, naming the offense: "red hair," and "curled—curled all over." His theatrical gesture of "extending his cane" with a "shaking" hand underscores this rudeness. Brocklehurst's accusatory sermon on the dangers of conforming to the world and allowing nature to have its way shows how narrow his religious tenets are, and how eager he is to force others to follow them. He calls Julia's beautiful hair an "excrescence," the ugliest connotation he can think of. He abruptly commands that she "turn round," and that all the older girls "rise up and direct their faces to the wall" so he can inspect their hair for indecent loveliness. Apparently he does not notice Miss Temple's handkerchief hiding her smile or consider that there might be "grimaces" on the faces of the girls. Brocklehurst's limited perceptions of others result from his rigid, narrow personality, deftly summed up in this scene by the sharp-eyed narrator.

2. In response to Mr. Brocklehurst's initial rude and dramatic outburst, Miss Temple's first reply is quiet, and her second "still more" quiet. She knows that she must humor this conceited boor. When he commands her to tell the girls to rise and face the wall, she must hide her amusement at his pomposity by placing her handkerchief over her lips. The narrator is able to see the faces of the girls, which are hidden from the great man. Their expressions reveal all too clearly what they think of the latest outburst of this bullying tyrant: by demanding total obedience to his arbitrary will, Brocklehurst forfeits even the most basic respect from the students.

3. The preacher does not understand that however clean a cup and platter might be on the outside, they may be far from spotless on the inside. It is ironic that Brocklehurst, who sees himself as a spiritual leader, is so ignorant of a powerful warning from the scripture. A further irony is that it is Jane, a young girl of no special piety, who aptly recalls this quotation. The metaphor compares the girls to the crockery: though they may be thoroughly scoured of all vanity until they look acceptably pious, no one can control the thoughts and emotions which lie deep inside. A further implication is that Brocklehurst should be far more concerned with the beliefs and feelings of his charges than with their outward appearance if he is really wishes to be their spiritual leader and save them from damnation.

4. There is a pivotal moment during which Mr. Brocklehurst is exposed as a hypocrite. If irony can be broadly defined as the *opposite* of what we expect, then this abrupt entrance of the fashionable Misses and Mrs. Brocklehurst in their elaborate clothing and hairdos represents irony of situation. Their entrance into the schoolroom immediately undercuts Brocklehurst's self-satisfied sermon on the evils of such worldly vanity, leaving the reader in no doubt as to the hollowness of his moral teachings.

Guidelines for Responding to the Essay Question

A successful essay will explore what the passage reveals about the class system and the attitude of the rich toward the poor. Develop each of the following points, using examples from the passage:

- Brocklehurst's double standard is displayed by the rules that he tries to impose on the charity students and by his manner of imposing them;

- The attitude of Miss Temple and the students toward the Brocklehursts, expressed in both words and gestures, reveals much about the double standard they live by.

A sound conclusion will summarize the implicit hypocrisy of Brocklehurst as a representative of his class, which aptly reflects the double standard that creates the tension in the passage.

6 *from* The Toughest Indian in the World

Sherman Alexie

Analysis of Skill Questions

1. Through the passage, we learn that Roman Fury is highly intelligent, resourceful, and filled with resentment toward the white culture that has victimized his people. Despite many obstacles, he has managed to educate himself and to achieve remarkable scores on the standardized aptitude test. Roman's achievement is a mark of his intelligence and ambition, because his circumstances are not conducive to success. Poverty and bitter experience have helped to form his character. Although life on the reservation is hard, Roman is proud of his heritage. Aware of the cultural bias of the CAT, he knows that he must be a warrior of a different kind if he is to defeat the white man during this confrontation.

2. The source of the external conflict in the story is cultural. Mr. Williams represents mainstream American culture, while Roman represents a minority perspective. Roman knows that Williams is stereotyping him by assuming that a poor Indian could never have achieved such a high test score on his own. The attitude of a man like Williams deals Roman a double injustice. Grappling all his life with poverty and a poor educational system, he now must contend with the contempt of a man who is his intellectual inferior. As an American Indian, Roman is made to feel marginalized; that makes his triumph all the more meaningful when he beats the white man at his own game of verbal and psychological intimidation. The test is one enemy, which he defeats handily. He then goes on to vanquish Williams with the white man's own weapon: the English language. The Mont Blanc pen and threatening body language are no match for Roman's anger and verbal brilliance. Further, when faced with a real antagonist, Roman forgets his internal conflict, the tension that comes of identifying with his own culture yet wanting success in the mainstream culture.

3. The author uses specific details to show that Roman, the poor boy from the reservation, is pitting himself against the powerful white culture of America. The man in the pin-striped suit wields a pen that is a status symbol and hides behind a ten-volume set of books that deal with intimidation. As Roman recognizes, the cir-

cumstances are designed to deprive a poor student of comfort, assurance, and a sense of being in command.

The private school is not convenient to a student living on a rural reservation. Its security guard is suspicious of an Indian, thinking him a potential vandal. The examination room is full of whites, except for the black student and the "ambiguously ethnic chick." The testing situation, most comfortable for private school students, is potentially frightening for minorities and rural students. The city setting contrasts sharply with the reservation. Roman and his grandmother have no dependable car, so Roman had ostensibly walked the 75 miles from the reservation to the private school. When his father died, he had to be buried in a brown suit, which must have been the only one he owned. His mother was buried in a purple dress, suggesting her own limited wardrobe. On the reservation, no one has much power.

4. Throughout the passage, language is used as a weapon to attack, disarm, or humiliate the enemy. Roman consistently uses sophisticated language and formal diction. The first sound Mr. Williams makes is "Hmmm," and the narrator comments, "as if the guttural were an important part of his vocabulary." The narrator seems to ask, who is the savage here? Roman, who knows that his extensive vocabulary is one of his great strengths, "wanted to be the first one to use a word actually found in *Webster's Dictionary*, Ninth Edition." A hostile, antagonistic tone is established, and the battle begins. When Williams learns that Roman's grandmother doesn't speak much English, he comments that Roman speaks it "well enough to score in the ninety-ninth percentile in the verbal section" of the CAT. Roman senses the suspicion underlying this remark and realizes that Williams has summoned him here to accuse him of cheating on the test. Williams then "picked up a Mont Blanc pen as if it were a weapon."

Roman strikes back by playing with Williams' words, turning the neutral "modest background" into "I've never been accused of modesty" and the insulting "calculating" into mathematical ability. Williams, on the other hand, relies largely on body language, puffing himself up and using the diminutive "son" to make Roman feel small. Roles are reversed: the white man uses a savage's physical power to "destroy" his "enemies" while the Indian uses the power of the white man's language. Roman has read Williams' body language bible and found it "derivative and ambiguous." His counter-attack is not physical; he uses hyperbole to take over the encounter as he spins a magical tale of a 75-mile walk, a 30-block run, a confrontation with the security guard, and his "fear" when he finds himself the only "Injun" in the testing room.

5. Throughout the passage, color is used to suggest vitality and authenticity, while lack of color is equated with deadness and insincerity. Mr. Williams is gray: "His teeth, skin, and pinstriped suit were all the same shade of gray. Roman couldn't tell where the three-season wool ended and where the man began." Williams is a suit, an empty figure of authority and power, colorless, not fully alive at his core, and so not to be trusted.

In contrast, Roman's "distracting" test-taking apparel is his "red, yellow, white, and blue grass-dance outfit." He explains that "My grandmother told me your little test was culturally biased, and that I might need a little extra power to do my best." The bright color of the Indian costume is a source of power for those who know what it symbolizes.

Roman's flashbacks of his parents' deaths and funerals are largely of color: yellow headlights, red truck, blue Chevy, brown suit; red blood, white handkerchief, purple dress. He recognizes the power of color, showing his keen sensitivity to the world around him. The author indirectly suggests that this sensitivity is Roman's inheritance from his culture. Even in their poverty, even in death, his people seem more fully alive and real than the pale administrator he encounters in the city.

Guidelines for Responding to the Essay Question

The thesis will sum up the protagonist's characteristics as they illuminate the theme of the passage. A successful essay will analyze:

- Roman's awareness of the victimization of his people;

- The fury and pride that Roman is heir to;

- Roman's conflict with the dominant society in the person of Mr. Williams, and the danger that his anger will get in the way of his goals;

- Roman's expert and aggressive use of language to undermine the power of his antagonist.

The conclusion will identify Roman's internal conflict, which is central to the meaning of the passage.

7

from Pride and Prejudice

Jane Austen

Analysis of Skill Questions

1. Collins' formal speech reflects his rigid, snobbish personality. Elizabeth comes close to laughing at him because he says, with "solemn composure," that he is afraid that he will be "run away with by his feelings." His words don't match his manner, and this ironic incongruity invites her ridicule.

2. Collins first refers to Lady Catherine as "the very noble lady whom I have the honour of calling patroness." He is in awe of her because of her social position, unconsciously painting her as a snob who doesn't let people forget her title. Collins is also impressed with Lady Catherine's power: she chose him to be the rector of the parish church, and apparently reminds him often that he owes his livelihood to her. She gives advice, unasked, that he should find a wife, but rather than resenting this impertinence, he says that she "condescended" to give him this invaluable recommendation. The second time she does so, she specifies that the wife must be a gentlewoman for her sake (so she will have suitable companionship other than a servant) as well has for his own: she must be "able to make a small income go a good way." Her major concession if he follows her advice will be to honor the new wife with a social call—another condescension that he thinks will thrill Elizabeth. Lady Catherine would doubtless agree that her "notice and kindness" are huge inducements to any prospective wife. Collins also tells his lively cousin that her "wit and vivacity I think must be acceptable to her, especially when tempered with the silence and respect which her rank will inevitably excite." The incongruity of this statement shows that Collins has learned from her ladyship that the most demure respect should be paid her. In short, Lady Catherine is an aristocratic snob with an inflated notion of her personal worth; she can easily dominate a social climber like Collins.

3. The pompous clergyman is the perfect vehicle for satire. As a suitor, there is nothing acceptable about Collins. His first reason for proposing to Elizabeth is impersonal and unemotional. To "set the example of matrimony" is the "right" social and moral action for a clergyman to take; Collins is nothing if not proper. His second reason is entirely selfish: "it will add very greatly to my happiness." A wife will make him more comfortable than a servant would, and requires no wages! His third reason, which he thinks is too low on the list, is that Lady Catherine has advised him to marry, and he values above all her good opinion. Because there is no other male heir to inherit the family estate, this dull cousin gets the entire fortune but intends to make up for the financial "loss to them, when the melancholy event takes place," through a marriage. This fourth reason is hardly a sound basis for a happy union between a man and a woman.

Finally, last on the list is "the violence of [his] affection," but the assurance Collins offers is flat, without any genuine emotion. Austen humorously has the clergyman refer to his wooden speech as "the most animated language." Collins undercuts even this tepid declaration of love by first blaming Elizabeth for her poverty, and then declaring that "no ungenerous reproach shall ever pass my lips" after the marriage has taken place. Has he forgotten that Elizabeth has no dowry because he himself gets all her father's fortune? Would anyone believe that he would not continue to reproach her?

4. In this passage, Austen gently satirizes the superficiality of conventional courtship and the marriage of convenience. She also challenges the prevailing assumption that a woman is always better off married than single. In Austen's world, marriage is a way to ally oneself with someone with social position and money. Austen's readers would have concurred that it is also not quite proper for a gentleman to remain unmarried, especially when the gentleman is a member of the clergy. Any woman of good family with the correct social graces would be a suitable marriage prospect. So Collins is typical in believing that no matter how modest a suitor's income or ridiculous his manner, a woman without a dowry will accept the gentleman's offer rather than remain unmarried.

Guidelines for Responding to the Essay Question

A successful essay will provide ample relevant evidence in support of the thesis, which is implied in the prompt: The dramatic irony of this passage is largely produced by Collins's use of language, such as diction, connotation, hyperbole, and syntax. The essay may be organized around several of these literary elements or in the order in which the evidence is presented in the passage. Consider:

- The effect of Collins's diction on the production of dramatic irony;

- The effect of Collins's hyperbole on the reader;

- The complicated syntax of Collins's sentences and its unintended effect on the reader.

A conclusion will sum up the disparity between the impression Collins intends to make and what he actually reveals about his character through his use of language.

8

from When the Emperor Was Divine
Julie Otsuka

Analysis of Skill Questions

1. The boy had been reassuring himself by smelling his father's scent, still lingering in the shoes he left behind, but this night the smell is gone. The detailed and intimate imagery of the passage conveys the immensity of the boy's loss and suggests the enormity of the government's action in separating them.

2. The FBI agents are dressed in "suits and ties and black fedoras," whereas his father is led away in bathrobe and slippers. The contrast suggests their power and his powerlessness. The description of the white house on the wide street near the sea, which smells of pine because the Christmas tree is up, suggests an all-American family. Ironically, in spite of his identification with American culture, the father is taken away in an ominously black car to be interrogated about his loyalty to the United States.

   Another contrast or incongruity lies in the way his father is dressed on this fateful day; his usual clothing is dignified, but he is forced from his home without proper shoes or hat. The boy sees his father as vulnerable without his hat, a symbol of white-collar status. The shabby slippers he wears also represent a loss of dignity and power, as well as a violation of privacy.

3. The boy remembers the agents' exact words with pain because they are so insulting to his father as well as to his mother. The racial slur "Papa-san" is the worst insult, appropriately delivered last.

4. Before she gets the father's note from the detention center, the mother had set the table for four and had hidden the house key outside the door in the hope that her husband would return home at any time. After her visit, she has lost that hope, and sets the table for three.

5. The mother takes seriously the information that "eighty-three Japanese have already been sent away on a train," so although the father asks only that she visit, she packs what he will need to get him through a long incarceration. There is pathos in the very ordinariness of the items, the little comforts that will not be available in the prison. What she *does not* pack is the proverbial file to aid his escape. Both husband and wife are passive and resigned to their fate—ironically, they are the opposite of dangerous enemy aliens. The mother's smiling in spite of her anxiety reassures her small son. She is able to consider his feelings and to try to make a mild joke about his father's humiliating circumstances.

6. The Sunday-best suit gives the father dignity to counteract his bathrobe. He asks to be remembered at his most formal and respectable, knowing how humiliating to his family his arrest has been. The boy remembers the bare head and the bathrobe and slippers because they accord with his father's disappointing behavior: no protests, no heroics, no efforts to protect his family or to even to stay with them.

   The silhouette in the back window of the car is "stiff and unmoving." His father does not look back, "not even once. Just to see if he was there." The boy very badly needs his father to act differently, to acknowledge his love and sorrow. But the father behaves with the stiff resolve of a proud man and remains the stoic.

Guidelines for Responding to the Essay Question

A successful essay will provide evidence that the boy's fantasy of reunion with his father reveals not only his deepest desires, but the depth of his loss and longing. It would include analysis of evidence such as:

- The details of how his father made the trip, including a description of his clothing;

- The imagined physical contact between father and son;

- The topics of conversation: the letters and the slippers;

- The imagery contained in the passage;

- The father's final words and actions;

- The use of understatement.

The conclusion will show that the fantasy represents the boy's attempt to resolve his fears and return his life to its normal state.

9 *from* The Adventures of Huckleberry Finn

Mark Twain

Analysis of Skill Questions

1. In this passage, Twain satirizes morbid romantic sentiments about death and mourning, particularly as expressed through bad art. Huck makes some amusing understatements about these lugubrious portraits, such as "They was different from any pictures I ever seen before—blacker, mostly than is common." Later he comments, "These was all nice pictures, I reckon, but I didn't somehow seem to take to them. . . ." He is damning the sentimental artwork with faint praise. His laconic comments show that Huck has correctly assessed the pictures even though he is just a country boy, supposedly ignorant and unformed in his opinions. These offhand observations achieve a satiric effect when contrasted with the family's worship of Emmeline's work.

2. Huck is unaware of how unromantic and thus inappropriate his word choices are. In his description of the first picture, Huck mentions "armpits" in the same breath as "slim black dress," undercutting the romantic picture. His mention of the "bulges" in the sleeves, which he compares to that lowly vegetable, a cabbage, take all the romance out of the image, as does the "scoop-shovel" shape of the bonnet. And the black ribbons around the slim ankles are attached to very wee black slippers, but the slippers are shaped "like a chisel." The second picture features a comb holding up a young lady's knot of hair, and Huck compares it to a chair back, an ordinary, if not grotesque, object of comparison. The occasion of the lady's grief, the death of a pet bird, also underscores the sense of the ridiculous in the passage. The bird is in her hand, "laying on its back . . . with its heels up." Those ludicrous stiff feet are as unappealing as the slippers like chisels.

Like a dousing in cold water, these clumsy words force the reader to see the false feeling in the pictures for what it is.

3. Huck does not recognize the clichés of romantic fiction and visual art, so he is impressed by the seriousness of Emmeline's chosen subjects. The mourner in each case is a young woman, a romantic heroine most susceptible to sentimentality. In describing the first picture, Huck mentions the young lady's black mourning dress, complete with black veil, her posture ("leaning pensive"), and the setting ("on a tombstone"), as well as her props, a white handkerchief (the better to weep), and a reticule, which may hold many more hankies. The second picture is of a young lady weeping over the death of her pet bird. Surely her response is unwarranted by the occasion—out of proportion to the situation—and thus comic. Huck reports that the third picture features a moon, tears running down cheeks, a letter with black sealing-wax (announcing a death), and a locket (containing a picture of the dear departed and/or a lock of his hair). The "greatest picture," the incomplete one, features "a long white gown," an incipient suicide from a bridge, another moon, and a mention of "her breast." Every cliché reminds the reader of the dishonesty of a sentimentalist, and gently mocks the conventions of romance.

4. The Grangerfords are convinced that their dead daughter's unfinished picture was her "greatest," which implies that they consider her an artist of remarkable talent. They keep the picture over her bed, "hid with a little curtain," and hang flowers on it to honor her birthdays. Twain leaves it to Huck to deflate this grandiosity. After describing the first three pictures, the young narrator admits that he "didn't somehow seem to take to them," and that "they always gave me the fan-tods," or fits. He reports that "a body could see by what she had done what they had lost," but his praise is indirect: does he see artistic talent in these portraits, or is he merely echoing the family's belief? Huck answers this question with his next remark: "But I reckoned that with her disposition she was having a better time in the graveyard." His final comment, about the unfinished fourth picture, is a fitting conclusion to the satire: "but there were so many arms it made her look too spidery, seemed to me."

Guidelines for Responding to the Essay Question

A successful essay will provide evidence of Emmeline's sentimentality and the way in which Huck's ignorance and honesty produce dramatic irony.

- Emmeline's pictures are the major evidence of her sentimentality, especially her choice of subject, her selection of detail, and the words she has provided under each picture.

- Huck's description of the pictures produces the dramatic irony through his use of figurative language, especially his metaphorical vehicles, his ignorance of clichés, his understatement, his attempt to share the family's taste, and his unguarded sharing of his true opinion.

The conclusion will show that in attempting to learn the appropriate response to death and in his honest responses to the pictures, Huck's is the perfect voice for exposing sentimentality.

10 *from* As I Lay Dying

William Faulkner

Analysis of Skill Questions

1. As Addie Bundren lies dying, Cash, who is a good carpenter, is making her coffin with hand tools right outside her bedroom window. From this section, we learn that Cash is skilled at his work and can infer that he is either out of touch with his emotions or that he suppresses his feelings so that he can work calmly in the hours before his mother's death.

2. Darl admires Cash's skill and the care he takes in making their mother's coffin. He notices the color and texture of the boards, and is sensitive to their beauty in the "shadow spaces." He has no doubt that Cash is doing a good thing, that such a well-built coffin will bring their mother "confidence and comfort." The sound made by the adze, "Chuck. Chuck. Chuck," comforts him as well. His reflections on his brother reveal that Darl makes the best of the situation and accepts people for what they are.

3. Jewel's hot temper, jealousy, and negativity are revealed in this section of the novel. He reads the same scene from a completely different angle, becoming outraged at the sight and sound of Cash's carpentry "right under her window," where their dying mother cannot ignore it. Jewel assumes that Cash's motive is to call Addie's attention to what a loving son and skillful carpenter he is: "See what a good one I am making for you." He is convinced that Cash wants their mother to die so he can see her body in his wonderful coffin. He compares the coffin-making to Cash's childhood attempt to please his mother by bringing her cow dung from the barn when she wished to plant flowers. Knowing Jewel's negative bias, we are left to infer that in his longing to be everything to his mother, he judges Cash much too harshly.

   Jewel's interior monologue shows that his animosity is not directed solely at Cash. He calls the visiting neighbors "buzzards," hovering over the dying woman. He reveals that the noise of the "sawing and nailing" keeps *him* awake. He objects to his sister's fanning, assuming that the breeze it creates is hard for their dying mother to breathe. He hears the sound of the adze as an unpleasant reminder of time passing ("one lick less"), and considers it Cash's attempt to call the attention of passersby to himself and his fine carpentry.

   Jewel wishes above all to be alone with his mother, isolated on a high hill, hurling rocks in the faces of those who attempt to approach. He fantasizes a scene in which she is at peace, alone with him. Jewel is jealous of anyone else's claims on her attentions, especially those of his siblings.

4. When Cash announces that he is going to bevel the edges of the planks, Vernon Tull protests that beveling will take more time, but, after studying Cash, hands him the plane with no further protest. There's no point in arguing: Cash cannot be talked out of his perfectionism. He does the beveling "with the tedious and minute care of a jeweler" in the heavy rain and the dark, after working nearly around the clock.

   When Mrs. Tull comes to the porch and asks not the taciturn Cash but her husband Vernon when the coffin will be finished, Vernon does not look up, evading the conflict between those in the house who want Addie's body put in the coffin immediately and the son who is using all his skill and patience to do a fine piece of carpentry for his mother. She makes the practical suggestion that they use planks from the barn to finish quickly and get out of the rain. Vernon stands with Cash, and, after watching the two for a while, Mrs. Tull goes back into the house in defeat. Cash continues his work, ignoring the rain and the dark and the wishes of everyone else. Tull repeats the suggestion to Cash, but Cash ignores it.

When he finally finishes, the others watch him: he doesn't speak much, so they have trained themselves to look for clues about what's going on inside of him. They are rewarded with a facial expression and a gesture: "his face is calm, musing; slowly he strokes his hands on his raincoated thighs in a gesture deliberate, final, and composed." As soon as the coffin has been carried inside, while Peabody is speaking of a snack, Cash goes back outside to gather and clean his tools "carefully," evidence that the tools are a part of him and that their care is of far more practical import than the need of a snack. All of these details reveal that his emotional range is quite narrow, and that he keeps his focus on his carpentry, his way of expressing his feelings.

Guidelines for Responding to the Essay Question

The thesis invites several ways of organizing an essay, but if the three passages are treated in turn, attitudes toward the brothers can be presented in order. In your essay, consider the following points:

- Darl's interior monologue in the first passage shows his character traits directly, and his diction, use of understatement, and selection of detail indirectly begin to engage our interest in his family and their situation.

- Jewel's interior monologue shows both how he feels about his siblings and others and how he responds to his mother's dying. His diction, figurative language, and selection of detail create a strong impression.

- Darl's omniscient description of the finishing of the coffin on the night of Addie's death characterizes Cash through his diction, selection of detail, and indirect comparison of Cash and the others.

The conclusion will evaluate the effects of Faulkner's techniques for engaging us with his characters. It may also explore why the author took pains to create differences in our responses to the three brothers.

11

from Somebody's Luggage

Charles Dickens

Analysis of Skill Questions

1. The waiter is kindly giving instructions about "his calling," assuming, with comic effect, that his audience is eager to know how to become a waiter. Only a naive narrator would make the assumption that his experiences are of universal interest, or use such an informal narrative mode. A high degree of intimacy with the reader is achieved, and we are entertained as well as enlightened.

2. Paraphrase: In early infancy, when all you understood was hunger, you were smuggled into the pantry of a restaurant to be nursed by your waitress mother.

    The complex syntax is quite formal and elevated, to say the least. The diction is similarly elevated: "conveyed," "harbour vacancy," "surreptitious," "healthful sustenance," "female constitution." The overall effect is mixed because the meaning of the sentence is simple and the actions it describes are easily understood, but the style is quite pompous. The manner (formal, elevated) and the matter (a waitress secretly nursing her baby while at work) are so at odds that Dickens creates comedy with this incongruity. A satiric tone is suggested by the contrast between appearance and reality as the plain meaning of the sentence deflates the high tone of the narrator.

3. The grandmother is four times called "unwilling," a direct contradiction of the usual stereotype of doting care. She uses her shawl to smother your infant cries instead of offering comfort. She shakes you when you have colic instead of rocking you, and her death is the occasion of thanksgiving. This hyperbolic contrast between appearance and reality is both comic and satiric.

4. The setting is first described by its smells: "roast and boiled, and soup, and gas, and malt liquors": not a very wholesome mixture. Furthermore, the pantry is littered with "cruets, dirty plates, dish-covers, and cold gravy," sights that are unappetizing, to say the least. The sound of your mother's voice is not "soothing you with nursery rhymes," but rather "calling down the pipe for veals and porks" as she loudly puts in her orders to the kitchen.

    The tone created by this imagery lies in the contrast between what an infant needs (a quiet, peaceful atmosphere for nursing), and what this one gets (a noisy, smelly, cluttered place), thus creating both comedy and satire.

5. Once "your brothers began to appear," and the mother could no longer work as a waitress, her reason for showing up at the back door "was of a housekeeping character." This can only mean that she needed money to support the household. The best evidence is that the restaurant was "going down then," losing its popularity (no wonder: it's "shabby" and has a dreadful name), and "your father took but little," meaning that he didn't earn much, so money was tight. But if the father "took" few tips, he "took" plenty "from a liquid point of view," suggesting that he was drinking up his earnings.

6. Again Dickens uses incongruity to produce a comic and satiric tone. To be unacknowledged by one's own father, having to loiter at the back door of the restaurant in order to beg for sustenance, being unwilling to confess even "under torture" that you know your father, all are hyperbole that produce humor, albeit of a pathetic sort. That the narrator, rather than suffering from the neglect inherent in the secrecy, is attracted to the mystery of being a "close secret," produces irony and satire.

    The hyperbole in the description of the father's living quarters produces comedy as well as satire: "a damp compartment," "behind a leaky cistern," in "a sort of cellar," with a "sink in it, and a smell, and a plate-rack and a bottle-rack, and three windows . . . , and no daylight." This dark, dank, smelly hole sounds like a dungeon. Nobody deserves to live in these conditions, but, ironically, the waiter's children are all attracted to his occupation by the living conditions.

Guidelines for Responding to the Essay Question

A successful essay will provide ample and relevant evidence in support of the thesis.

A close analysis of the narrator's syntax and diction and their effect on the reader will establish Dickens' use of comedy and irony in producing his satire. Devices such as hyperbole, imagery, and choice of details are also useful evidence.

The comic tone produced by the diction and syntax will be described, then illustrated with one or two strong examples.

Several examples of imagery and hyperbole will be offered in support of the thesis.

An analysis of the mildly comic effect and poignant tone of Dickens' satire utilizes the details selected as evidence.

The conclusion will sum up the satiric effect produced by the mixture of comedy and irony.

12 *from* The Dubliners

James Joyce

Analysis of Skill Questions

1. The evening "invades" the avenue, as darkness and shadow mirror Eveline's sadness and fatigue. She smells "the odor of dusty cretonne," of the layers of dirt and grime, suggesting years of unchanging stagnation in the house. At the end of the street there used to be a field where she played, but it is now a row of "bright brick houses with shining roofs," not like her "little brown house." Its size and color sum up its atmosphere, yet she remembers that "they seemed to have been rather happy then." As she looks around the room, she sees the same objects "which she had dusted once a week for so many years," and though this detail may suggest stagnation to the reader, Eveline thinks regretfully that "Perhaps she would never see again those familiar objects from which she had never dreamed of being divided." The "yellowing" photograph of the priest and the "colored print" of an Irish saint suggests that religion is central to this house, but long ago the priest emigrated, and she seems to regret that she has never learned his name, suggesting that her religious devotion has not left with him. The "broken harmonium" suggests that what pleasure might once have come from music and a harmonious family life is long in the past, but Eveline seems to cling to her memories of that past.

2. "Their father used often to hunt them in out of the field with his blackthorn stick": if this behavior is "not so bad" compared to his current behavior, and if the children "seemed to have been rather happy then," things must have worsened considerably in the years following her mother's death, yet Eveline seems to find pleasure remembering the days when "her father was not so bad." She finds nothing good about the changes: "Her mother was dead. Tizzie Dunn was dead, too, and the Waters had gone back to England. Everything changes. Now she was going to go away like the others, to leave her home."

   Without her brothers to take the beatings and thus protect her, she is far more vulnerable to her father's violent and abusive threats, especially "of a Saturday night" when he is "especially bad," yet her thoughts about this drunken and violent man's behavior are only that this regular abuse, which she understates by calling a "squabble," "had begun to weary her unspeakably." She seems to take as her rightful duty the handing over of "her entire wages" to her father, working outside her home, and doing all the marketing, cooking, cleaning, and childcare. Eveline is clearly conflicted about her father. She is afraid of his threats of violence ("She knew it was that that had given her the palpitations"), yet he demands of her what he did of his wife—to consider his needs before her own—and she never questions his expectations.

3. Eveline's mother was a dutiful wife and mother. She was not treated with respect by her husband. She died leaving young children. Dutiful in the extreme, taking abuse from her husband, she does not get his respect in return, and her plight should be a strong warning to Eveline to get away at the first opportunity. Yet Eveline accepts her duty as the oldest daughter to take on the role of her dead mother, not only accepting her tasks, but also her poor treatment by the head of the household.

4. Eveline is treated disrespectfully both by her supervisor at work and her father at home. She imagines that she will not be working outside her home once she is a wife, and that her husband will not become drunken and violent. "In her new home, in a distant unknown country," everything would be different: with the change would come the absence of the old expectations of her and the weight of responsibilities, offering the possibility of more options than her job as a shop girl, and, in her new role as a wife, respectful treatment. She would put distance between herself and her father's violence.

Guidelines for Responding to the Essay Question

The thesis will make a clear statement about what we learn from the first half of the story that foreshadows Eveline's decision to stay home. The memories and feelings that come to Eveline on the eve of her departure are clues to her eventual decision. In your essay, refer to the following:

- Evidence of Eveline's acquiescence to the values and mores of her home, including her duty as the eldest daughter, supports an interpretation of her character;

- Evidence of Eveline's devotion to the past and to her mother's memory supports the general characterization;

- Examples of Eveline's ambivalent attitude toward her father's behavior helps to explain her decision;

- Eveline's level of comfort in her present situation and her fear of the unknown provides evidence of her timidity.

The conclusion will weigh the evidence in favor of staying against the promise and potential problems of a new life.

13 *from* The Witness

Katherine Ann Porter

Analysis of Skill Questions

1. The first two paragraphs supply many details that reveal the setting. Since Uncle Jimbilly is repairing harness, carriage tops, and plows, he lives on a farm that is not particularly prosperous ("making them over and making them do"): we are told that he was born into slavery and understand that the farm is somewhere in the South. Because he is now very old, but carriages and plows are still used, the time must be during the first few decades of the twentieth century.

2. The first half of the story focuses on Uncle Jimbilly, its protagonist, with only a brief and indirect reference to those who try to open his stiff hands and who request tombstones for their ceremonial funerals of little creatures. The reader can make the inference that they are children, but they are not characterized until later. The children come to Uncle Jimbilly to ask a favor, and they listen to his stories.

3. The story is told by a narrator who seems to share the naivete of the children and should not be considered wholly reliable; certainly the narrator is not omniscient. This type of narrator is appropriate here because the story hinges upon our awareness that Uncle Jimbilly is not the faintly ridiculous figure perceived by the children (and the narrative voice so closely identified with them) but rather a tragic witness to horrors beyond the imagination. The narrative voice refers to those who interact with Uncle Jimbilly as "a child," "one," "you," "a credulous child," "somebody," and "everybody." In every case the narrator is identified with the three white children and reveals nothing to the reader but what the children grasp about the situation. Their naivete produces the tensions and ironies in the story. The gap between what the narrator understands and what the reader is meant to understand results in dramatic irony.

4. The author's attitude toward the subject of slave atrocities is not implicit in the narrative voice, nor in the responses of the children. It can be found by examining the patterns of imagery, the connotations of the vivid diction, and the syntax of the protagonist, as well as the structure of the text. These elements reveal the compassion of the author for Uncle Jimbilly, the survivor of the inhuman institution of slavery. Uncle Jimbilly's centrality to the story—it is his voice that predominates and sets the tone—reflects Porter's condemnation of whites who fostered the institution or merely stood by and allowed the abuses to take place. Thus, while the narrator's tone is ingenuous and naïve, the overall tone of the story is one of outrage.

   The title suggests that Uncle Jimbilly is literally witnessing to the atrocities perpetrated on the very soil owned by the white children's family. But "The Witness" may also suggest that the descendents of the slaveholders are on trial: they "wiggle" and feel "guilty." Uncle Jimbilly was powerless to complain to the perpetrators of the murders much less bring them to justice: he was owned by them.

5. Because the story has no clear plot, it must be structured in some other way. The author describes habitual action (what Uncle Jimbilly typically did or said

when the children were with him) with representative examples. The story's meaning is revealed by this structure, in which the trivial alternates with the tragic. Two very different situations are juxtaposed: the natural deaths of a few little creatures, and the torture and murder of tens of thousands of human beings under the slave system. The children's pets are given the dignity of "proper ceremonies" with "the cart draped as a hearse, a shoe-box coffin with a pall over it, a profuse floral outlay, and, of course, a tombstone." Uncle Jimbilly joins in with their play, taking trouble to carve a flower, "smoothing the back and sides" of the "tombstone," refusing only to carve "Safe in Heaven" for a "tame jackrabbit." While he is doing so, he speaks to the children of the deaths of humans, first in vague ghost stories, next of slaves beaten nearly to death, and finally of those tortured to death in the swamps. And he does so, we are told, "in a low, broken, abstracted murmur, as if to himself"; but the narrator is careful to make us understand that "he was really saying something he meant one [i.e., the children] to hear." Uncle Jimbilly's young audience is unable to grasp the significance of the stories told in earnest about real events, and the dramatic irony is produced by the narrator's having no more understanding than they.

6. The children's embarrassed, confused response to the former slave's tales is symbolic of the white South in later years: vaguely uneasy, disbelieving, and finally culpable of suppressing a tragic history. Uncle Jimbilly is himself a symbol of dehumanization; he has been transmuted from slave to servant. Like the symbolic tame jackrabbit, Uncle Jimbilly has been subdued and is now an entertainer of children, a type of pet. Yet, as with the rabbit, a creature originally wild, there is much more in the man's nature than the children comprehend.

   The symbolic power of the narrative lies in Uncle Jimbilly's reports. Long ago, he was powerless to complain to the perpetrators of the murders much less bring them to justice: he was their property and as such had no voice. His murmurings symbolize this lack of voice, of power over his fate, and Uncle Jimbilly represents many thousands of slaves. He is just as powerless to express his horror and outrage to the children's parents. So he is indirect: he tells his stories to the children.

7. What Uncle Jimbilly doesn't say has great significance. Does he or anyone know the names and numbers of the dead, even on this one farm? Were there funeral ceremonies of any kind? Was any human dignity awarded to them at their deaths? Are there tombstones for them out in the swamp? The specific facts are not told, perhaps because they are shrouded by the passage of time, perhaps because even now, the black man with the secrets is powerless to accuse the descendants of white slaveholders. The ironic juxtaposition of the bunny's funeral and the deaths of uncounted anonymous human beings is central to the story. Uncle Jimbilly is trying to make the descendants of the slaveholders understand and care about "the horrors of slave times." He is the witness, and he is witnessing to the children, challenging the social order and the complacency of whites. The author's judgment of slaveholders is indirect, but clear. The rambling narration and seemingly random nature of Uncle Jimbilly's stories serve to lead the reader to confront the full horror of slavery.

Guidelines for Responding to the Essay Question

A successful essay will posit that characterization is key to the story's theme, and will analyze the effects of both direct and indirect characterization. It will focus on Uncle

Jimbilly and the narrator, but consider also the scenes in which Uncle Jimbilly and the children interact.

- Direct characterization provides a wealth of detail about Uncle Jimbilly as well as a basic understanding of the relationship he has with the children;

- Uncle Jimbilly and the children are characterized indirectly by their dialogue and actions;

- Uncle Jimbilly's motivation is suggested by his interaction with the children;

- The narrator's point of view and its limitations are a source of dramatic irony;

- The narrator comes between Uncle Jimbilly and the author, but the two share the same motivation.

The conclusion will consider how the author's viewpoint reveals the theme.

English Literature

Drama

Part II of this book offers practice in how to approach a scene from a play. Drama shares with fiction such key elements as plot, characterization, and dialogue. However, readers of a play have only a script in hand and so must imagine the fully realized production of the drama on stage. The script is like a musical score containing notes and instructions that direct the artist to perform the piece appropriately. Our task is to learn to read cues so that we see and hear in our imaginations an approximation of the playwright's vision for a stage production.

Conventions of the Drama — The dramatic action is divided into acts and scenes, which indirectly indicate the passage of time or a change of place. Within each act, there is a variable number of scenes. Stage productions cannot depend on car chases, panoramic views, close-ups, or more than a very few changes of scene; flashbacks and antecedent action are conveyed only through dialogue or changes of scenery and costume. Serious drama in particular tends to shun the use of flashy and elaborate stage sets, which, although entertaining for popular audiences, distract from meaning.

When all else is stripped away from theater, dialogue and action remain. Few modern plays employ narrators to provide exposition. Accordingly, the drama is an enactment of words and actions without direct commentary or explanation. Older forms of drama often relied on the prologue, in which an actor explains the occasion of the play or recapitulates the antecedent action. In most contemporary theater, speeches, gestures, and movements must carry the burden of meaning. Modern playwrights rarely depend on the highly artificial conventions of the aside or the soliloquy, devices that allow a character to speak to the audience directly. So we must interpret the characters' thoughts and motivations through the cues provided by the dramatist.

Theatrical Properties, or "Props" — The stage directions in a script provide vital information about the theatrical components used in producing the play on stage. The author usually indicates how the set must look and provides directions about the kinds of stage properties that create a sense of place and time. Lighting and music may convey the time, mood, and atmosphere. Such useful cues as costuming and makeup may be specified. Some sets are realistic representations, some are stark, merely hinting at the locale, whereas others are simply bare stages. Plays written when theaters had no sets at all require us to listen closely to the words that help us imagine the setting. Some theaters have seating in the round. Shakespeare's had no curtain. Historically, dramatists have had to consider physical limitations that affect no other literary genre.

Stage Directions — The playwright's notes are important to stagecraft because these help actors to understand the author's intent and to interpret their characters using verbal and nonverbal communication effectively. Stage directions often specify speech rhythm and intonation as well as pacing: adverbs abound as actors are directed about how to say their lines. Gesture, facial expression, and movement are often specified in stage directions, too.

A Useful Note — From the point of view of the actor facing the audience, stage directions refer to upstage and downstage (away from and toward the audience, respectively), stage right and left, center stage, stage apron (in front of the curtain), and proscenium (the arch that forms the fourth wall).

If we read a play with the attention we give to fiction or poetry, pausing to consider the significance of all stage directions, we will be able to come to a reasonable interpretation of the dramatic whole. A play on stage is already interpreted for us. No two productions are alike, and we may forever picture and hear the voice of the first Hamlet or Nora that we see. A reader, on the other hand, has the opportunity to be producer and director, and to play all the roles in his or her imagination.

14 *from* The Glass Menagerie

Tennessee Williams

lesson

Background and Purpose

Tennessee Williams is one of the giants of the American theater. His young adulthood was in some ways like Tom's in *The Glass Menagerie*: he worked in a shoe factory while trying to make a name for himself as a writer. But in the play, Tom's father has long ago abandoned the family, and Tom's salary is his family's main support. Tom lives with his mother, Amanda, and his shy and withdrawn sister, Laura. According to the stage directions, their apartment *"faces an alley and is entered by a fire-escape."* Along with the alleys, garbage cans, and tangled clotheslines, which are visible at the start and close of the play, the fire-escapes provide *"an accidental poetic truth, for all of these huge buildings are always burning with the slow and implacable fires of human desperation."*

The play opens with Tom in the uniform of a merchant sailor, addressing the audience in the theatrical convention of narrator. The setting is the Great Depression of the 1930s, when workers in St. Louis were striking, sometimes violently. The audience understands that Tom has enlisted in the armed services and has left his troubled family behind. Further stage directions in the passage explain the context of the quarrel between mother and son, the positions of the actors on the stage, and the lighting: *"Before the scene is lighted, the violent voices of TOM and AMANDA are heard. They are quarreling behind the portieres. In front of them stands LAURA with clenched hands and a panicky expression. A clear pool of light is on her figure throughout this scene."*

	AMANDA:	What is the matter with you, you—big—big—IDIOT!
	TOM:	Look!—I've got *no thing*, no single thing—
	AMANDA:	Lower your voice.
Line	TOM:	In my life here that I can call my OWN! Everything is—
5	AMANDA:	Stop that shouting!
	TOM:	Yesterday you confiscated my books! You have the nerve to—
	AMANDA:	I took that horrible novel back to the library—yes! That hideous book by that insane Mr. Lawrence. [*TOM laughs wildly.*] I cannot control the output of diseased minds or people who cater to them—[*TOM laughs still more wildly.*] BUT I WON'T ALLOW SUCH FILTH BROUGHT INTO MY HOUSE! No, no, no, no, no!
10		
	TOM:	House, house! Who pays rent on it, who makes a slave of himself to—
15		

Using Skills to Understand the Passage

1. What do the stage directions for the actors' speaking parts add to your understanding of how the scene would be performed? How do these directions illuminate the emotional content of the words and the attitude with which they should be spoken?

9 **Mr. Lawrence:** D.H. Lawrence's novels, which had been banned, were newly published and considered by many to be shockingly explicit about human sexuality.

AMANDA	[*fairly screeching*]:	Don't you DARE to—
TOM:		No, no *I* mustn't say things. *I've* got to just—
AMANDA:		Let me tell you—
TOM:		I don't want to hear any more! [*He tears the portieres open. The upstage area is lit with a turgid smoky red glow.* AMANDA's *hair is in metal curlers and she wears a very old bathrobe, much too large for her slight figure, a relic of the faithless Mr. Wingfield. An upright typewriter and a wild disarray of manuscripts is on the drop-leaf table. The quarrel was probably precipitated by* AMANDA's *interruption of his creative labor. A chair lies overthrown on the floor. Their gesticulating shadows are cast on the ceiling by the fiery glow.*]
AMANDA:		You *will* hear more, you—
TOM:		No, I won't hear more, I'm going out!
AMANDA:		You come right back in—
TOM:		Out, out, out! Because I'm—
AMANDA:		Come back here, Tom Wingfield! I'm not through talking to you!
TOM:		Oh, go—
LAURA	[*desperately*]:—Tom!	
AMANDA:		You're going to listen, and no more insolence from you! I'm at the end of my patience.
TOM	[*comes back toward her*]:	What do you think I'm at? Aren't I supposed to have any patience to reach the end of, Mother? I know, I know. It seems unimportant to you, what I'm *doing*—what I *want* to do—having a little *difference* between them. You don't think that—
AMANDA:		I think you've been doing things that you're ashamed of. That's why you act like this. I don't believe that you go every night to the movies. Nobody goes to the movies night after night. Nobody in their right minds goes to the movies as often as you pretend to. People don't go to the movies at nearly midnight, and movies don't let out at two A.M. Come in stumbling. Muttering to yourself like a maniac! You get three hours' sleep and then go to work. Oh, I can picture the way you're doing down there. Moping, doping, because you're in no condition.
TOM	[*wildly*]:	No, I'm in no condition!
AMANDA:		What right have you got to jeopardize your job? Jeopardize the security of us all? How do you think we'd manage if you were—
TOM:		Listen! You think I'm crazy about the *warehouse*? [*He bends fiercely toward her slight figure.*] You think I want to spend fifty-five *years* down there in that—*celotex interior!* With—*fluorescent—tubes!* Look! I'd rather somebody picked up a crowbar and battered out my brains—than go back mornings! I *go!*

Line numbers in left margin: 20, 25, 30, 35, 40, 45, 50, 55, 60

Using Skills to Understand the Passage

2. Stage directions also help us imagine what we would be seeing the actors do on stage. How do directions about movements and gestures increase our understanding of the scene?

3. Directions are also given about scenic design, stage properties, and costumes as well as lighting. How do these technical directions establish the mood of the play and determine our reactions to the scene?

4. Characterize Amanda. What does her language tell you about her personality, her values, and her motivations? How do these factors clarify Tom's conflict and point toward its resolution?

Essay Question

Analyze the complex nature of Tom's conflict and the clues provided by the passage that foreshadow how he will resolve it.

15 lesson

from Pygmalion
George Bernard Shaw

Background and Purpose

George Bernard Shaw is best known for his eccentricity and for his fifty-three witty plays; he won the Nobel Prize for Literature in 1925. Shaw founded the major socialist organization in Britain. Like Ibsen, whose work he admired, Shaw wrote dramas that called into question the rigid morality of his audiences and addressed social problems, especially those caused by the class system. Shaw's plays, unlike Ibsen's, are full of humor and gentle satire.

Pygmalion (1912) was an immediate success throughout Europe and America. During his lifetime, Shaw resisted pressure to reduce the drama to a popular musical; *My Fair Lady*, which gave the story a sentimental ending, was composed six years after the author's death in 1950. *Pygmalion* concerns one of Shaw's pet causes: language reform (notice that he omits certain pesky marks of punctuation). Professor Higgins is an expert in phonetics. The exposition which precedes the passage below sets up the plot: the evening before, Higgins was out in public making notes of the accents of people in a crowd, and explaining to his colleague Pickering that he makes a good living by helping people to rise in social class by improving their accents. He uses a flower girl's speech as an example of "English that will keep her in the gutter to the end of her days." Eliza Doolittle, the flower girl, overhears him boast to his colleague that within three months "I could pass that girl off as a duchess at an ambassador's garden party." The passage, which displays the wit and humor that runs throughout the play, begins as Eliza shows up at the professor's door requesting elocution lessons. Mrs. Pearce is his housekeeper.

HIGGINS	[*brusquely, recognizing her with unconcealed disappointment, and at once, babylike, making an intolerable grievance of it*]: Why, this is the girl I jotted down last night. Shes no use: Ive got all the records I want of Lisson Grove [her neighborhood's] lingo; and I'm not going to waste another cylinder on it. [*To the girl*] Be off with you: I don't want you.

Line 5

THE FLOWER GIRL: Don't you be so saucy. You aint heard what I come for yet. [*To MRS PEARCE, who is waiting at the door for further instructions*] Did you tell him I come in a taxi?

10

MRS PEARCE: Nonsense, girl! What do you think a gentleman like Mr Higgins cares what you came in?

THE FLOWER GIRL: Oh, we are proud! He aint above giving lessons, not him: I heard him say so. Well, I aint come here to ask for any compliment; and if my money's not good enough I can go elsewhere.

15

HIGGINS: Good enough for what?

THE FLOWER GIRL: Good enough for ye-oo. Now you know, don't you?

Using Skills to Understand the Passage

1. Who has better manners, the flower girl or the professor? Cite the evidence. How does the contrast produce humor?

2. What do Eliza's misunderstandings contribute to the humor of the scene?

20   I'm come to have lessons, I am. And to pay for em too: make no mistake.

HIGGINS   [*stupent*]: Well!!! [*Recovering his breath with a gasp*] What do you expect me to say to you?

THE FLOWER GIRL: Well, if you was a gentleman, you might ask me to sit down, I think. Don't I tell you I'm bringing you business?

25   HIGGINS: Pickering: shall we ask this baggage to sit down, or shall we throw her out of the window?

THE FLOWER GIRL: [*running away in terror to the piano, where she turns at bay*]: Ah-ah-oh-ow-ow-ow-oo! [*Wounded and whimpering*] I wont be called a baggage when Ive offered
30   to pay like any lady.

[*Motionless, the two men stare at her from the other side of the room, amazed.*]

PICKERING [*gently*]:   What is it you want, my girl?

THE FLOWER GIRL: I want to be a lady in a flower shop stead of selling
35   at the corner of Tottenham Court Road. But they wont take me unless I can talk more genteel. He said he could teach me. Well, here I am ready to pay him—not asking any favor—and he treats me as if I was dirt.

MRS PEARCE: How can you be such a foolish ignorant girl as to think
40   you could afford to pay Mr Higgins?

THE FLOWER GIRL: Why shouldn't I? I know what lessons cost as well as you do; and I'm ready to pay.

HIGGINS: How much?

THE FLOWER GIRL [*coming back to him, triumphant*]: Now youre
45   talking! I thought youd come off it when you saw a chance of getting back a bit of what you chucked at me last night. [*Confidentially*] Youd had a drop in, hadn't you?

HIGGINS   [*peremptorily*]: Sit down.

THE FLOWER GIRL: Oh, if youre going to make a compliment of it—

50   HIGGINS   [*thundering at her*]: Sit down.

MRS PEARCE [*severely*]: Sit down, girl. Do as youre told.

[*She places the stray chair near the hearthrug between* HIGGINS *and* PICKERING, *and stands behind it waiting for the girl to sit down*].

THE FLOWER GIRL: Ah-ah-ah-ow-ow-oo! [*She stands, half rebellious,*
55   *half bewildered*].

PICKERING [*very courteous*]: Wont you sit down?

LIZA   [*coyly*]: Don't mind if I do. [*She sits down.* PICKERING *returns to the hearthrug*].

HIGGINS: Whats your name?

60   THE FLOWER GIRL: Liza Doolittle.

HIGGINS [*declaiming gravely*]:
          Eliza, Elizabeth, Betsy and Bess,
          They went to the woods to get a bird's nes':

PICKERING: *They found a nest with four eggs in it:*

65   HIGGINS: *They took one apiece, and left three in it.*

[*They laugh heartily at their own wit.*]

LIZA: Oh, don't be silly.

Using Skills to Understand the Passage

3. The following stage directions describe Liza's dress and manner when she appears at Higgins's drawing room door: "*She has a hat with three ostrich feathers, orange, sky-blue, and red. She has a nearly clean apron, and the shoddy coat has been tidied a little.*" Her manner is of "*innocent vanity and consequential air.*" What do these details add to her characterization? How does her language match her appearance?

MRS PEARCE: You mustn't speak to the gentleman like that.

LIZA: Well, why wont he speak sensible to me?

70 HIGGINS: Come back to business. How much do you propose to pay me for the lessons?

LIZA: Oh, I know whats right. A lady friend of mine gets French lessons for eighteenpence an hour from a real French gentleman. Well, you wouldnt have the face to ask me the

75 same for teaching me my own language as you would for French; so I wont give more than a shilling. Take it or leave it.

Essay Question

In what ways are Liza and Higgins alike? How might their similarities represent the source of their conflict? Does this conflict promise the audience tears or laughter? Why?

16 lesson

from The Importance of Being Earnest
Oscar Wilde

Background and Purpose

Irish playwright Oscar Wilde was educated at Oxford and lived in London for most of his life. A sophisticated man, Wilde was primarily a satirist; his best-known play, *The Importance of Being Earnest* (1895) mocks the middle class that dominated the industrial age with its earnestness about work and morality. The play pits the values of this class against those of the lazy and lax aristocracy, who were all too ready to enter the marriage exchange of social superiority for middle-class money. As with most satire, the characters are types, and exaggeration is the rule. Among other literary devices, Wilde makes use of verbal irony and rhetorical devices such as parallelism to make us laugh at the follies of Lady Bracknell. In the following scene, she has just discovered that Jack (who wishes to be known as Earnest) wants to marry her daughter. She is about to interview him for the position of son-in-law.

LADY BRACKNELL [*pencil and notebook in hand*]: I feel bound to tell you that you are not down on my list of eligible young men, although I have the same list as the dear Duchess of Bolton has. We work together, in fact. However, I am quite
Line
5   ready to enter your name, should your answers be what a really affectionate mother requires. Do you smoke?

JACK: Well, yes, I must admit I smoke.

LADY BRACKNELL: I am glad to hear it. A man should always have an occupation of some kind. There are far too many idle men
10   in London as it is. How old are you?

JACK: Twenty-nine.

LADY BRACKNELL: A very good age to be married at. I have always been of opinion that a man who desires to get married should know either everything or nothing. Which do you know?

15   JACK   [*after some hesitation*]: I know nothing, Lady Bracknell.

LADY BRACKNELL: I am pleased to hear it. I do not approve of anything that tampers with natural ignorance. Ignorance is like a delicate exotic fruit; touch it and the bloom is gone. The whole theory of modern education is radically
20   unsound. Fortunately in England, at any rate, education produces no effect whatsoever. If it did, it would prove a serious danger to the upper classes, and probably lead to acts of violence in Grosvenor Square. What is your income?

JACK: Between seven and eight thousand a year.

25 LADY BRACKNELL [*makes a note in her book*]: In land, or in investments?

Using Skills to Understand the Passage

1. Make inferences about Lady Bracknell's scale of values. Consider that the order in which her questions are asked provides a clue to her priorities when assessing a prospective husband for her daughter.

2. What use does Wilde make of verbal irony to reverse values, trivializing serious matters and and vice versa? In this scene, what purpose is served by reversing conventional wisdom?

3. What evidence is presented of Lady Bracknell's social snobbery?

JACK: In investments, chiefly.

LADY BRACKNELL: That is satisfactory. What between the duties
expected of one during one's life-time, and the duties exacted
30   from one after one's death, land has ceased to be either a
profit or a pleasure. It gives one position, and prevents one
from keeping it up. That's all that can be said about land.

JACK: I have a country house with some land, of course, attached
to it, about fifteen hundred acres, I believe; but I don't
35   depend on that for my real income. In fact, as far as I can
make out, the poachers are the only people who make
anything out of it.

LADY BRACKNELL: A country house! How many bedrooms? Well, that
point can be cleared up afterwards. You have a town house, I
40   hope? A girl with a simple, unspoiled nature, like Gwendolen,
could hardly be expected to reside in the country.

JACK: Well, I own a house in Belgrave Square, but it is let by the
year to Lady Bloxham. Of course, I can get it back
whenever I like, at six months' notice.

45 LADY BRACKNELL: Lady Bloxham? I don't know her.

JACK: Oh, she goes about very little. She is a lady considerably
advanced in years.

LADY BRACKNELL: Ah, now-a-days that is no guarantee of respectability
of character. What number in Belgrave Square?

50 JACK: 149.

LADY BRACKNELL [*shaking her head*]: The unfashionable side. I
thought there was something. However, that could easily
be altered.

JACK: Do you mean the fashion, or the side?

55 LADY BRACKNELL [*sternly*]: Both, if necessary, I presume. What are
your politics?

JACK: Well, I am afraid I really have none. I am a Liberal Unionist.

LADY BRACKNELL: Oh, they count as Tories. They dine with us. Or
come in the evening, at any rate. Now to minor matters.
60   Are your parents living?

JACK: I have lost both my parents.

LADY BRACKNELL: Both? . . . That seems like carelessness. Who was
your father? He was evidently a man of some wealth. Was
he born in what the Radical papers call the purple of
65   commerce, or did he rise from the ranks of aristocracy?

JACK: I am afraid I really don't know. The fact is, Lady Bracknell, I
said I had lost my parents. It would be nearer the truth to
say that my parents seem to have lost me . . . I don't actually
know who I am by birth. I was . . . well, I was found.

Using Skills to Understand the Passage

4. How does Wilde use language to wittily reveal the economic problems of the landed aristocracy? Identify and analyze the pun, the epigram complete with antithesis, and the most unexpected and incongruous diction in the passage.

Essay Question

Satire is broadly classified after its earliest practitioners in ancient Rome: either Horatian (gentle, urbane, witty, and sympathetic) or Juvenalian (biting, bitter, angry, and contemptuous). Which type of satire is employed in this passage, and on what evidence do you base your opinion?

17
lesson

from MASTER HAROLD . . . and the boys
Athol Fugard

Background and Purpose

Athol Fugard's play, *MASTER HAROLD . . . and the boys*, is set in his native South Africa. The play was first produced in 1982, during Apartheid (racial segregation), but its theme of racism, shown through characterization, irony, and symbolism, makes it universal.

This passage occurs toward the end of the play. Hally, a white boy, has just spat in the face of his old friend and mentor, Sam, and has told Sam to start calling him Master Harold. Sam has long been employed as a waiter in the tea room run by Hally's mother. Earlier Hally had been reminiscing about when the two had made and flown a kite. Willie, the other waiter, is a simple man, though not without understanding.

	SAM	[*Taking out a handkerchief and wiping his face*]: It's all right, Willie.
		[*To* HALLY] Ja, well, you've done it . . . Master Harold. Yes, I'll
Line		start calling you that from now on. It won't be difficult
5		anymore. You've hurt yourself, Master Harold. I saw it
		coming. I warned you, but you wouldn't listen. You've just
		hurt yourself *bad*. And you're a coward, Master Harold. The
		face you should be spitting in is your father's . . . but you used
		mine, because you think you're safe inside your fair skin . . .
10		and this time I don't mean just or decent. [*Pause, then moving violently towards* HALLY]. Should I hit him, Willie?
	WILLIE	[*Stopping* SAM]: No, Boet Sam.
	SAM	[*Violently*]: Why not?
	WILLIE:	It won't help, Boet Sam.
15	SAM:	I don't want to help! I want to hurt him.
	WILLIE:	You also hurt yourself.
	SAM:	And if he had done it to you, Willie?
	WILLIE:	Me? Spit at me like I was a dog? [*A thought that had not occurred to him before. He looks at* HALLY] Ja. Then I want
20		to hit him. I want to hit him hard!
		[*A dangerous few seconds as the men stand staring at the boy.* WILLIE *turns away, shaking his head*]. But maybe all I do is go cry at the back. He's little boy, Boet Sam. Little *white* boy. Long trousers now, but he's still little boy.
25	SAM	[*His violence ebbing away into defeat as quickly as it flooded*]: You're right. So go on, then: groan again, Willie. You do it better than me. [*To* HALLY] You don't know what you've just done . . . Master Harold. It's not just that you've made me feel

Using Skills to Understand the Passage

1. After you have read the passage, consider the use of capitalization and punctuation in the play's title and throughout the body of the text. For example, why is the white boy's name in capital letters with the label "Master"? Why is there an ellipsis (. . .) before the mention of the other characters and before each address of Hally as "Master" Harold? Why are the Black adults called "boys," and why is this noun *not* capitalized, even though it is part of a title? What can you infer about the subtext of Sam's words from these mechanical devices?

2. Sam tells Hally at the start of the passage that what he has been trying to do has failed. By the end of the scene he has revealed his goal and the reasons for his failure to achieve it. Explain what you have inferred from Sam's words.

30

35

40

45

50

dirtier than I've ever been in my life . . . I mean, how do I wash off yours and your father's filth? . . . I've also failed. A long time ago I promised myself I was going to try and do something, but you've just shown me . . . Master Harold . . . that I've failed. [*Pause*] I've also got a memory of a little white boy when he was still wearing short trousers and a black man, but they're not flying a kite. It was in the old Jubilee days, after dinner one night. I was in my room. You came in and just stood against the wall, looking down at the ground, and only after I'd asked you what you wanted, what was wrong, I don't know how many times, did you speak and even then so softly I almost didn't hear you. "Sam, please help me to go and fetch my Dad." Remember? He was dead drunk on the floor of the Central Hotel Bar. They'd phoned for your Mom, but you were the only one at home. And do you remember how we did it? You went in first by yourself to ask permission for me to go into the bar. Then I loaded him onto my back like a baby and carried him back to the boarding house with you following behind carrying his crutches. [*Shaking his head as he remembers*] A crowded Main Street with all the people watching a little white boy following his drunk father on a nigger's back! I felt for that little boy . . . Master Harold. I felt for him. After that we still had to clean him up, remember? He'd messed in his trousers, so we had to clean him up and get him into bed.

HALLY: [*Great pain*] I love him, Sam.

55 SAM:

60

65

70

75

I know you do. That's why I tried to stop you from saying these things about him. It would have been so simple if you could have just despised him for being a weak man. But he's your father. You love him and you're ashamed of him. You're ashamed of so much! . . . And now that's going to include yourself. That was the promise I made to myself: to try and stop that happening. [*Pause*] After we got him to bed you came back with me to my room and sat in a corner and carried on just looking at the ground. And for days after that! You hadn't done anything wrong, but you went around as if you owed the world an apology for being alive. I didn't like seeing that! That's not the way a boy grows up to be a man! . . . But the one person who should have been teaching you what that means was the cause of your shame. If you really want to know, that's why I made you that kite. I wanted you to look up, be proud of something, of yourself . . . [*Bitter smile at the memory*] . . . and you certainly were that when I left you with it up there on the hill. Oh, ja . . . something else! . . . If you ever do write it as a short story, there *was* a twist in our ending. I couldn't sit down there and stay with you. It was a "Whites Only" bench. You were too young, too excited to notice then. But not anymore. If you're not careful . . . Master Harold . . . you're going to be sitting up there by yourself for a long time to come, and there won't be a kite in the sky.

Using Skills to Understand the Passage

3. Explain the many ironies in Sam's story of the night when Hally's drunken father has to be carried home. What is ironic in the fact that Hally must ask permission for a black man to enter the bar at all? In what ways is the father characterized by this story, and how is he a foil for Sam? Why does Sam repeat, "I felt for that little boy"? What effect does the repetition have on the hearer?

4. Hally says only four words in this passage. Judging from Sam's response, what can you infer about what Hally had been saying earlier about his father? Why did Sam try to stop him? What is the significance of Sam's failure to stop him?

5. What is the symbolic significance of the kite? How does the kite episode stand in stark contrast to the scene that has just occurred between Sam and the boy?

6. What is the ironic and symbolic significance of Sam's revelation about why he left Hally alone on the bench?

Essay Question

Based on your reading of the rest of the passage, explicate the dialogue between Sam and Willie with which the passage begins.

18 lesson

from The School for Scandal
Richard Brinsley Sheridan

Background and Purpose

Richard Brinsley Sheridan's play, *The School for Scandal*, was first performed in 1777. In mocking the behavior of polite society, Sheridan's witty comedy delivers a pointed social critique. The play displays many of the devices essential to satire, including the satiric use of diction and connotation, verbal irony, syntactical devices, caricature, and hyperbole. This passage is from the beginning of the play. Lady Sneerwell is busy at her dressing-table (this was the era of elaborate powdered wigs, beauty marks atop generous layers of makeup, and satin and lace for both genders). Her servant, Snake, drinks chocolate as she quizzes him about his latest chore, delivering items to a gossip column.

LADY SNEERWELL: The paragraphs, you say, Mr. Snake, were all inserted?

Line
5

SNAKE: They were, madam, and as I copied them myself in a feigned hand, there can be no suspicion whence they came.

LADY SNEERWELL: Did you circulate the reports of Lady *Brittle's* intrigue with Captain *Boastall*?

10

SNAKE: That is in as fine a train as your ladyship could wish,—in the common sense of things, I think it must reach Mrs. *Clackit's* within four-and-twenty hours; and then, you know, the business is as good as done.

LADY SNEERWELL: Why, truly, Mrs. *Clackit* has a very pretty talent, and a great deal of industry.

15

20

SNAKE: True, madam, and has been tolerably successful in her day:—to my knowledge, she has been the cause of six matches being broken off, and three sons being disinherited, of four forced elopements, as many close confinements, nine separate maintenances, and two divorces;—nay, I have more than once traced her causing a *Tete-a-Tete* in the *Town and Country Magazine*, when the parties perhaps had never seen each other's faces before in the course of their lives.

LADY SNEERWELL: She certainly has talents, but her manner is gross.

25

SNAKE: 'Tis very true,—she generally designs well, has a free tongue, and a bold invention; but her coloring is too dark, and her outline often extravagant. She wants that *delicacy* of *hint*, and *mellowness* of *sneer*, which distinguish your ladyship's scandal.

Using Skills to Understand the Passage

1. Make inferences about the characters of Sneerwell, Snake, Brittle, Boastall, and Clackit based on their names, and discuss how the use of caricature sets the tone of the scene.

2. Paraphrase Snake's long catalog of Mrs. Clackit's achievements, beginning with "She has been the cause of . . ."

3. In the catalog of disgrace and ruin, what does syntax contribute to the satire? Consider the content of the discussion, the order in which the items are listed, and the effect of this presentation.

4. What is ironic about Mrs. Clackit's talents and the uses she makes of them? What metaphor is implied?

5. How does Lady Sneerwell's talent compare to Mrs. Clackit's, according to Snake? What is ironic about her superior talent? Why does Snake use hyperbole in his praise of Lady Sneerwell?

LADY SNEERWELL: Ah! You are partial, Snake.

30 SNAKE: Not in the least; everybody allows that Lady *Sneerwell* can do more with a *word* or a *look* than many can with the most labored detail, even when they happen to have a little truth on their side to support it.

Essay Question

Consider the use of irony and caricature as they contribute to the satiric effect of the passage. How do these devices establish the tone of the play?

19 *from* The Crucible
Arthur Miller

lesson

Background and Purpose

This passage from Arthur Miller's *The Crucible* dramatizes the prelude to the famous witch-hunt in Salem, Massachusetts, in 1692. The witchcraft hysteria in Europe had already caused the deaths of up to 100,000 people, many of them old and poor, single, or widowed women. It should be noted that Miller premiered the play in 1953, at the height of the Cold War, which pitted the United States and its NATO allies in Western Europe against the Communist bloc in Eastern Europe. Senator Joe McCarthy, now a notorious figure in American history, held hearings in which he publicly accused army officials, members of the media, and public figures of being Communists. He gives his name to McCarthyism, the use of unfair or accusatory methods to suppress opposition. Another name for this practice is *witch-hunt*.

In the play, clergy and government officials work together in the Puritan theocracy to examine those accused of witchcraft. Betty Parris, the local clergyman's daughter, has started exhibiting alarming symptoms. The Reverend Samuel Parris sends for Hale, a clergyman who purports to be a specialist in witchcraft. As Hale prepares to examine Betty, Rebecca Nurse, a wise and gentle town matriarch, subtly suggests her doubts about the proceedings.

Miller's play is faithful to the trial records: the Putnams will be the chief accusers, and Giles Corey's wife will be one of the scapegoats who are hanged. Lengthy stage directions which directly characterize him are omitted from this passage from the first act of the play.

	PARRIS	[*quickly*]: Will you look at my daughter, sir? [*Leads* HALE *to the bed.*] She has tried to leap out the window; we discovered her this morning on the highroad, waving her arms as though she'd fly.
Line		
5	HALE	[*narrowing his eyes*]: Tries to fly.
	PUTNAM:	She cannot bear to hear the Lord's name, Mr. Hale; that's a sure sign of witchcraft afloat.
	HALE	[*holding up his hands*]: No, no. Now let me instruct you. We cannot look to superstition in this. The Devil is precise;
10		the marks of his presence are as definite as stone, and I must tell you all that I shall not proceed unless you are prepared to believe me if I should find no bruise of hell upon her.
	PARRIS:	It is agreed, sir—it is agreed—we will abide by your
15		judgment.
	HALE:	Good then. [*He goes to the bed, looks down at* BETTY. *To* PARRIS]: Now, sir, what were your first warning of this strangeness?

Using Skills to Understand the Passage

1. What can you infer about the historical and cultural context of *The Crucible*? What do these people believe and fear? How do they see the world? Why do the clergymen encourage this world view?

	PARRIS:	Why, sir—I discovered her [*indicating* ABIGAIL] and my
20		niece and ten or twelve of the other girls, dancing in the forest last night.
	HALE	[*surprised*]: You permit dancing?
	PARRIS:	No, no, it were secret—
	MRS. PUTNAM	[*unable to wait*]: Mr. Parris's slave has knowledge of
25		conjurin', sir.
	PARRIS	[*to* MRS. PUTNAM]: We cannot be sure of that, Goody Ann—
	MRS. PUTNAM	[*frightened, very softly*]: I know it, sir. I sent my child— she should learn from Tituba who murdered her sisters.
	REBECCA	[*horrified*]: Goody Ann! You sent a child to conjure up the
30		dead?
	MRS. PUTNAM:	Let God blame me, not you, not you, Rebecca! I'll not have you judging me any more! [*To* HALE]: Is it a natural work to lose seven children before they live a day?
	PARRIS:	Sssh!
35	[REBECCA, *with great pain, turns her face away. There is a pause.*]	
	HALE:	Seven dead in childbirth.
	MRS. PUTNAM	[*softly*]: Aye. [*Her voice breaks; she looks up at him. Silence.* HALE *is impressed.* PARRIS *looks to him. He goes to his books, opens one, turns pages, then reads. All wait,*
40		*avidly.*]
	PARRIS	[*hushed*]: What book is that?
	MRS. PUTNAM:	What's there, sir?
	HALE	[*with a tasty love of intellectual pursuit*]: Here is all the invisible world, caught, defined, and calculated. In these
45		books the Devil stands stripped of all his brute disguises. Here are all your familiar spirits—your incubi and succubi; your witches that go by land, by air, and by sea; your wizards of the night and of the day. Have no fear now—we shall find him out if he has come among us, and I mean to
50		crush him utterly if he has shown his face! [*He starts for the bed.*]
	REBECCA:	Will it hurt the child, sir?
	HALE:	I cannot tell. If she is truly in the devil's grip we may have to rip and tear to get her free.
55	REBECCA:	I think I'll go, then. I am too old for this. [*She rises.*]
	PARRIS	[*striving for conviction*]: Why, Rebecca, we may open up the boil of all our troubles today!
	REBECCA:	Let us hope for that. I go to God for you, Sir.
	PARRIS	[*with trepidation—and resentment*]: I hope you do not
60		mean we go to Satan here! [*slight pause*].
	REBECCA:	I wish I knew. [*She goes out; they feel resentful of her note of moral superiority*]
	PUTNAM	[*abruptly*]: Come, Mr. Hale, let's get on. Sit you here.
	GILES:	Mr. Hale, I have always wanted to ask a learned man—
65		what signifies the readin' of strange books?
	HALE:	What books?
	GILES:	I cannot tell; she hides them.

Using Skills to Understand the Passage

2. Who is Tituba, and what does her presence in the background of this scene represent?

3. Hale's plan to "save" Betty is expressed in the forms of personification and metaphor. What is being personified and compared in this passage? What makes each literary device apt, in light of the world view of these people?

4. How do Ann Putnam and Parris as well as the assembled villagers feel about the saintly old woman, Rebecca Nurse? What might these feelings foreshadow?

HALE: Who does this?

GILES: Martha, my wife. I have waked at night many a time and
70   found her in a corner, readin' of a book. Now what do you
               make of that?

HALE: Why, that's not necessarily—

GILES: It discomfits me! Last night—mark this—I tried and tried
               and could not say my prayers. And then she close her book
75   and walks out of the house, and suddenly—mark this—I
               could pray again!

                    . . . [*stage directions omitted here*]

HALE: Ah! The stoppage of prayer—that is strange. I'll speak
               further on that with you.

GILES: I'm not sayin' she's touched the Devil, now, but I'd admire
80   to know what books she reads and why she hides them.
               She'll not answer me, y' see.

HALE: Aye, we'll discuss it. [*To all*]: Now mark me, if the Devil is
               in her you will witness some frightful wonders in this
               room, so please to keep your wits about you. Mr. Putnam,
85   stand close in case she flies. Now, Betty, dear, will you sit
               up? [*PUTNAM comes in closer, ready-handed. HALE sits BETTY
               up, but she hangs limp in his hands.*] Hmmm. [*He observes
               her carefully. The others watch breathlessly.*] Can you hear
               me? I am John Hale, minister of Beverly. I have come to
90   help you, dear. Do you remember my two little girls in
               Beverly? [*She does not stir in his hands.*]

PARRIS   [*in fright*]: How can it be the Devil? Why would he choose
               my house to strike? We have all manner of licentious
               people in the village!

95 HALE: What victory would the Devil have to win a soul already
               bad? It is the best the Devil wants, and who is better than
               the minister?

GILES: That's deep, Mr. Parris, deep, deep!

PARRIS   [*with resolution now*]: Betty! Answer Mr. Hale! Betty!

100 HALE: Does someone afflict you, child? It need not be a woman,
               mind you, or a man. Perhaps some bird invisible to others
               comes to you—perhaps a pig, a mouse, or any beast at all.
               Is there some figure bids you fly? [*The child remains limp
               in his hands. In silence he lays her back on the pillow.
105   Now, holding out his hands toward her, he intones*]: In
               nomine Domini Sabaoth sui filiique ite ad infernos. [*She
               does not stir.*]

**Using Skills
to Understand the Passage**

5. What does Hale's method of
   investigation reveal about his
   beliefs? How might readers of
   today react to his line of
   questioning?

Essay Question

What does this passage foreshadow about the unfolding action of *The Crucible* as
the characters prepare to play their parts in the witchcraft trials? Consider their possible motivations as you formulate a thesis about the forces that lead neighbor to
accuse neighbor of witchcraft.

105–106 **In nomine . . . ad infernos:** In the Name of the Lord of Hosts and His Son, go back
to Hell. [an exorcism]

20 *lesson*

from **Tartuffe**
Molière

Background and Purpose

Molière uses his witty comedies to satirize the foibles of seventeenth-century French society. In *Tartuffe* (1669) the title character, a hypocritical opportunist, gets a foolish middle-aged man under his power and persuades him to give him his daughter, Mariane, in marriage. When the father authoritatively orders the girl to marry Tartuffe, she looks to her beloved fiancé, Valere, for help and succor. But when Valere hears the sudden news, his response is not what she expects. In this passage from Act Two, Scene Four of the play, the young lovers nearly allow pride and anger to divide them. Only the intervention of Dorine, the clever maid, saves the situation.

Tartuffe was translated from Molière's French verse into English heroic couplets in 1963 by the distinguished American poet Richard Wilbur. Molière's wit and satire are well served by Wilbur's use of heroic couplets. Our expectation of a rhyme is always met, often in surprising and witty ways. Except for one couplet, every pair of rhymes in this scene is perfect (not slant). Much of the humor is created by the formal march of iambic pentameter lines, the perfectly rhyming couplets, and the use of double rhymes.

	VALERE:	Madam, I've just received some wondrous news
		Regarding which I'd like to hear your views.
	MARIANE:	What news?
Line	VALERE:	You're marrying Tartuffe.
5	MARIANE:	I find
		That Father does have such a match in mind.
	VALERE:	Your father Madam . . .
	MARIANE:	. . . has just this minute said
		That it's Tartuffe he wishes me to wed.
10	VALERE:	Can he be serious?
	MARIANE:	Oh, indeed he can;
		He's clearly set his heart upon the plan.
	VALERE:	And what position do you propose to take,
		Madame?
15	MARIANE:	Why—I don't know.
	VALERE:	For heaven's sake—
		You don't know?
	MARIANE:	No.
	VALERE:	Well, well!
20	MARIANE:	Advise me, do.
	VALERE:	Marry the man. That's my advice to you.

Using Skills to Understand the Passage

1. What does Valere expect Mariane's response to her father's edict to be? How does she respond instead? Why? The scene works only if this basic motivation is clear.

2. Describe the role of Dorine in breaking the stalemate. Consider her physical action as well as her diction.

MARIANE:	That's your advice?	
VALERE:	Yes.	
MARIANE:	Truly?	
25 VALERE:	Oh, absolutely.	

MARIANE: That's your advice?

VALERE: Yes.

MARIANE: Truly?

25 VALERE: Oh, absolutely.
You couldn't choose more wisely, more astutely.

MARIANE: Thanks for this counsel; I'll follow it, of course.

VALERE: Do, do; I'm sure 'twill cost you no remorse.

MARIANE: To give it didn't cause your heart to break.

30 VALERE: I gave it, Madam, only for your sake.

MARIANE: And it's for your sake that I take it, Sir.

DORINE [*withdrawing to the rear of the stage*]:
Let's see which fool will prove the stubborner.

VALERE: So! I am nothing to you, and it was flat
Deception when you . . .

35 MARIANE: Please, enough of that.
You've told me plainly that I should agree
To wed the man my father's chosen for me,
And since you've deigned to counsel me so wisely,
I promise, Sir, to do as you advise me.

40 VALERE: Ah, no, 'twas not by me that you were swayed.
No, your decision was already made;
Though now, to save appearances, you protest
That you're betraying me at my behest.

MARIANE: Just as you say.

45 VALERE: Quite so. And now I see
That you were never truly in love with me.

MARIANE: Alas, you're free to think so if you choose.

VALERE: I choose to think so, and here's a bit of news:
You've spurned my hand, but I know where to turn
50 For kinder treatment, as you shall quickly learn.

MARIANE: I'm sure you do. Your noble qualities
Inspire affection . . .

VALERE: Forget my qualities, please.
They don't inspire you overmuch, I find.
55 But there's another lady I have in mind
Whose sweet and generous nature will not scorn
To compensate me for the loss I've borne.

MARIANE: I'm no great loss, and I'm sure that you'll transfer
Your heart quite painlessly from me to her.

60 VALERE: I'll do my best to take it in my stride.
The pain I feel at being cast aside
Time and forgetfulness may put an end to.
Or if I can't forget, I shall pretend to.
No self-respecting person is expected
65 To go on loving once he's been rejected.

MARIANE: Now, that's a fine, high-minded sentiment.

VALERE: One to which any sane man would assent.
Would you prefer it if I pined away
In hopeless passion till my dying day?
70 Am I to yield you to a rival's arms
And not console myself with other charms?

3. Consider the effect of the rhymes in lines 27–32, 54–57, and 72–77. These sound devices can enhance the meaning by either satisfying our expectations or surprising us with incongruity. Verbal irony and witty modifications of clichés may also be produced by rhymes.

4. Consider the double rhymes in the passage, such as "expected"/"rejected" in lines 64–65. What is their effect? Hint: Double rhymes are rare in serious poems because they tend to be inherently humorous.

5. How does the regularity of meter and rhyme contribute to the swift and humorous pacing of the dialogue? What reasons do the lovers have for interrupting each other so often and what is the effect of such interruptions? Consider lines 34–35, 45–46, 76–80, and 90–93 in your analysis.

MARIANE:	Go then: console yourself; don't hesitate.
	I wish you to; indeed, I cannot wait.
VALERE:	You wish me to?
75 MARIANE:	Yes.
VALERE:	That's the final straw.
	Madam, farewell. Your wish shall be my law.
	[*He starts to leave, and then returns; this repeatedly*]
MARIANE:	Splendid.
VALERE:	[*Coming back again*]
	This breach, remember, is of your making;
80	It's you who've driven me to the step I'm taking.
MARIANE:	Of course.
VALERE:	[*Coming back again*]
	Remember, too, that I am merely
	Following your example.
MARIANE:	I see that clearly.
85 VALERE:	Enough. I'll go and do your bidding, then.
MARIANE:	Good.
VALERE:	[*Coming back again*]
	You shall never see my face again.
MARIANE:	Excellent.
VALERE:	[*Walking to the door, then turning about*]
90	Yes?
MARIANE:	What?
VALERE:	What's that? What did you say?
MARIANE:	Nothing. You're dreaming.
VALERE:	Ah. Well, I'm on my way.
95	Farewell, *Madame*.
	[*He moves slowly away*]
MARIANE:	Farewell.
DORINE:	[*To MARIANE*]
	If you ask me,
	Both of you are mad as mad can be.
	Do stop this nonsense, now. I've only let you
100	Squabble so long to see where it would get you.
	Whoa there, Monsieur Valere!
	[*She goes and seizes VALERE by the arm; he makes a great show of resistance*]

Essay Question

What tone is created in this passage by Wilbur's choice of diction and prosody? How does this tone determine our reaction to the quarrelling lovers?

21 lesson

from Othello
William Shakespeare

Background and Purpose

Iago, the villain in Shakespeare's tragedy *Othello*, is one of the most fiendish characters in all of literature. Under the pretense that he is a faithful aide to the great Moorish general Othello, Iago is determined to destroy him. His motives are slight and insubstantial: anger that he was passed over for a promotion by Othello and some vague, groundless fears that his wife Emilia has been unfaithful to him with Othello. Iago plots his evil cunningly. He insinuates to Othello that his new wife Desdemona has been unfaithful to him with the very man, Cassio, who got the lieutenancy Iago wanted. Thus with one blow he can destroy the two men he envies and hates. He does not hesitate, though he destroys Desdemona as well and causes his wife Emilia's suicide in remorse for her part in the plot.

Act 3, Scene 3 is the turning point in the action, the start of the denouement. Iago's success is secured through a brief ballet in which the principals interact, and Emilia and Iago take turns revealing their intentions through the device of the soliloquy. Iago has already caused Othello to doubt the honor of his new lieutenant and the fidelity of his bride; Othello is wracked with doubt and jealousy as Desdemona enters. Because the audience is privy to Iago's thoughts, the passage is rife with dramatic irony. This device was perfected by the Greek tragedians, in particular Sophocles, in the fifth century B.C. Though it is used in fiction and poetry as well, it is especially wrenching in the theater, where the entire audience shares the horror of watching the characters ignorantly acting against their own best interests.

In this scene, Othello suffers the torments of jealousy, while Iago advances his deadly plot. Emilia unwittingly becomes Iago's tool, with tragic consequences for all of the principals.

[*Enter* DESDEMONA *and* EMILIA.]

OTHELLO: If she be false, heaven mocks itself!
          I'll not believe 't.

DESDEMONA: How now, my dear Othello?

Line
          Your dinner, and the generous islanders

   5   By you invited, do attend your presence.

OTHELLO: I am to blame.

DESDEMONA:
          Why do you speak so faintly? Are you not well?

OTHELLO: I have a pain upon my forehead, here.

DESDEMONA:
          Faith, that's with watching. 'Twill away again.

  10   Let me but bind it hard; within this hour

---

9 **with watching:** from lack of sleep

Using Skills to Understand the Passage

1. What is Othello's mental and physical condition as the passage begins? What motivates Desdemona to offer her husband the handkerchief and what is ironic in her not noticing its loss?

It will be well.

OTHELLO: Your napkin is too little.

Let it alone.   *[The handkerchief falls, unnoticed.]*

Come, I'll go in with you.

DESDEMONA:

15   I am very sorry that you are not well.

[OTHELLO and DESDEMONA exit.]

EMILIA *[picking up the handkerchief]*:

I am glad I have found this napkin.

This was her first remembrance from the Moor.

My wayward husband hath a hundred times

Wooed me to steal it. But she so loves the token

20   (For he conjured her she should ever keep it)

That she reserves it evermore about her

To kiss and talk to. I'll have the work ta'en out

And give 't Iago. What he will do with it

Heaven knows, not I.

25   I nothing but to please his fantasy.

[Enter IAGO.]

IAGO: How now? What do you here alone?

EMILIA: Do not you chide. I have a thing for you.

IAGO: You have a thing for me? It is a common thing—

EMILIA: Ha?

30   IAGO: To have a foolish wife.

EMILIA: O, is that all? What will you give me now

For that same handkerchief?

IAGO: What handkerchief?

EMILIA: Why, that the Moor first gave to Desdemona,

35   That which so often you did bid me steal.

IAGO: Hast stol'n it from her?

EMILIA: No, faith, she let it drop by negligence,

And to th' advantage I, being there, took 't up.

Look, here 'tis.

40   IAGO: A good wench! Give it me.

EMILIA: What will you do with 't, that you have been so earnest

To have me filch it?

IAGO *[snatching it]*:   Why, what is that to you?

EMILIA: If it be not for some purpose of import,

45   Give 't me again. Poor lady, she'll run mad

When she shall lack it.

IAGO: Be not acknown on 't.

I have a use for it. Go, leave me.   *[EMILIA exits.]*

I will in Cassio's lodging lose this napkin

---

17 **remembrance:** keepsake

21 **reserves it evermore:** always keeps it

22 **work:** needlework, embroidery pattern; **ta'en out:** taken out, copied

25 **nothing but to:** only; **fantasy:** fancy, whim

38 **to th' advantage:** important purpose

47 **Be not acknown on 't:** do not admit to knowing about it

Using Skills to Understand the Passage

2. What do you learn from Emilia's soliloquy about her understanding of the symbolic importance of the handkerchief to the marriage?

3. What is Emilia's motive in giving the handkerchief to her husband? Is she conflicted about whether to do so? How does she rationalize not returning it to Desdemona?

4. What is Iago's reason for asking Emilia to steal the handkerchief? What part will the handkerchief play in his plan to ruin Othello and Cassio? Paraphrase and explicate Iago's soliloquy. Keep in mind that he understands jealousy because he also is its victim. Comment on the aptness of the analogies suggested by the words *poison* and *sleep*.

50　　　　　　And let him find it. Trifles light as air
　　　　　　　Are to the jealous confirmations strong
　　　　　　　As proofs of holy writ. This may do something.
　　　　　　　The Moor already changes with my poison.
　　　　　　　Dangerous conceits are in their natures poisons,
55　　　　　　Which at the first are scarce found to distaste,
　　　　　　　But with a little act upon the blood
　　　　　　　Burn like the mines of sulfur.

[*Enter* OTHELLO.]

　　　　　　　　　　　　　　　　　　　I did say so.
　　　　　　　Look where he comes. Not poppy nor mandragora
60　　　　　　Nor all the drowsy syrups of the world
　　　　　　　Shall ever medicine thee to that sweet sleep
　　　　　　　Which thou owedst yesterday.

Essay Question

Consider the many ironies of the scene as Iago manipulates Othello, Emilia, and Desdemona. How and why do these three work against their best interests? Is any of them responsible for his or her own downfall? Is poetic justice at work?

---

54 **conceits:** conceptions, ideas

55 **are . . . distaste:** scarcely offend the taste

57 **the mines of sulfur:** sulfur mines, once on fire, seemed unquenchable

59 **poppy:** opium; **mandragora:** a narcotic syrup

60 **drowsy:** sleep-inducing

62 **owedst:** did own, did experience

22
lesson

from Twelfth Night
William Shakespeare

Background and Purpose

This popular comedy has a subplot that is as much fun as the main plot. Countess Olivia's waiting-gentlewoman, the clever and witty Maria, decides to make a fool of Malvolio, the self-important and ambitious steward, head of the servants. Forging Olivia's handwriting, Maria has written a love letter addressed to Malvolio, hoping that when he finds it he will be deceived by its flattery.

Only a self-deluded egoist such as Malvolio could fall for such a ploy, for Olivia is a wealthy and aristocratic young woman, mourning the death of her brother. Indulging in her melancholy, Olivia is displeased with her several aristocratic suitors and would hardly have accepted the romantic attentions of a servant. Furthermore, she sees Malvolio clearly. Earlier in the play she has remonstrated with him over his vanity: "O, you are sick of self-love, Malvolio, and taste with a distempered appetite." Those who have assembled to enjoy the sport and comment upon the spectacle of the steward's self-regard are Sir Toby, Olivia's drunken kinsman; the easily led Sir Andrew, flattered by Sir Toby into believing that the fair Olivia will marry him; and Fabian, a witty gentleman in Olivia's household.

In order to appreciate the trick, a reader must imagine the play as a performance and stage this scene in the imagination. Both direct and indirect stage directions are important. We must picture where the letter is planted and where the characters are on stage when Malvolio finds and reads the letter. The asides of the eavesdroppers help characterize them: the tone of each remark, the implication and subtleties of the language, and the subtext that is often unspoken but felt—each is important. The notes offer help with unfamiliar words and phrases as well as those that have different meanings today, but the syntax requires some effort, especially Malvolio's pompous sentence structure and diction. Metaphor is an important device in ridiculing Malvolio.

[*Enter* MARIA.]

TOBY: Here comes the little villain.—How now, my metal of India?

Line
5

MARIA: Get you all three into the boxtree. Malvolio's coming down this walk. He has been yonder i' the sun practicing behavior to his own shadow this half hour. Observe him, for the love of mockery, for I know this letter will make a contemplative idiot of him. Close, in the name of jesting!

Using Skills to Understand the Passage

1. How does Malvolio reveal his character? Consider both his initial posturing and his response to the letter.

1–2 **villain:** here, a term of affection; **metal of India:** golden one (the "Indies"—Americas—were a source of gold)

3 **boxtree:** boxwood shrubbery

7 **close:** stay hidden

[*They hide.*] Lie thou there [*putting down the letter,*] for here comes the trout that must be caught with tickling.

[*She exits.*]

[*Enter MALVOLIO.*]

10   MALVOLIO: 'Tis but fortune, all is fortune. Maria once told me she did affect me, and I have heard herself come thus near, that should she fancy, it should be one of my complexion. Besides, she uses me with a more exalted respect than anyone else that follows her. What should I think on 't?

15   TOBY   [*aside*]: Here's an overweening rogue.

FABIAN   [*aside*]: O, peace! Contemplation makes a rare turkeycock of him. How he jets under his advanced plumes!

ANDREW   [*aside*]: 'Slight, I could so beat the rogue!

TOBY   [*aside*]: Peace, I say.

20   MALVOLIO: To be Count Malvolio.

TOBY   [*aside*]: Ah, rogue!

ANDREW   [*aside*]: Pistol him, pistol him!

TOBY   [*aside*]: Peace, peace!

MALVOLIO: There is example for 't. The lady of the Strachy married
25   the yeoman of the wardrobe.

ANDREW   [*aside*]: Fie on him, Jezebel!

FABIAN   [*aside*]: O, peace, now he's deeply in. Look how imagination blows him.

MALVOLIO: Having been three months married to her, sitting in my
30   state—

TOBY   [*aside*]: O, for a stone-bow, to hit him in the eye!

MALVOLIO: Calling my officers about me, in my branched velvet gown, having come from a daybed, where I have left Olivia sleeping—

35   TOBY   [*aside*]: Fire and brimstone!

FABIAN   [*aside*]: O, peace, peace!

MALVOLIO: And then to have the humor of state; and after a demure

Using Skills to Understand the Passage

2. How is Sir Toby characterized through both his own words and those of Malvolio?

3. We can form our estimate of Sir Andrew's character only through his own words. He is both a minor and a flat character, and so he does not develop throughout the drama. What is Sir Andrew's role in the unfolding plot, and how do his traits enhance the humor of the scene?

4. Fabian serves several functions in the scene, supplying needed commentary on the action, helping to facilitate the plot against Malvolio, and contributing metaphors that describe Malvolio. Provide evidence of these contributions to the plot against the vain steward.

5. How is Maria characterized? Consider what she has written as well as what she does and says during the scene, along with the epithets the others use for her.

9 **trout . . . tickling:** These fish can be lured from hiding places by stroking their gills.

10–11 **she did affect me:** Olivia loved me; **come . . . near:** say something close to this

12 **fancy:** fall in love; **complexion:** nature, appearance

14 **follows:** serves

16 **contemplation:** anticipation, expectation

17 **jets . . . plumes:** struts like a turkeycock with feathers spread

18 **'Slight:** By God's light (a strong oath)

22 **Pistol:** shoot

25 **yeoman:** servant, officer

26 **Jezebel:** a proud queen in the Bible

27 **deeply in:** mired in his fantasy

28 **blows:** swells

30 **state:** chair of state (as Count Malvolio)

31 **stone-bow:** a crossbow that propels stones

32 **officers:** underlings who manage the estate; **branched:** embroidered with flowers

37 **have . . . state:** assume a haughty manner fitting my position

		travel of regard, telling them I know my place, as I would they should do theirs, to ask for my kinsman Toby—
40	TOBY	[*aside*]: Bolts and shackles!
	FABIAN	[*aside*]: O, peace, peace, peace! Now, now.
	MALVOLIO:	Seven of my people, with an obedient start, make out for him. I frown the while, and perchance wind up my watch, or play with my—some rich jewel. Toby approaches;
45		curtsies there to me—
	TOBY	[*aside*]: Shall this fellow live?
	FABIAN	[*aside*]: Though our silence be drawn from us with cars, yet peace.
	MALVOLIO:	I extend my hand to him thus, quenching my familiar
50		smile with an austere regard of control—
	TOBY	[*aside*]: And does not Toby take you a blow o' the lips then?
	MALVOLIO:	Saying "Cousin Toby, my fortunes, having cast me on your niece, give me this prerogative of speech—"
	TOBY	[*aside*]: What, what?
55	MALVOLIO:	"You must amend your drunkenness."
	TOBY	[*aside*]: Out, scab!
	FABIAN	[*aside*]: Nay, patience, or we break the sinews of our plot.
	MALVOLIO:	"Besides, you waste the treasure of your time with a foolish knight—"
60	ANDREW	[*aside*]: That's me, I warrant you.
	MALVOLIO:	"One Sir Andrew."
	ANDREW	[*aside*]: I knew 'twas I, for many do call me fool.
	MALVOLIO	[*seeing the letter*]: What employment have we here?
	FABIAN	[*aside*]: Now is the woodcock near the gin.
65	TOBY	[*aside*]: O, peace, and the spirit of humors intimate reading aloud to him
	MALVOLIO	[*taking up the letter*]: By my life, this is my lady's hand!
	. . .	
70		Soft, here follows prose. [*He reads.*] *If this fall into thy hand, revolve. In my stars I am above thee, but be not afraid of greatness. Some are born great, some achieve greatness, and some have greatness thrust upon 'em. Thy fates open their hands. Let thy blood and spirit embrace them. And, to inure thyself to*

37–38 **a demure . . . regard:** soberly surveying my officers

47 **drawn . . . cars:** forced from us through torture; **cars:** chariots

50 **regard of control:** look of mastery

51 **take . . . o':** give you a blow on

57 **break . . . plot:** cripple, destroy, our scheme

64 **woodcock:** a proverbially stupid bird; **gin:** trap

65 **spirit of humors:** that which controls moods

65–66 **intimate . . . him:** suggest to him that he read aloud

67 **hand:** handwriting

69 **revolve:** consider; **stars:** destiny

72 **open their hands:** have become generous

73 **inure:** accustom

75

80

what thou art like to be, cast thy humble slough and appear fresh. Be opposite with a kinsman, surly with servants. Let thy tongue tang arguments of state. Put thyself into the trick of singularity. She thus advises thee that sighs for thee. Remember who commended thy yellow stockings and wished to see thee ever cross-gartered. I say, remember. Go to, thou art made, if thou desir'st to be so. If not, let me see thee a steward still, the fellow of servants, and not worthy to touch Fortune's fingers. Farewell. She that would alter services with thee.

The Fortunate-Unhappy

85

90

95

100

Daylight and champion discovers not more! This is open. I will be proud, I will read politic authors, I will baffle Sir Toby, I will wash off gross acquaintance, I will be point-devise the very man. I do not now fool myself, to let imagination jade me; for every reason excites to this, that my lady loves me. She did commend my yellow stockings of late, she did praise my leg being cross-gartered, and in this she manifests herself to my love and, with a kind of injunction, drives me to these habits of her liking. I thank my stars, I am happy. I will be strange, stout, in yellow stockings, and cross-gartered, even with the swiftness of putting on. Jove and my stars be praised! Here is yet a postscript.

[*He reads.*] *Thou canst not choose but know who I am. If thou entertain'st my love, let it appear in thy smiling; thy smiles become thee well. Therefore in my presence still smile, dear my sweet, I prithee.*

Jove, I thank thee! I will smile. I will do everything that thou wilt have me.   [*He exits.*]

105

FABIAN: I will not give my part of this sport for a pension of thousands to be paid from the Sophy.

TOBY: I could marry this wench for this device.

ANDREW: So could I, too.

TOBY: And ask no other dowry with her but such another jest.

ANDREW: Nor I neither.

[*Enter* MARIA.]

---

74 **like:** likely; **cast . . . slough:** discard your humble attitude (as a snake sloughs off its old skin)

75 **opposite:** confrontational

76 **tang . . . state:** ring out with political opinions

76–77 **Put . . . singularity:** adopt idiosyncrasies

79 **cross-gartered:** wearing ribbons tied around the knees; **Go to:** an expression of protest

85 **champion:** open country; **discovers:** reveals; **open:** perfectly clear

86 **politic:** political and/or wise; **baffle:** publicly humiliate

87 **gross:** base

87–88 **point-devise . . . man:** precisely the man described in the letter

89 **jade:** dupe, delude

93–94 **these . . . liking:** wear the kind of clothes that she likes; **strange:** extraordinary, exceptional

95 **stout:** proud, arrogant

99 **thou entertain'st:** you accept

105 **Sophy:** ruler of Persia

110	FABIAN:	Here comes my noble gull-catcher.
	TOBY:	Wilt thou set thy foot o' my neck?
	ANDREW:	Or o' mine either?
	TOBY:	Shall I play my freedom at tray-trip and become thy bondslave?
115	ANDREW:	I' faith, or I either?
	TOBY:	Why, thou hast put him in such a dream that when the image of it leaves him he must run mad.
	MARIA:	Nay, but say true, does it work upon him?
	TOBY:	Like aqua vitae with a midwife.
120	MARIA:	If you will then see the fruits of the sport, mark his first approach before my lady. He will come to her in yellow stockings, and 'tis a color she abhors, and cross-gartered, a fashion she detests; and he will smile upon her, which will now be so unsuitable to her disposition, being addicted to a
125		melancholy as she is, that it cannot but turn him into a notable contempt. If you will see it, follow me.
	TOBY:	To the gates of Tartar, thou most excellent devil of wit!
	ANDREW:	I'll make one, too. *[They exit.]*

Essay Question

Considering Maria's final words, the plans we overhear Malvolio make, and Olivia's disposition and attitude, write an essay in which you hypothesize about the next meeting of Malvolio and his employer.

---

110 **gull-catcher:** A gull is a person easily cheated (gullible).

113 **play:** bet; **tray-trip:** a gambling game

119 **aqua vitae:** strong drink, brandy

126 **notable contempt:** well-known object of contempt

127 **Tartar:** Tartarus, hell

128 **make one, too:** join you

Independent Analysis

from Fences
August Wilson

Background and Purpose

August Wilson's play *Fences* (1986) is the second drama in a cycle about life in an African-American neighborhood in Pittsburgh. The play is set in 1957. Its protagonist, Troy Maxson, is much like Wilson's stepfather, a gifted athlete who was a teenager in the 1930s. At that time, few colleges offered scholarships to minorities. He turned to crime, killed someone during a robbery, and was imprisoned for twenty years. He married Wilson's mother on his release. Wilson's own experiences in a mostly white suburb also contribute to the portrait of Troy as a "proud soul battered by racism." A third influence is the Negro Baseball League, and the amazing prowess of its star players, who were banned from major league play by the color barrier until well into the 1940s.

In this passage, Troy confronts his son Cory about the boy's aspirations to play college football. At the end of the scene, he reveals the disappointments of a thwarted life: a star player in the former Negro League who was too old to join the majors once they were integrated, he has served a long prison term, and now, at age 54, holds a job as a garbage collector. Despite the hard knocks, Troy has character; at another point in the play we learn that a friend admires him for his honesty, strength, and capacity for hard work. The passage begins with father and son working together on a fence for the back yard on a Saturday afternoon.

	TROY:	Your mama tell me you done got recruited by a college football team? Is that right?
	CORY:	Yeah. Coach Zellman say the recruiter gonna be coming by to talk to you. Get you to sign the permission papers.
Line 5	TROY:	I thought you was supposed to be working down there at the A&P. Ain't you suppose to be working down there after school?
	CORY:	Mr. Stawicki say he gonna hold my job for me until after the football season. Say starting next week I can work weekends.
10	TROY:	I thought we had an understanding abut this football stuff? You suppose to keep up with your chores and hold that job down at the A&P. Ain't been around here all day on a Saturday. Ain't none of your chores done . . . and now you telling me you done quit your job.
15	CORY:	I'm gonna be working weekends.
	TROY:	You damn right you are! And ain't no need for nobody coming around here to talk to me about signing nothing.

	CORY:	Hey, Pop . . . you can't do that. He's coming all the way from North Carolina.
20	TROY:	I don't care where he coming from. The white man ain't gonna let you get nowhere with that football noway. You go on and get your book-learning so you can work yourself up in that A&P or learn how to fix cars or build houses or something, get you a trade. That way you have something
25		can't nobody take away from you. You go on and learn how to put your hands to some good use. Besides hauling people's garbage.
	CORY:	I get good grades, Pop. That's why the recruiter wants to talk with you. You got to keep up your grades to get recruited.
30		This way I'll be going to college. I'll get a chance. . . .
	TROY:	First you gonna get your butt down there to the A&P and get your job back.
	CORY:	Mr. Stawicki done already hired somebody else 'cause I told him I was playing football.
35	TROY:	You a bigger fool than I thought . . . to let somebody take away your job so you can play some football. Where you gonna get your money to take out your girlfriend and whatnot? What kind of foolishness is that to let somebody take away your job?
40	CORY:	I'm still gonna be working weekends.
	TROY:	Naw . . . naw. You getting your butt out of here and finding you another job.
	CORY:	Come on, Pop! I got to practice. I can't work after school and play football too. The team needs me. That's what
45		Coach Zellman say. . . .
	TROY:	I don't care what nobody else say. I'm the boss . . . you understand? I'm the boss around here. I do the only saying that counts.
	CORY:	Come on, Pop!
50	TROY:	I asked you . . . did you understand?
	CORY:	Yeah . . .
	TROY:	What?!
	CORY:	Yessir.
	TROY:	You go on down there to that A&P and see if you can get your
55		job back. If you can't do both . . . then you quit the football team. You've got to take the crookeds with the straights.
	CORY:	Yessir.

Essay Question

What assumptions about race and culture motivate Troy in his confrontation with his son? Is father or son more realistic about the value of a college education and the opportunities offered minorities by colleges and professional sports teams in 1957? Why?

from Los Vendidos
Luis Valdez

Background and Purpose

Author Luis Valdez is the son of Mexican farmworkers, born and reared in California. He began his career as a dramatist working with an experimental theater company, then formed his own company of farmworkers. During a strike, Valdez's company improvised short, satirical plays dramatizing their oppression. The stock characters who exemplify Anglo stereotypes of Mexicans and the mixture of Spanish and English spoken by the characters help to dramatize Valdez' theme. The title, *Los Vendidos*, may be translated either as "The Sellouts" or "Those Who are Sold."

The analogy of a used car lot, which provides the framework of the play, is central to the theme. Honest Sancho, the proprietor of the Used Mexican Lot, has four models for sale. His customer, Miss Jimenez (who insists on the Anglo pronunciation JIM-enez), is from the office of the Governor of California. She is looking for "a Mexican type for the administration." Sancho first offers the farmworker model, and when this one is rejected, displays three more models: the urban tough, the romantic revolutionary, and the bilingual college graduate.

	SANCHO:	Well, you come to the right place, lady. This is Honest Sancho's Used Mexican Lot, and we got all types here. Any particular type you want?
Line	SECRETARY:	Yes, we were looking for somebody suave . . .
5	SANCHO:	Suave.
	SECRETARY:	Debonaire.
	SANCHO:	De buen aire.
	SECRETARY:	Dark.
	SANCHO:	Prieto.
10	SECRETARY:	But of course, not too dark.
	SANCHO:	No muy prieto.
	SECRETARY:	Perhaps, beige.
	SANCHO:	Beige, just the tone. Asi como cafecito con leche, ¿no?
	SECRETARY:	One more thing. He must be hard-working.
15	SANCHO:	That could only be one model. Step right over here to the center of the shop, lady. [*They cross to the FARMWORKER.*] This is our standard farmworker model. As you can see, in the words of our beloved Senator George Murphy, he is "built close to the ground." Also, take special notice of his
20		4-ply Goodyear huaraches, made from the rain tire. This

---

13 **Asi . . . leche:** like coffee with milk

20 **huaraches:** sandals

---

wide-brimmed sombrero is an extra added feature; keeps off the sun, rain and dust.

SECRETARY: Yes, it does look durable.

SANCHO: And our farmworker model is friendly. Muy amable. Watch.
25 [*snaps his fingers.*]

FARMWORKER [*lifts up head*]: Buenos dias, señorita. [*His head drops.*]

SECRETARY: My, he is friendly.

SANCHO: Didn't I tell you? Loves his patrones! But his most attractive feature is that he's hard-working. Let me show
30 you. [*Snaps fingers. FARMWORKER stands.*]

FARMWORKER: ¡El jale! [*He begins to work.*]

SANCHO: As you can see he is cutting grapes.

SECRETARY: Oh, I wouldn't know.

SANCHO: He also picks cotton. [*Snaps. FARMWORKER begins to pick*
35 *cotton.*]

SECRETARY: Versatile, isn't he?

SANCHO: He also picks melons. [*Snaps. FARMWORKER picks melons.*] That's his slow speed for late in the season. Here's his fast speed. [*Snap. FARMWORKER picks faster.*]

40 SECRETARY: Chihuahua . . . I mean, goodness, he sure is a hardworker.

SANCHO [*pulls the FARMWORKER to his feet*]: And that isn't the half of it. Do you see these little holes on his arms that appear to be pores? During those hot sluggish days in the field when the vines or the branches get so entangled, it's almost
45 impossible to move, these holes emit a certain grease that allows our model to slip and slide right through the crop with no trouble at all.

SECRETARY: Wonderful. But is he economical?

SANCHO: Economical? Señorita, you are looking at the Volkswagen
50 of Mexicans. Pennies a day is all it takes. One plate of beans and tortillas will keep him going all day. That, and chile. Plenty of chile. Chile jalepeños, chile verde, chile colorado. But, of course, if you do give him chile [*Snap. FARMWORKER turns left face. Snap. FARMWORKER bends over*],
55 then you have to change his oil filter once a week.

SECRETARY: What about storage?

SANCHO: No problem. You know these new farm labor camps our Honorable Governor Reagan has built out by Parlier or Raisin City? They were designed with our model in mind.
60 Five, six, seven, even ten in one of those shacks will give you no trouble at all. You can also put him in old barns, old cars, riverbanks. You can even leave him out in the field overnight with no worry!

---

24 **Muy amable:** Very friendly

28 **patrones:** bosses

32 **El jale:** The job

40 **Chihuahua:** Wow!

SECRETARY: Remarkable.

65 SANCHO: And here's an added feature: every year at the end of the season, this model goes back to Mexico and doesn't return, automatically, until next spring.

SECRETARY: How about that. But tell me, does he speak English?

SANCHO: Another outstanding feature is that last year this model
70 was programmed to go out on STRIKE! [*Snap.*]

FARMWORKER: ¡Huelga! ¡Huelga! Hermandos, salganse de esos files. [*Snap. He stops.*]

SECRETARY: No! Oh no, we can't strike in the State Capitol.

SANCHO: Well, he also scabs. [*Snap.*]

75 FARMWORKER: Me vendo barato, ¿y qué? [*Snap.*]

SECRETARY: That's much better, but you didn't answer my question. Does he speak English?

SANCHO: Bueno . . . no, pero he has other . . .

SECRETARY: No.

80 SANCHO: Other features.

SECRETARY: No! He just won't do!

SANCHO: Okay, okay, pues. We have other models.

Essay Question

Consider the stereotype of the farmworker: what attitudes and preconceptions are being satirized? What is added to the satire by the machine analogy?

---

71 **Huelga . . . files:** Strike, strike, brothers, leave those rows

75 **Me vendo . . . qué:** My price is cheap, so what?

78 **Bueno . . . pero:** Well, no, but

82 **pues:** then

from The Rover
Aphra Behn

Background and Purpose

The Rover (1677) was written by that rarity, a female dramatist of the seventeenth century. Behn succeeded in bringing to the stage at least seventeen plays; her prolific output and successful productions were remarkable in an era which did not consider women writers respectable. Restoration comedy, of which *The Rover* is a fine example, is not known for its tameness. It typically explores love and intrigue, with broad characters such as the rake, the charming young lady, and the restless wife. Four of the roles in *The Rover* were played by women, among the first to appear on the English stage.

The play has a feminist theme: women as commodities in the marriage market. An issue in *The Rover* is the practice of "jointure," a stipend for widows. Although a husband pocketed his bride's dowry, her father could in part protect her by offering her an income upon her husband's death; such monies were essential because women could not inherit their husbands' estates. In *The Rover*, Florinda, the older daughter, has been offered jointure if she will marry according to her father's wishes, and the younger, Hellena, is meant to take vows as a nun; what would have been her dowry can instead be her sister's jointure.

The play is set in Naples during Carnival or Mardi Gras, a time of masked revelry. The masks donned by the revellers provide a measure of anonymity and thus encourage bold, flirtatious behavior. What unfolds is a comedy of romantic intrigue whose end is, of course, marriage. Note that the language is closer to modern English than Shakespeare's, but that the second-person familiar *thee* and *thou* is still used between intimates. A few words have a different meaning now than they did in the 17th century, but the frank expression of the feelings, plans, and hopes of these young women should be quite clear. This passage begins the play:

FLORINDA: What an impertinent thing is a young girl bred in a nunnery! How full of questions! Prithee no more, Hellena; I have told thee more than thou understand'st already.

Line 5 HELLENA: The more's my grief. I would fain know as much as you, which makes me so inquisitive; nor is't enough I know you're a lover, unless you tell me too who 'tis you sigh for.

FLORINDA: When you're a lover I'll think you fit for a secret of that nature.

HELLENA: 'Tis true, I never was a lover yet, but I begin to have a
10 shrewd guess what 'tis to be so, and fancy it very pretty to sigh, and sing, and blush, and wish, and dream and wish, and long and wish to see the man, and when I do look pale and tremble, just as you did when my brother brought home the fine English colonel to see you. What do you call
15 him? Don Belvile?

FLORINDA: Fie, Hellena.

HELLENA: That blush betrays you. I am sure 'tis so. Or is it Don Antonio the Viceroy's son? Or perhaps the rich old Don Vincentio, whom my father designs you for a husband? Why do you blush again?

20

FLORINDA: With indignation; and how near soever my father thinks I am to marrying that hated object, I shall let him see I understand better what's due to my beauty, birth, and fortune, and more to my soul, than to obey those unjust commands.

25

HELLENA: Now hang me, if I don't love thee for that dear disobedience. I love mischief strangely, as most of our sex do who are come to love nothing else. But tell me, dear Florinda, don't you love that fine *Anglese*? For I vow, next to loving him myself, 'twill please me most that you do so, for he is so gay and so handsome.

30

FLORINDA: Hellena, a maid designed for a nun ought not to be so curious in a discourse of love.

HELLENA: And dost thou think that ever I'll be a nun? Or at least till I'm so old I'm fit for nothing else? Faith no, sister; and that which makes me long to know whether you love Belvile, is because I hope he has some mad companion or other that will spoil my devotion. Nay, I'm resolved to provide myself this Carnival, if there be e'er a handsome proper fellow of my humour above ground, though I ask first.

35

40

FLORINDA: Prithee be not so wild.

HELLENA: Now you have provided yourself of a man you take no care of poor me. Prithee tell me, what dost thou see about me that is unfit for love? Have I not a world of youth? A humour gay? A beauty passable? A vigor desirable? Well shaped? Clean limbed? Sweet breathed? And sense enough to know how all these ought to be employed to the best advantage? Yes, I do and will; therefore lay aside your hopes of my fortune by my being a devote, and tell me how you came acquainted with this Belvile. For I perceive you knew him before he came to Naples.

45

50

Essay Question

From the evidence of their own words, what can you infer about the characters of these sisters? What evidence foreshadows that their father's plans will be thwarted?

---

29 **Anglese:** Englishman

49 **devote:** nun

Drama

Anlayses of Skill Questions and Guidelines for Essays

14 *from* The Glass Menagerie

Tennessee Williams

Analysis of Skill Questions

1. The stage directions indicate to the actors that they must speak their lines with a specific degree of intensity. For instance, although we know from her words that Amanda is upset by Tom's loud voice, her preoccupation with what the neighbors will think is overridden by her anger. The actress playing this role is told that she is to be *"fairly screeching"* her next lines. The actor playing Tom's role is directed to laugh *"wildly"* and *"still more wildly."* He is later directed to speak words *"wildly."* We can interpret his mood with the help of these clues. Laura's single word is to be said *"desperately."* We are reminded of how frightened she is by the quarrel and what it may foreshadow. She interrupts because she does not want Tom to say anything irrevocable to their mother.

2. Gestures help convey the emotional content of the dialogue. Early in the quarrel, Tom *"tears the portieres open."* This action demonstrates how badly he wants to break free of the immediate as well as the long-term situation. We are told that both Tom and Amanda are *"gesticulating,"* making large physical gestures that express emotion. Tom responds to Laura's warning by moving back toward his mother in what might be a conciliatory way. However, in his last speech, at the height of his anger and resentment, he *"bends fiercely toward her slight figure"* in a threatening stance. Though movement and gesture are important, it is just as important to notice that Laura *does not* move during the scene.

3. The physical aspects of staging reinforce meaning and contribute to the emotional impact of the play. We know that the quarrel takes place where Tom does his writing because of the "wild disarray of manuscripts" on the table. The chair "overthrown on the floor" tells us that he is angry about the interruption to his work. Lighting also reinforces meaning and sets a distinctive atmosphere. In this passage, the playing area has "a turgid smoky red glow," the very color of rage. The "fiery glow" casts the actors' shadows on the ceiling. That apartment is hellish and Amanda, in "metal curlers" and a "very old bathrobe, much too large" which once belonged to her faithless husband, is a devil. By clinging so obstinately to her past and constantly asserting her claims on her son's future, she is torturing Tom. The light on Laura's still figure, in contrast, is "a clear pool," reminding Tom starkly of his obligation to her: innocent and undemanding, she is helpless without him.

4. Judging from her reasons for confiscating the Lawrence novel, Amanda is narrow, prudish, and judgmental. She calls the novel "hideous" and "filth," its author "insane," and his mind "diseased." When she accuses Tom of unspeakable behavior under cover of darkness, she speaks from her own narrow understanding of the world: "Nobody" behaves that way. "Nobody in their right minds"; "People don't. . . ." It's true that her kind of people are bound within the safe margins of their little lives, forgetting the healthy desire of young adults to claim independence and leave home.

  Amanda uses clichés liberally as she tries to impose her will on her son: "You come right back in—" and "Come back here, Tom Wingfield! I'm not through talking to you!" Her rhetorical questions get to the heart of the matter—"What right have you. . . ." —and bring about the turning point, the crux of Tom's conflict: does he have the right to live his own life and act on his ambitions? If he does anything other than stay miserably at home in order to feed and shelter his feckless mother and helpless sister, he flouts his mother's will. Amanda's overriding concern is security; even her strong desires for decency and keeping up appearances are overridden by her concern for Laura's future and her own. Because she misunderstands what her son wants and why he needs to escape from the apartment at night, her vituperative attack on his motives precipitates the very crisis she fears.

Guidelines for Responding to the Essay Question

The thesis will state that Tom is frustrated and conflicted by his situation, and that in this passage he moves closer to resolving his conflict by leaving home. A successful essay will:

Analyze the several sides of his conflict: Tom's conflicting needs and feelings and the claims of others;

Present evidence of his frustration with the present situation: his job, his mother's demands, his ambitions;

Present evidence of his feelings for Laura and the conflict these feelings cause;

Present evidence of the alternating action and paralysis caused by his conflict with his mother.

The conclusion will show that Tom comes closer to resolving his conflicts as a result of the quarrel.

from Pygmalion

George Bernard Shaw

Analysis of Skill Questions

1. In this passage, the customary manners of highborn and lowborn are reversed. Higgins rudely speaks of Eliza in the third person, saying "shes no use" and then orders her, "Be off with you: I don't want you." Eliza stands up for herself and points out the professor's rudeness, calling him "saucy." When Higgins asks, "What do you expect me to say to you?" she gives him a lesson in basic manners: "Well, if you was a gentleman, you might ask me to sit down, I think." Higgins continues to give his guest orders: "Hold your tongue" and "Sit down." Eliza's feelings are hurt. She is acting with what she believes to be refinement in offering to pay for the lessons and continues to remind Higgins that she is not asking for any favors. Higgins insults and frightens the girl with rude names like "baggage," and sends her, *"wounded and whimpering,"* across the room, while she utters her first frightful sound.

    Eliza protests, "I wont be called a baggage when Ive offered to pay like any lady," making clear that she intends to behave with gentility. She responds well to Pickering's courtesy, finally sitting down when politely invited to do so. She calls the gentlemen "silly" when they mockingly recite the childish rhyme, and when Mrs. Pearce reproves her she asks, "Why wont he speak sensible to me?" again pointing out Higgins' poor manners. Ironically, the gentleman who is the flower girl's host is rude and abusive, while in contrast, the lowly guest is forthright, but never rude, recognizing the difference between good and bad manners. We are provoked by the incongruity into laughter, at ourselves as well as at the characters, as we are forced to admit that good grammar and genteel elocution are not the same as good manners.

2. Eliza makes a series of miscalculations that contribute to the humor of the scene. She has arrived at the professor's door in a taxi, spending money she can ill afford in order to behave correctly and to impress him so he will accept her as a student. She is unaware that Higgins does not know or care how people arrive at his doorstep; his housekeeper sizes up and screens visitors. When Higgins brusquely tells her to leave, she assumes that Mrs. Pearce has failed to tell him that "I come in a taxi." She then takes the housekeeper's response, "What do you think a gentleman like Mr Higgins cares what you came in?" as proof of Higgins' pride, and assumes that a mere teacher has a lot of nerve pretending to be a gentleman: "Oh, we are proud! He aint above giving lessons, not him: I heard him say so."

    A still more telling error stems from Eliza's certainty that her friend's French lessons from "a real French gentleman" should rightly cost more than "teaching me my own language." The point of Higgins' boast is precisely that the girl with the lower class accent must be taught the elements of language that are foreign to her: standard genteel English grammar and pronunciation. If he can transform her slum girl's speech into that of a duchess, he will have proven his talent to Pickering and to the world at large. Eliza, however, has not grasped that the professor's interest was originally engaged by the challenge of transforming the discordant sounds coming out of her mouth. She thinks that a shilling per lesson is worth the famous professor's time.

3. Eliza's costume and mode of address are part of her effort to impress Higgins in order to convince him to take her on as a pupil. Her hat shows her idea of fine taste—plenty of bold color and ostentatious display. She is apparently not acquainted with subtlety. Compared to their first meeting, when she was selling flowers on a street corner, she is cleaner, if not perfectly clean, and she has made an effort to improve her "shoddy coat." Thinking that she looks very much the gentlewoman, she tries to talk like one, using the word *lady* to refer to herself and her friend no fewer than three times in a few minutes. Her efforts to speak like a lady have the same inadvertent results as the feathers in her hat: she can't get hired in a flower shop "unless I can talk more genteel." Just as her dirty apron reveals her lowly social class and its realities, so does her remark that Higgins must have tossed her coins the evening before because "Youd had a drop in, hadn't you?" She assumes that he must have been intoxicated at the time.

Eliza is also trying to appear worldly and businesslike. Her pathetic attempt to make her coat presentable accords with what she considers a businesslike manner. She repeatedly says that she should be welcomed because "I'm bringing you business," and "I am ready to pay him—not asking any favor." Her manner deteriorates until she is reduced to haggling: "You wouldnt have the face to ask me the same for teaching me my own language . . . so I won't give you more than a shilling. Take it or leave it." Eliza does not seem to realize that ladies do not conduct business—that the two just don't mix—so when she says, "Ive offered to pay like any lady," she is uttering one of the funniest lines in the play.

Guidelines for Responding to the Essay Question

The thesis will state the source of the conflict and the anticipated tone and action of the developing plot. A successful essay will consider the following similarities between Liza and Higgins:

- An excessive degree of self-involvement;
- Ample evidence of pride and arrogance;
- Unconventional views about gender, class, and social proprieties;
- Honesty to the point of bluntness.

The conclusion will sum up the kind of play that is produced by the clash of these seemingly dissimilar persons.

16

from The Importance of Being Earnest

Oscar Wilde

Analysis of Skill Questions

1. Lady Bracknell begins the interview by broaching those topics that are really important to her: Jack's relationship to tobacco, his age, and his education. She moves on to specifics about his income and its source, then examines him about his

real estate holdings. She is more interested in the respectability of Jack's tenant than in his political views. And finally she comes to "minor matters": Jack's pedigree and social status. Lady Bracknell would prefer Jack to be aristocratically idle and ignorant, suitably wealthy with sound investments, and possessed of a house in a socially acceptable part of London, on the more fashionable side of the square. If Jack's financial background is solid, his class background becomes a minor matter, especially if he behaves like an aristocrat and values style over substance.

2. In the character of Lady Bracknell, Wilde offers a satiric portrait of the aristocracy. In her simile in praise of "natural ignorance," Lady Bracknell asserts that, "like a delicate and exotic fruit," ignorance must not be tampered with. Her ironic reversal of values is seen in her assertion that "the whole theory of modern education is radically unsound." She adds, "Fortunately . . . education produces no effect whatsoever." Such a foolish statement makes her a figure of fun and adds to the satiric effect of her speeches.

    Lady Bracknell hears first about Jack's country house, but fervently hopes that he also has a town house, for "a girl with a simple, unspoiled nature . . . could hardly be expected to reside in the country." Conventional wisdom says that it is the sophisticated city, not the unpretentious countryside, that corrupts the naïve, so here, again, Lady Bracknell's interpretation of experience leaves her open to ridicule. Jack assures Lady Bracknell that he doesn't depend on his country acres for his "real income." His witty irony should be delivered deadpan: "the poachers are the only people who make anything out of it."

    Bracknell then turns the usual social scale upside down by asking whether Jack's father was "born in . . . the purple of commerce," or whether he rose "from the ranks of aristocracy." Purple is the color of royalty, and commerce is beneath those with inherited wealth, yet here she suggests that the sons of businessmen are born into wealth. The basis of the aristocracy is that one is born into one's place and can neither rise nor fall in rank of one's own volition. By making Lady Bracknell invert values in this preposterous fashion, Wilde reveals that at the heart of this character lies a complete disdain for reality coupled with an utter complacency about her own illusions.

3. Lady Bracknell provides ample evidence of her ingrained snobbery throughout the interview. She has joined forces with "the dear Duchess of Bolton" to marry off their daughters, and she feels bound to tell Jack at the outset that he is not "down on my list of eligible young men." She graciously concedes that she is "quite ready to enter your name, should your answers be what a really affectionate mother requires." This is code for the fact that young men on the list are socially acceptable and rich.

    Lady Bracknell is vitally interested in the respectability of Jack's tenant, who though she has a title and is "considerably advanced in years," is not known to Lady Bracknell, and, therefore, may be socially beyond the pale. In that case, her slight business connection to Jack might sully his social position.

    Jack is in grave danger of being kept off the list when Lady Bracknell discovers that his townhouse is on the unfashionable side of Belgrave Square: she "sternly" insists that both the fashion and the side could be altered, if necessary. She has a firm grasp of what high society views as vital in a prospective bridegroom.

    Politics is far down on Lady Bracknell's list of vital concerns. She lumps the Liberal Unionists in with the Tories, but indicates that they are second-best, barely socially acceptable: "They dine with us. Or come in the evening, at any rate." An invitation to dine of course trumps a mere invitation to visit after dinner.

4. Wilde's use of highly stylized language throughout this scene exemplifies his wit and rhetorical finesse. When Lady Bracknell expresses satisfaction that Jack's money is in investments rather than land, she succinctly points out the economic realities of the times. She uses parallelism and alliteration in the sentence that also delivers a pun: "What between the duties expected of one during one's lifetime, and the duties exacted from one after one's death, land has ceased to be either a profit or a pleasure." Landowners in an agrarian economy were expected to provide for their tenants. That is one kind of duty. The other "duty" is inheritance taxes, which were enormous. The epigram, with beautifully balanced antithesis, follows: "It [land] gives one position, and prevents one from keeping it up." As for diction, surely a most startling word in the context is Lady Bracknell's accusation of "carelessness" when Jack admits to having lost both his parents.

Guidelines for Responding to the Essay Question

The thesis must make a claim about whether Wilde's satire is Horatian or Juvenalian, and preview the supporting evidence from Lady Bracknell's speeches. Consider the following:

- The order of Lady Bracknell's list of questions as these determine the structure of the passage and the thrust of the satire;

- Lady Bracknell's irreverence for things usually deemed sacred;

- The snobbery evidenced by many of Lady Bracknell's comments;

- Lady Bracknell's ignorance of politics, as contrasted with her keen understanding of economic realities.

The conclusion must clinch the argument for the overall tone of the satire.

17 *from* MASTER HAROLD . . . and the boys
Athol Fugard

Analysis of Skill Questions

1. The author's use of capitalization and punctuation are significant devices because they reveal the underlying racial determination of the relationship between the characters. Sam is doing Hally's bidding in calling him Master Harold. The boy is insisting on this unearned mark of respect from grown men. The two waiters are black South Africans, and their lack of status is shown by their being called "boys" by whites. They are an afterthought in the title, as shown by the ellipsis, as though they have little importance compared to the self-absorbed white boy, and their kindly friendship means nothing to him. The actor playing Sam is directed by the ellipses to pause before and after he says "Master Harold" every time he uses the name. This strongly implies his disgust with Hally's behavior, and the sarcasm with which he uses the title of respect. Other uses of the ellipsis slow down his words and render them more ominous, making us hear them as warnings.

2. Sam has tried to act as a father to Hally, to make up for his biological father's shaming lack of responsibility and dignity. Sam has been trying to give Hally the self-respect he needs in order to become a decent man. But now Sam knows that he has failed because Hally has insulted and humiliated him by insisting on being called Master Harold, and by spitting in his face. Hally has taken on the racism of his father, chosen it over the love and decency offered by Sam.

3. Apartheid laws in South Africa were based on the belief that the most debased white person was superior to the best Black person. Ironically, Sam is acting with fatherly compassion, whereas Hally's real father is humiliating the boy by drunkenly groveling on the floor. The father is characterized as a baby in that he cannot stand or walk without aid; he is a cripple and he is also emotionally immature. He has responded to his handicap in an infantile way by becoming an alcoholic, and on this occasion he has messed in his trousers, so he must be cleaned up and put to bed. It is ironic, the opposite of what the onlookers expect, that the procession home is led by a little boy, while the father, who should be in charge of boy and servant, is helplessly being carried by his "inferior." Sam's repetition serves to emphasize his love and compassion for Hally and is especially poignant considering what Hally has just done to repay his fatherly kindness.

4. Hally must have been saying disrespectful things about his father, as though he "just despised him for being a weak man." But Sam knows that it is not that simple and wants to teach the boy a lesson of compassion: "He's your father. You love him and you're ashamed of him." Hally is failing in Sam's eyes; furthermore, Hally has now done irrevocable things to Sam, which will make him ashamed of himself. Sam knows that a boy with no self-respect cannot become a man.

5. The kite was made by Sam, his gift to Hally, and was meant to help the boy "look up, be proud of something, of yourself. . . ." As Hally succeeds in proudly launching the kite, he is symbolically looking at himself with pride and respect, thus beginning to grow to manhood. The kite episode contrasts starkly with the scene that has just taken place in that Hally, having seemed to launch his own life with the help of his mentor, has now betrayed both that mentor and himself.

6. Sam's revelation that a black man is not permitted to sit on a bench designated for whites is symbolic of the entirely destructive and inhuman system of Apartheid. The tragic irony of the play lies in the fact that racism deprives the boy of the surrogate father he desperately needs, even as it dehumanizes the black man who is in every way superior to the boy's biological father. A further dismal result is that Hally, who has every reason to know better, has taken on the bigotry of his family and white society; in doing so he has rejected the loving man who could have saved him from isolation and shame. Hally may have been sitting high on a hill (above black people), but he is alone—his father is not a father to him, and Sam is not permitted to be there. Consequently, Hally is without a source of pride and self-respect.

Guidelines for Responding to the Essay Question

An explication calls for a careful analysis of the meanings, relationships, paradoxes, and ironies of a text. Your thesis will suggest that the opening dialogue contains all the significant meanings of the rest of the passage. Address the following points in your discussion:

- Why it will not now be difficult for Sam to address Hally as "Master Harold";

- What is implied in the statement, "you've just hurt yourself *bad*";

- What is cowardly about Hally's spitting in Sam's face;

- The sense in which Hally's real target is his father;

- What makes Hally feel safe and why this is despicable;

- The significance of Sam's pun on "fair";

- The wish of both Sam and Willie to do physical violence.

The conclusion might comment on the significance of Willie's final words, which dissipate the threat of violence and sum up the consequences of Hally's act for all three characters.

18 *from* The School for Scandal

Richard Brinsley Sheridan

Analysis of Skill Questions

1. Each character's name is highly suggestive of an unpleasant trait or two. As Snake's last line indicates, Lady Sneerwell is a genius at "sneering" and ruining reputations with "a word or a look" only. Snake's first words indicate that he is sly: he disguises his handwriting in the gossipy report Lady Sneerwell has ordered him to circulate. He is also insinuating, and like the snake in the Garden of Eden, flatters his employer greatly. Lady Brittle, as her name suggests, must be snappish and easily offended, as well as cold and lacking in feeling. Captain Boastall also deserves what he gets, because he is a braggart. Mrs. Clackit's name describes the hen-like noises she makes. Her appellation implies that she chatters thoughtlessly and at great length, and thus hers is the perfect name for a gossip. Throughout the scene, the use of caricature establishes an ironic tone that points up the disagreeable nature of the characters and their business.

2. Mrs. Clackit's vicious gossip has caused six engagements to be broken, three sons to be disinherited, four elopements, four secret pregnancies, nine separations, and two divorces; in a contribution to a gossip column, she claims that two people who had never even met are having a love affair.

3. The significance of the content and ordering of these items is that, ironically, the *least* painful and ruinous is mentioned last, the position usually reserved for the *strongest* example. These gossips have upside-down values and a complete disregard for the feelings of others; the most delicious use of slander and defamation of character is that which is made public in the gossip columns of a high-society magazine.

4. Mrs. Clackit has a talent for spreading scandal. Snake says that she "generally designs well," and has "a bold invention." If she were an artist, this would be a worthwhile and socially useful talent, but ironically, she uses her talent to tell lies and thus ruin reputations. She works industriously at this business. The successes that Snake catalogs are all human tragedies caused by her malicious gossip.

5. Lady Sneerwell hints more delicately and her sneering is more mellow, but ironically, her hints are just as untrue and just as malicious as Clackit's. She is more talented because she is more subtle, but uses her talent for the same vicious ends. Mediocre liars overdo the detail, but Lady Sneerwell can outdo them with her subtlety, even when they have "a little truth on their side" and she has none. The sycophantic Snake becomes hyperbolic in his praise of Lady Sneerwell because he is afraid that in praising Mrs. Clackit's talents so lavishly, he has offended his employer.

Guidelines for Responding to the Essay Question

The thesis will state the effects of caricature and of ordinary words as they are used in the context of the dialogue. The latter might include:

- Words that denote ordinary business transactions;
- Words that usually describe the arts and artists;
- Words that denote secrecy.

A conclusion will more generally describe how the use of irony and caricature create satire.

19

from The Crucible

Arthur Miller

Analysis of Skill Questions

1. The folk of Salem tend to be superstitious and fearful of the extraordinary. They follow their clergy in viewing the world as a battleground between the forces of good and evil. Hale reassures the villagers that his books contain "all the invisible world, caught, defined, and calculated." The Devil and all his familiar spirits as well as witches and wizards are all believed to be real, if invisible, presences. The people believe that witches fly: Betty's most alarming symptom is her attempt to leap out the window. Putnam believes that Betty's refusal to hear God's name spoken is evidence that she has been bewitched, but Hale, the expert, claims that this belief is superstition. His books are from Europe, where for several centuries learned men and clerics have been studying the subject—and drowning, hanging, and burning "witches."

   The Crucible provides authentic details that reveal contemporary thinking about witchcraft. Hale's interrogation of Betty focuses directly on the form of assault used by the Devil, whether bird or beast. Because Betty has supposedly tried to throw herself from the housetop, Hale believes that the Devil has urged the girl to fly. He prays over her in Latin, invoking the Christian God to send the Devil back to hell. We begin to understand that the clergy increased their moral authority and produced conformity among the pious and largely ignorant colonists through the manipulation of fear.

2. The shadowy figure in the background is the slave Tituba. The dancing in the forest suggests to Mrs. Putnam and even to Hale that the slave Tituba is a witch, for, after all, she is of African descent and, therefore, may worship the Devil instead of God; any god but their particular one must be a devil. Tituba may be teaching the girls how to commune with the Devil, believed to inhabit the untamed and godless wilderness that surrounds the tiny settlement of Salem. Other forms of independent thinking are also suspect; Martha Corey reads "strange books" at night: unusual behavior, especially for a woman, in that time and place. Her husband claims that this reading "discomfits" him and makes him unable to say prayers, possible "proof" that the books contain satanic knowledge and spells.

3. Hale says that "if she is truly in the Devil's grip" it will be necessary to "rip and tear" to free the child. This picture of physical violence, a tug of war between a man of God and the Devil himself, personifies evil, making it very real and powerful. It suggests that the battle for the child's soul is of great import. When Rebecca Nurse is unwilling to witness the physical violence upon a little girl that will ensue, Parris, *"striving for conviction,"* uses an image of foul infection: "Why, Rebecca, we may open up the boil of all our troubles today." To cut open a boil is painful, but is necessary to relieve the body of the disease that is making it ill. Betty Parris represents the greater community; the body politic of Salem is threatened with an epidemic of witchcraft and must purge itself of the germ.

4. The villagers, in particular Ann Putnam and Parris, seem to begrudge Rebecca Nurse her moral authority over the townspeople. When Rebecca expresses her astonishment that Ann sent a child "to conjure up the dead," Ann Putnam responds, "Let God blame me, not you, not you, Rebecca! I'll not have you judging me any more!" Clearly Rebecca has been a moral arbiter in the village, and Mrs. Putnam resents being judged by the saintly old woman. She uses the pretext of witchcraft in the village to shift the blame for her disappointments onto Rebecca.

   Parris, too, fears and resents Rebecca. Her unwillingness to witness Hale's attempt to "crush" the Devil "utterly" by ripping and tearing the body and spirit of his child gives Parris pause, so that as Rebecca leaves, he is having second thoughts about having sent for Hale. When Rebecca says, "I go to God for you, sir," she is saying that she is going off to pray for Parris, rather than for his daughter. He responds "*(with trepidation—and resentment)*:" "I hope you do not mean we go to Satan here!" The elderly woman's wisdom and insight hint that Parris has started a terrible process that will take on its own momentum. He asks Hale, *(in fright)*: "How can it be the Devil? Why would he choose my house to strike?" He is afraid for himself at least as much as for his daughter, for his job and his position in the community. The rest join Parris in feeling *"resentful of her note of moral superiority"* in leaving them to go and pray. All of this evidence foreshadows that Rebecca Nurse may be accused of witchcraft.

5. Hale's method of investigation reveals that he is doctrinaire and rigid in his interpretation of evil and possession. He offers his expert testimony when Putnam points to "a sure sign of witchcraft" in Betty's not being able to "bear to hear the Lord's name." Hale asserts that "The Devil is precise; the marks of his presence are definite as stone. . . ." Hale thus shows that he believes that there is a science to the discovery of witchcraft. His attitude toward the authorities who wrote his books is indicated in the stage direction, *"with a tasty love of intellectual pursuit,"* and the books themselves are scholarly tomes, completely defining and cataloguing the world of evil spirits. Hale has complete faith in the "knowledge" to be found in the books. Today's more sophisticated readers, on the other hand, know the pitfalls of such superstitious thinking. When Hale asks the child whether the Devil

has appeared to her in the form of a bird, mouse, or other harmless creature, we react with disgust and pity for the ignorance the question reveals.

The beginning of Hale's interrogation of the child shows another glaring flaw in methodology, which will have terrible results: he is instructing her, putting words into her mouth that accord with what his books have taught him. If she agrees that she is being afflicted by the Devil in the form of a bird or beast, she cannot be held responsible for her own behavior. Why would she resist? Hale is apparently unaware that he is leading the witness, and thus making her "confession" worthless. The reader understands this as the prelude to the tragedy that was the Salem witch-hunt.

Guidelines for Responding to the Essay Question

The thesis will state that there are several distinct and understandable motives for accusing one's neighbors. A successful essay will analyze:

- The powerful motive of a girl such as Betty Parris, and by extension, her peers;
- Tituba's possible motivation in speaking with the girls about ancient practices;
- Ann Putnam's major grievance and general outlook on life;
- Parris' strong motivation to retain the power conferred by his position as clergyman.

The conclusion should consider how all of these human motivations produce the tragic consequences with which history has made us familiar: the murder of innocents who become the victims of superstition and pettiness.

20 *from* Tartuffe

Molière

Analysis of Skill Questions

1. Valere would undoubtedly expect Mariane to fall into his arms in tears and beg him to save her from a fate worse than death. Because he begins the interview rather coldly ("Madam, I've just received some wondrous news / Regarding which I'd like to hear your views"), the tone of the discussion is formal and brittle, rather than impassioned and warm. Moreover, instead of showing that he is distraught or else taking charge in fine manly fashion and telling her what to do, Valere asks Mariane what she proposes to do. Disappointed that he does not take command, she wavers, and by the time she asks his advice, neither can trust in the other's love. Hurt pride makes it impossible to resort to romantic reassurances, so their anger escalates.

2. Dorine's first comment is an aside to the audience: "Let's see which fool will prove the stubborner." This tells us all we need to know about her good sense and understanding of the situation. She allows the quarrel to go on until Valere has made five gestures to leave, and only then intervenes. Her diction

is strongly realistic: she not only calls the lovers foolish and stubborn, but "mad as mad can be." She tells them to stop the "nonsense," and calls their tragic scene a mere "squabble." Yelling "Whoa, there," as if to a runaway horse, she uses physical action, grabbing Valere's arm to keep him from leaving, thus deflating his romantic gesture and making a farce out of the couple's anger and hurt pride.

3. Perfect rhymes fulfill expectation in a satisfying way *or* surprise us by the incongruity of the rhyming word. Lines 15–20 provide the expected tone as the lovers' quarrel takes a competitive and sarcastic turn, but Mariane's use of the formal word *Sir* to refer to her lover is matched by Dorine's aside to the audience, in which *stubborner* is a surprise, an infrequently used adjective which deflates the high seriousness of the quarrel.

In lines 51–52, Valere has announced that he can easily replace Mariane with a young woman who would welcome his devotion. Mariane responds with verbal irony which Valere chooses to take literally, thus escalating the quarrel.

The finality of the following exchange in lines 72–77 is reinforced by the rhymes. The wry verbal irony is produced by Mariane's not only claiming to wish her lover gone, but hurrying him on his way: "don't hesitate" and "I cannot wait." Valere angrily produces variations on clichés: "the last straw" and "your wish is my command." The clever modification of the clichés to fit the poetic form increases the amusement of the audience.

4. Double rhymes produce witty or comic effects because they are surprising and clever. The following couplets produce this effect especially well: lines 25–26, 38–39, 64–65, and 99–100. There is inherent wit and humor in the sounds of "lutely" / "stutely," "wisely" / "vise me," "pected" / "jected," and "let you" / "get you."

5. The very regularity of the meter adds to the humor. The fact that two people so at odds work this closely to keep the rhythm going creates the fun. Sometimes Mariane and Valere are so desperate to hear the fond words that would break the tension, they try to anticipate one another's thoughts and speech. At other times they break in with angry retorts.

In the case of Mariane's interruption in line 35, she doesn't miss a beat because she doesn't want to hear Valere's accusation that she was deceiving him all along.

In lines 45–46, Valere seems to interrupt in order to agree, but actually advances a new grievance.

In lines 76–80, as Valere repeatedly begins to leave but always returns, Mariane's responses force him to repeat his intentions, but also allow him to delay the final break. The double rhyme contributes to the humor.

This exchange is followed by the most desperate one of all, when, in lines 90–93, Valere again pauses in his retreat and this time pretends that he has heard Mariane speak.

"Ah. Well" indeed. The two have reached the climax of their argument, and need to be saved from themselves by Dorine. The very fact that they read each other's minds so well is a measure of their sincere attachment.

Guidelines for Responding to the Essay Question

Your thesis will clearly identify the tone of the passage and explicate the devices that create that tone. A successful essay will analyze the effects of the following:

- The effect of the rhyming couplets, considering especially double rhymes and lines and couplets which are shared by several speakers;

- The effect of the diction;
- The effect of the rapid pacing of the quarrel.

A conclusion will sum up the ways in which Wilbur's use of prosody and diction sets the tone and puts it at variance with the attitudes of the quarreling lovers.

21

from Othello

William Shakespeare

Analysis of Skill Questions

1. Othello is full of doubt and indecision and raging with jealousy. His emotions are causing "a pain upon [his] forehead." Desdemona's focus is entirely on soothing the headache by binding Othello's brow with the handkerchief. In dramatic terms, it is ironic that when he brushes it aside, she is so concerned about his discomfort that she does not notice that the handkerchief, her cherished love token, falls to the ground.

2. Emilia explains in a soliloquy that the handkerchief was the first gift that Othello gave to Desdemona during their courtship. Furthermore, Othello was explicit about its importance, strongly imploring his beloved to keep it always. Desdemona does not put it away, but keeps it with her at all times, kissing it and talking to it as though it were Othello himself.

3. Emilia's actions are motivated solely by her desire to please her husband. Iago has been asking her to steal the handkerchief for him, and although Emilia knows that Iago is "wayward," she is glad she found it and plans to give it to him. Because she assumes that Desdemona "let it drop by negligence," she has less compunction about stealing it. When she asks what Iago wants with the handkerchief, she does explain that she hopes it is "for some purpose of import" because, "Poor lady, she'll run mad/When she shall lack it." But in the end Emilia obeys her husband's wishes.

4. Iago's soliloquy lets us know that he now has the key to his plot: He will plant Desdemona's handkerchief in Cassio's bedroom, where Cassio will find it. Iago comments that even though the handkerchief is scant evidence of adultery, a jealous person will accept it as though it were a sacred truth from the Bible. Othello is already jealous, the victim of Iago's insinuations. Iago says that dangerous ideas (in this case, Othello's notion that Desdemona may be unfaithful to him) are like poison: at first they hardly taste bad, but once they begin to work in the body they burn insufferably. This analogy is worked out through the remainder of the passage. When Othello enters, he looks so distraught that Iago comments, "I did say so," meaning that the burning has begun—Othello is being tortured by the poison of jealousy. Iago then uses the analogy of sleep: no medicine will ever give the jealous Othello the sleep (peace and contentment) that he had only yesterday.

Guidelines for Responding to the Essay Question

The thesis will state that with Iago's manipulation, Othello, Desdemona, and Emilia each make a fatal mistake that leads to the tragic denouement, while the audience is excruciatingly aware of the dramatic irony involved.

Analysis will demonstrate the change in Othello from the beginning of his scene with Desdemona to its end, despite the loving concern of his wife.

Analysis will also demonstrate that Desdemona's fatal loss of the handkerchief is not the "negligence" that Emilia supposes, and that Emilia secures the handkerchief for Iago in spite of caring for Desdemona and knowing that its loss will upset her.

The conclusion will comment on Iago's soliloquy, which tells us what the three still do not know: how he will use the handkerchief to undo them all.

22 *from* Twelfth Night

William Shakespeare

Analysis of Skill Questions

1. Malvolio reveals his enormous ego through the delusion, encouraged by Maria, that Olivia favors him. He imagines that Olivia treats him with "more exalted respect" than she does her other servants. These slight hints of preferment have gone to Malvolio's head: in his imagination, he is already Count Malvolio. He cites an example of another highborn lady who married beneath her, as though breaking the social order is natural where the servant is a superior individual. Malvolio's fantasy of treating his fellow servants haughtily and forcing his minions to do his will suggests that he is a petty tyrant in his present role as steward. The imagined scene reveals his enormous personal vanity and his belief in his personal attractions. He pictures himself in a velvet gown, frowning and gesturing with the self-importance (winding his watch and playing with "some rich jewel") which he imagines suitable to a person of consequence. In this daydream, Malvolio bullies and insults his wife's uncle, Sir Toby, who curtsies to him and he calls Toby "cousin" instead of "sir."

   Malvolio instantly believes even the grossest flattery in the letter and resolves to take on the characteristics he mistakenly believes "noble": pride and arrogance, political punditry, snobbery, and a preference for extreme and foolish fashions. He is prepared to do the lady's bidding in all things but only because he knows that once he is safely married, he will wield power over her. It never occurs to Malvolio that the letter's last words are the most preposterous of all, in which Olivia supposedly "would alter services with thee," or gladly consent to be his servant.

2. Malvolio's speech points out Sir Toby's flaws: the nobleman is a drunkard who wastes his time with the foolish Sir Andrew. Sir Toby's own words reveal his disposition: he is flirtatious toward Maria, greatly enjoying her wit, and is ready to propose marriage by the end of the scene. As the uncle of the Countess Olivia, he is outraged by Malvolio's pretensions to aristocracy. He is especially angered when

Malvolio, fantasizing that he is already allied to the noble family, drops the "Sir," referring to him as simply "Toby." He is incited to violence, offering to "beat the rogue," and "hit him in the eye" with a stone from a crossbow. He asks, "Shall this fellow live?" and consigns him to the "fire and brimstone" of hell and the "bolts and shackles" of imprisonment. But he also greatly enjoys the trick and often hushes the others so that Malvolio will remain unaware of their presence, wanting the villain to have ample opportunity to get into trouble with his mistress. He displays some wit of his own as he tells Maria at the end of the scene that he will follow her "to the gates of Tartar, thou most excellent devil of wit!"

3. Sir Andrew is Sir Toby's sidekick. He merely echoes the sentiments of Sir Toby, and thus indirectly tells us more about the other character. Sir Andrew uses the same insulting names for Malvolio and takes the cue that the "rogue" should be shot. He stupidly chooses his allusion to a proud person in the Bible without bothering to find one of the same gender as Malvolio: a "Jezebel" has the irrelevant connotations of being an evil and scheming woman. Sir Andrew foolishly calls the attention of the others to Malvolio's insult to himself, "a foolish knight," and says, "I knew 'twas I, for many do call me fool," and he seems resigned to being thus characterized. At the end of the scene, Sir Andrew repeats every remark that Sir Toby makes: he, too, wants to marry Maria, and he too would "ask no other dowry" but her wit, though he is too dimwitted himself to understand most of the fun. He ends the scene following his more clever friend in pursuit of Maria.

4. Fabian supplies stage directions and commentary by remarking that Malvolio is deeply involved in his fantasy, his ego swelling by the minute. He implores his fellow eavesdroppers to be quiet so that Malvolio will not notice them. He wants to see to what extent Malvolio will be tricked, so his requests for silence become stronger. He warns the other eavesdroppers metaphorically that their talking will "break the sinews of our plot," crippling and thus weakening it. He correctly attributes the success of "this sport" to Maria, and admires her for her wit though he is not so foolish as to decide that he wants to marry her on the strength of it.

Fabian's chief contributions to the scene are his animal metaphors. Maria first compares Malvolio to a "trout that must be caught with tickling." These shy fish can be stroked into capture by wily fishermen, as Malvolio will be lured by the flattering letter into making a fool of himself with Olivia. Fabian takes up the motif, observing that Malvolio's presumptuous anticipation of becoming a count "makes a rare turkeycock of him." Like the bird, Malvolio spreads his feathers and struts his conceit for all to see, but he is really only a turkey. Third, when Malvolio finds the letter, Fabian remarks, "Now is the woodcock near the gin," comparing him to another foolish bird, easily caught in a trap. When Maria appears at the end of the scene, Fabian calls her "my noble gull-catcher," an expression that functions as a pun for a gullible person and suggests yet another bird, in an echo of the metaphor comparing the letter to an animal trap.

5. Maria's character is displayed through the letter itself. She knows exactly how to appeal to Malvolio because she understands that his pretensions and ambitions make him vulnerable to flattery. Maria is not only fun-loving; she is motivated to teach Malvolio a lesson about his true social status. She has such faith in her scheme that she does not stay to hear her victim be taken in by the letter, exiting before he finds it and not reentering until he is gone. Her final remarks, which prophecy "the fruits of the sport," also show faith in her abilities.

Maria is further characterized by the flattering epithets others use in speaking to and of her. Toby calls her "the little villain," and "my metal of India," affectionately anticipating the success of her scheme and estimating her value highly.

Fabian reveals his admiration by calling her "my noble gull-catcher," and Toby ends the scene by naming her "thou most excellent devil of wit!"

Guidelines for Responding to the Essay Question

The thesis will show how Malvolio's open display of his character traits will affect Olivia. A successful essay will include specific analysis of Malvolio's new attire, manner, and style of address and Olivia's presumable reaction to her servant's incomprehensible behavior.

The conclusion should consider how well-prepared we are for that reaction and how satisfying it is—whether, in fact, it is poetic justice.

Poetry

Part III of this book provides practice in explicating different poetic forms. Some of the poems are presented in pairs, and most of them represent the complete work of art. You will find that many of the skills and concepts you have been working with are essential in analyzing poetry. As you explore this section, you will add many more literary terms to your toolkit. Despite certain formal considerations, poetry shares many elements with fiction and drama. We read a poem with an eye to setting, atmosphere, plot, persona (narrator), character, and conflict. Figurative language, such as metaphor and symbol, comes to the fore, along with form and structure. On such a small canvas, compression supplies the richness and power. The poem requires our attention to each word, to its placement and sound qualities, and to the many elements that comprise prosody: versification, meter, rhythm, rhyme, and stanza.

Punctuation and Rhythm — Most poets are extremely sensitive to sound, and so is the ideal reader. It is of prime importance that you read a poem aloud, observing the usual rules for the inflection of English sentences. If there is no punctuation at the end of a line, make only the slightest of pauses before continuing; a comma demands a shorter pause than a semicolon or a period. In scanning a poem, you may exaggerate the rhythm to discover the right pattern of stresses and punch the rhyming sounds in search of the rhyme scheme, but a poem reveals its meaning and structure only when you read it sentence by sentence, carefully observing punctuation. When, after explication and analysis, you once again read a poem aloud, all the pieces will fall into place.

Scansion — Scansion is the system for describing conventional rhythms by dividing lines into feet. Metrical rhythm is a pattern of stronger and weaker stresses or accents in the syllables of a line. The meter is rarely perfect, nor is it meant to be, so the opening line is not necessarily a perfect example. The study of a few lines reveals which syllables are stressed in polysyllabic words and how a monosyllabic word functions; nouns, verbs, and adjectives are nearly always more significant (and thus more worthy of stress) than articles and prepositions. Rhetorical accent is also helpful in listening for the pattern because certain syllables receive greater emphasis in order to enhance meaning. Finally, we determine the predominant pattern, keeping in mind that perfectly regular meter is suitable only for a nursery rhyme, and that substitutions disturbing the regular rhythm are frequent and useful, not only for subtlety of sound but also for meaning and emphasis.

Meter and Line Length — The rhythmic patterns that prevail in English poetry are meters of two types. Duple feet have one accented syllable and one unaccented syllable, as musical time may be marked as two or four notes to the measure; triple feet have one accented and two unaccented syllables, as in 3/4 or 6/8 time in music. Each of these types may be either rising (accent at the end) or falling (accent at the beginning). This gives us four possibilities ("x" is the mark for unaccented syllables, "/" for accented ones):

> IAMB: the rising duple foot (x /   x /   x /   x /   x /)
>
> TROCHEE: the falling duple foot (/ x   / x   / x   / x)
>
> ANAPEST: the rising triple foot (x x /   x x /   x x /)
>
> DACTYL: the falling triple foot (/ x x   / x x)

The number of feet in a line should be added to the description of the meter, using familiar numeric prefixes:
   The first line above has five feet, called *iambic pentameter*.
   The second has four feet, called *trochaic tetrameter*.
   The third has three feet, called *anapestic trimeter*.
   The fourth has two feet, called *dactylic dimeter*.
   More rarely used meters are monometer (one foot), hexameter (six feet), heptameter (seven feet, often heard as four plus three), and octameter (eight feet).
   The most usual substitutions (variations) are feet that can rarely be sustained in English, but do provide emphasis in an iambic line:
   Trochee for iamb, especially at the start of a line (initial substitution);
   Spondee for any duple foot (a spondee is a duple foot containing two accented syllables).
   A caesura is a pause or break in the line, variously placed, that modifies the regularity of the meter.
   A line of poetry is either end-stopped (both sense and grammatical construction end with the line) or enjambed, a French term meaning "a striding over," for the continuation of the sense and grammatical construction into the next line.

The vast majority of poems in English fall into iambic meter because that is the natural rhythm of the language. We find that the pentameter line prevails in Shakespeare's plays and sonnets, and in the work of Chaucer, Milton, Dryden, and Pope. Iambic tetrameter has also been widely used for the past four centuries. The meter called "common" is just that, and consists of alternating lines of iambic tetrameter and trimeter, usually in four-line stanzas.

Rhyme Schemes — By convention, patterns of end-rhyme (sound correspondences at the ends of lines) are noted by giving each new sound a new letter of the alphabet, so that a sonnet by Shakespeare has the following rhyme scheme: *ababcdcdefefgg*. The last two, *gg*, indicate a rhymed couplet. Perfect or true rhyme is the strongest correspondence of sound. There are many names for more nuanced rhymes. (See Glossary.)

Stanzas — In contrast to the sonnet, a poem in continuous form with no breaks, many poems are formed of stanzas, regularly recurring groupings of two or more lines. Their length, metrical form, even rhyme scheme may be identical, but need not be. Common stanzas have numeric names, such as tercet and quatrain for a three- or four-lined stanza. Most fixed forms, such as the ballad, the sestina, and the villanelle (but not the sonnet) have a definite pattern of meter, rhyme, and stanza. Lines grouped in unequal blocks, called verse paragraphs, may, like prose paragraphs, be organized according to content.

Form — When we speak of form, we mean the organization of the parts of the poem in relation to its total effect. Verse form is the organization of rhythmic units; stanza form is the organization of lines in groups; generic form is the type of poem (elegy, ode, etc.). Conventional forms exist before the particular work is written; organic forms develop for the poem at hand, resulting in a nonce form (for the moment, or nonce—used only once).

Structure — The framework of a piece of literature, its general plan or outline, is easily seen in fiction, where chapter divisions or breaks in the text serve to organize plot; in drama, the action is divided into acts and scenes. The more subtle structures of poems are nonetheless important, and are often the most reliable key to the theme of the work. The sequence of images and ideas that carry meaning is conveyed via grammar, syntax, and rhetorical devices.

Poetic Diction — We must be attentive to the author's word choices and to the patterns created by these choices, the degree to which words, phrases, and figures are abstract or concrete, Latinate or Anglo-Saxon, colloquial or formal, technical or common, and especially whether they are intended to convey literal or figurative meaning.

Syntax — This component of grammar concerns the ordering, grouping, and placement of words in a sentence—the relation of words within the larger unit of the sentence.

Rhetoric — In classical times, rhetoric was the highly regarded and carefully studied art of persuasion, and a major part of a medieval education. It now has negative connotations, "empty rhetoric" being language that sounds good but is at best devoid of meaning and at worst a clever bit of lying. In the study of literature, rhetoric concerns the larger organization of the material, including such common devices as anaphora, antithesis, apostrophe, parallelism, the rhetorical question, and the pun. (See Glossary.)

Sound Devices — In addition to the sounds contributed by rhyme and meter, the more common sound devices include alliteration, assonance, consonance, and onomatopoeia. Their general effect may be called euphonious or cacophonous. (See Glossary.)

Figurative Language — A metaphor, from a Greek word meaning "to transfer," is an analogy identifying one object with another and ascribing to the first object one or more of the qualities of the second. It is useful to speak of the subject of the comparison as the "tenor," and the image by which the idea is conveyed as the "vehicle." Their similarities may be called the "grounds." The easiest figures are similes because both the tenor and vehicle are named, whereas in the various kinds of metaphor one or even both may be unnamed. The two essential questions to ask of any metaphor are: what two unlike things are being compared, and what do they have in common? Metaphors give us a fresh understanding of an ordinary thing or information about an unknown thing through the often surprising, unsuspected similarities the poet has perceived. Common types of metaphor include metonymy, personification, and synecdoche. (See Glossary.)

Five O'Clock Shadow
Sir John Betjeman

Background and Purpose

Sir John Betjeman, Poet Laureate of England from 1972 until his death in 1984, uses language in ways that make the ordinary seem very important. He suffered from Parkinson's Disease for the last ten years of his life.

Five O'Clock Shadow

This is the time of day when we in the Men's Ward
    Think, "One more surge of the pain and I give up the fight,"
When he who struggles for breath can struggle less strongly;
    This is the time of day which is worse than night.

Line
5   A haze of thunder hangs on the hospital rose-beds,
    A doctors' foursome out on the links is played,
Safe in her sitting-room Sister is putting her feet up:
    This is the time of day when we feel betrayed.

Below the windows, loads of loving relatives
10   Rev in the car park, changing gear at the bend,
Making for home and a nice big tea and the telly:
    "Well, we've done what we can. It can't be long till the end."

This is the time of day when the weight of bedclothes
    Is harder to bear than a sharp incision of steel.
15 The endless anonymous croak of a cheap transistor
    Intensifies the lonely terror I feel.

—Sir John Betjeman

---

7 **Sister:** in Britain, a nurse, not necessarily a nun

Using Skills to Understand the Poem

1. What do we learn from the title and first line about the speaker and setting of this poem? Is it morning or evening? How do we know? (Hint: Consider the pun in the title.) Is *shadow* literal only or also figurative? What tone does this word announce?

2. Considering the context, what is the double significance of *can* in line 3?

3. What is the purpose of the literal details about revving car engines and "changing gear" mentioned in line 10? What figurative meaning do these details suggest?

4. What is the effect of the comparisons in line 4 and lines 13–14?

Essay Question

The tone of "Five O'Clock Shadow" is largely produced by the poet's careful word choice. The study of diction includes consideration of the effect of a word's sound, as well as its connotations, and the possibility of double meanings. Analyze how the diction helps create the tone of the poem by considering such words and phrases as "haze of thunder hangs" (line 5), "safe in her sitting-room" (line 7), "betrayed" (line 8), "loads of loving relatives" (line 9), "Harder to bear" (line 14), "anonymous croak" (line 15).

24 lesson

The Sound of Night
Maxine Kumin

Background and Purpose

Maxine Kumin has published fifteen books of poetry, was awarded the Pulitzer Prize in 1973, and served as Consultant in Poetry to the Library of Congress before that post was renamed Poet Laureate of the United States. "The Sound of Night," published in 1961, plays with sound devices such as onomatopoeia, in which words imitate nonverbal sounds. The poet's diction is worth close analysis, as is her use of figurative language to convey ideas. Kumin lives on a horse farm in New Hampshire, where this poem is set.

The Sound of Night

And now the dark comes on, all full of chitter noise.
Birds huggermugger crowd the trees,
the air thick with their vesper cries,
Line   and bats, snub seven-pointed kites,
5   skitter across the lake, swing out,
squeak, chirp, dip, and skim on skates
of air, and the fat frogs wake and prink
wide-lipped, noisy as ducks, drunk
on the boozy black, gloating chink-chunk.

10   And now on the narrow beach we defend ourselves from dark.
The cooking done, we build our firework
bright and hot and less for outlook
than for magic, we lie in our blankets
while night nickers around us. Crickets
15   chorus hallelujahs; paws, quiet
and quick as raindrops, play on the stones
expertly soft, run past and are gone;
fish pulse in the lake; the frogs hoarsen.

Now every voice of the hour—the known, the supposed, the strange,

20   the mindless, the witted, the never seen—
sing, thrum, impinge, and rearrange
endlessly; and debarred from sleep we wait
for the birds, importantly silent,
for the crease of first eye-licking light,

25   for the sun, lost long ago and sweet.
By the lake, locked black away and tight,
we lie, day creatures, overhearing night.

—Maxine Kumin

Using Skills to Understand the Poem

1. Consider the poet's use of unusual words in this poem. What part of speech is *chitter* according to the dictionary, and how is it used in line 1? What do you notice about the placement and meaning of the word *huggermugger* in line 2? Finally, how does the use of *vesper* as an adjective in line 3 continue the mood created by the other images in the first stanza?

2. Air cannot be literally "thick" with sounds. How does the figurative device of synesthesia work in line three?

3. What do alliteration, assonance, and consonance add to the mood of the poem?

4. The bats are the subject of a metaphor in line 4. What do the bats have in common with kites? How does the kite reference help you to form a mental image of the bats? If necessary, use a photograph of a bat to help you answer the question.

5. Consider the poet's description of the frogs in lines 7–9. What is unusual about the word choice, and what is the effect of these choices? What is added by the sounds of the words?

6. Consider the verbs used in lines 5–6. What is the overall impression produced by this string of verbs?

7. Analyze the metaphors in lines 14–16. What connects these comparisons?

8. In line 23, what does the poet mean when she says that the birds are "importantly" silent? What two meanings of this adverb fit the poem?

Essay Question

Write an essay in which you consider the point of view of the humans spending the night beside the lake. Look especially at the poem's diction. What do the various sounds mean to the listeners? What variety of feelings do they evoke? How does the speaker underscore the idea that people are "day creatures" who find the night alien, even alarming?

25 lesson

Mosquito
John Updike

Background and Purpose

In the Preface to his *Collected Poems 1953–1993,* American writer John Updike says that writing poetry is for him "the highest kind of verbal exercise—the most satisfying. . . ." Justly famous for his many novels and admired for the wit and ingenuity of both his more serious poetry and his light verse, Updike says, "My poems are my oeuvre's beloved waif." Updike reveals in his notes that he is well aware that only female mosquitoes bite, needing protein-rich blood to mature their eggs. He explains that he tried the pronouns *she* and *it*, but that either of these choices "diminishes the music of the lines and falsifies the subjective experience." The mosquito felt, to the male poet as he lay there, "like a male antagonist. . . ." He nearly omitted the poem from the collection because the *he* makes it "hopelessly marred," but did not want to lose "the last two, gender-free stanzas."

Mosquito

On the fine wire of his whine he walked,
Unseen in the ominous bedroom dark.
A traitor to his camouflage, he talked
A thirsty blue streak distinct as a spark.

Line

5   I was to him a fragrant lake of blood
From which he had to sip a drop or die,
A reservoir, a lavish field of food,
I lay awake, unconscious of my size.

We seemed fair-matched opponents. Soft he dropped
10   Down like an anchor on his thread of song.
His nose sank thankfully in; then I slapped
At the sting on my arm, cunning and strong.

A cunning and strong Gargantua, I struck
This lover pinned in the feast of my flesh

15 Lulled by my blood, relaxed, half-sated, stuck,
Engrossed in the gross rivers of myself.

Success! Without a cry the creature died,
Became a fleck of fluff upon the sheet.
The small welt of remorse subsides as side

20 By side we, murderer and murdered, sleep.

—John Updike

Using Skills to Understand the Poem

1. Explain what the details in the poem reveal about the speaker, setting, occasion, conflict, and purpose of the poem.

2. What can we discover about the protagonist through both direct and indirect characterization? What motivates his actions and feelings?

3. Analyze any three of the similes and metaphors in the poem. Is there a pattern in the vehicles used? Are they appropriate to the purposes of the poem? How are the protagonist's feelings displayed through the choice of figurative language?

4. What tone is produced by the sound devices in the poem? Consider the uses and effect of rhyme, meter, metrical substitutions, enjambment, caesura, alliteration, assonance and consonance, and choose one example of each to comment on. What is the overall effect of the sound of the poem in relation to its meaning: is the sound primarily euphonious or cacophonous?

Essay Question

This poem is of a type called mock heroic, which uses the lofty and exalted style of an epic for a trivial subject, thus giving it a dignity it does not deserve. How do setting, plot, characters, and especially diction, create a mocking tone, one which ridicules the deeds related by comparing them with the high deeds of proud heroes in epic poems?

---

13 **Gargantua:** a gigantic man in a satiric work by Rabelais (French writer in the sixteenth century)

Question
May Swenson

Background and Purpose

May Swenson (1919–1989) whose journals are almost as well known as her poetry, was four times a finalist for the National Book Award. An annual competition for the May Swenson Poetry Award honors her as "one of America's most provocative, insouciant, and vital poets." "Question" was published in 1978. Like much of Swenson's work, it is especially notable for its evocation of the things of the physical world.

Question

Body my house
my horse my hound
what will I do
when you are fallen

Line
5 Where will I sleep
How will I ride
What will I hunt

Where can I go
without my mount
10 all eager and quick
How will I know
In thicket ahead
is danger or treasure
when Body my good
15 bright dog is dead

How will it be
to lie in the sky
without roof or door
and wind for an eye

20 With cloud for shift
how will I hide?

—May Swenson

Using Skills to Understand the Poem

1. Describe the prosody of the poem and comment on the effect of the initial substitutions of the meter.

2. Describe the structure and rhetorical devices of the poem, especially anaphora and parallelism.

3. Analyze the three metaphors in the poem: in each case, what is the speaker's body being compared to? What will be lost when the body is gone?

Essay Question

In what ways do the structure, rhetorical devices, and prosody of the poem contribute to its meaning?

27

Dolor
Theodore Roethke

lesson

Background and Purpose

Short poems compress much meaning in few words, largely because of careful use of diction. Consider how American poet Theodore Roethke (1898–1963) creates mood and atmosphere largely through his choice of words. He wrote the poem in 1948, but, surprisingly, huge changes in technology seem not to have changed the point of the poem.

Dolor

I have known the inexorable sadness of pencils,
Neat in their boxes, dolor of pad and paper-weight,
All the misery of manila folders and mucilage,

Line   Desolation in immaculate public places,

5   Lonely reception room, lavatory, switchboard,
The unalterable pathos of basin and pitcher,
Ritual of multigraph, paper-clip, comma,
Endless duplication of lives and objects.
And I have seen dust from the walls of institutions,

10   Finer than flour, alive, more dangerous than silica,
Sift, almost invisible, through long afternoons of tedium,
Dropping a fine film on nails and delicate eyebrows,
Glazing the pale hair, the duplicate grey standard faces.

—Theodore Roethke

Using Skills to Understand the Poem

1. How would you characterize the speaker in this poem?

2. What is the setting of the poem, and how does it encapsulate modern life?

3. How is the poem structured? Consider its two grammatical parts along with its rhetorical patterns of repetition and parallelism. What is the effect of this structure? How does line 8 give point and focus to the catalog that precedes it?

4. The mood of the poem is largely created by its diction. Examine the concrete nouns in the first seven lines: which are modified with adjectives? What mood do the modifiers create?

5. List the abstract nouns and the adjectives that modify them in the first eight lines, and consider their effect. How are they related to the concrete nouns? What mood is created?

6. In lines 9–13, consider the literal and figurative meanings of the dust. To what does the speaker compare it? How do verbs and adjectives suggest the relationship between the dust and those upon whom it settles?

7. How does the poem's final line reinforce the meaning of the whole? What does the speaker suggest about the people he has observed?

Essay Question

How does this poem provide an extended definition of its title?

28 lesson

Promises Like Pie-Crust
Christina Rossetti

Background and Purpose

Christina Rossetti (1830–1894) was born into a family of gifted Italians who had sought political asylum in England. Her brothers helped found the Pre-Raphaelite Brotherhood of painters and poets, aesthetes inspired by medieval art. Rossetti's first poems were published under a male pseudonym, and ironically, her *Goblin Market* (1862) was the first great success of the group. Though one of her brothers edited her work ten years after her death, her *Complete Poems* were not published until 1979. Now considered a significant, even major Victorian poet, Rossetti turned in her later years to writing children's stories and religious poems, several of which have been set to music by renowned composers and are now beloved carols for Christmas. Rossetti never married, though she turned down at least two suitors and broke an engagement. Her imagination transcended the narrow confines of the Victorian model of womanhood. The speaker in "Promises Like Pie-Crust" is at the very least unconventional in her response to a lover's entreaties.

Promises Like Pie-Crust

Promise me no promises,
        So will I not promise you;
Keep we both our liberties,
Line   Never false and never true:
5   Let us hold the die uncast,
        Free to come as free to go;
For I cannot know your past,
        And of mine what can you know?

You, so warm, may once have been
10   Warmer towards another one;
I, so cold, may once have seen
        Sunlight, once have felt the sun:
Who shall show us if it was
        Thus indeed in time of old?
15   Fades the image from the glass
        And the fortune is not told.

Promises Like Pie-Crust: An old English proverb: "Promises are like pie-crust, made to be broken."

If you promised, you might grieve
    For lost liberty again;
If I promised, I believe
20 I should fret to break the chain:
Let us be the friends we were,
    Nothing more but nothing less;
Many thrive on frugal fare
    Who would perish of excess.

—Christina Rossetti

Using Skills to Understand the Poem

1. Describe the form and structure of the poem. What is the occasion of the poem? What two reasons does the speaker give for refusing to promise a committed love? What compromise does she suggest at the end?

2. Analyze the effect on meaning of such devices as syntax, repetition, parallelism, and paradox.

3. Analyze the effect on meaning of the imagery and figurative language.

Essay Question

How persuasive is the poem? How powerful is its argument? Account for its effect.

29 Eve

Ralph Hodgson

lesson

Background and Purpose

This narrative poem by Ralph Hodgson retells the old story of Eve's seduction by Satan in the Garden of Eden, which was first found in *Genesis*. Hodgson's version begins after God has created Adam and Eve. God has given them freedom to do anything but eat the fruit of a certain tree, the Tree of Knowledge. Hodgson does not speculate about Adam's actions, nor mention God's visit to the garden or his reaction to the disobedience of the woman and the serpent, though Eve's expulsion from Eden, which ends the poem, reveals his judgment. The poet has added several settings and characters, using diction, figurative language, and sound devices to create the mood, tone, and meaning of the poem.

Eve

Eve, with her basket, was
Deep in the bells and grass,
Wading in bells and grass
Line   Up to her knees.
5   Picking a dish of sweet
Berries and plums to eat,
Down in the bells and grass
Under the trees.

Mute as a mouse in a
10   Corner the cobra lay,
Curled round a bough of the
Cinnamon tall. . . .
Now to get even and
Humble proud heaven and
15   Now was the moment or
Never at all.

"Eva!" Each syllable
Light as a flower fell,
"Eva!" he whispered, the
20   Wondering maid,
Soft as a bubble sung
Out of a linnet's lung,
Soft and most silvery

"Eva!" he said.
25 Picture that orchard sprite;
Eve, with her body white,
Supple and smooth to her
Slim fingertips;
Wondering, listening,
30 Listening, wondering.
Eve with a berry
Halfway to her lips.

Oh, had our simple Eve
Seen through the make-believe!
35 Had she but known the
Pretender he was!
Out of the boughs he came,
Whispering still her name,
Tumbling in twenty rings
40 Into the grass.

Here was the strangest pair
In the world anywhere,
Eve in the bells and grass
Kneeling, and he
45 Telling his story low. . . .
Singing birds saw them go
Down the dark path to
The Blasphemous Tree.

Oh, what a clatter when
50 Titmouse and Jenny Wren
Saw him successful and
Taking his leave!
How the birds rated him,
How they all hated him!
55 How they all pitied
Poor motherless Eve!

Picture her crying
Outside in the lane,
Eve, with no dish of sweet
60 Berries and plums to eat,
Haunting the gate of the
Orchard in vain. . . .
Picture the lewd delight
Under the hill tonight—
65 "Eva!" the toast goes round,
"Eva!" again.

—Ralph Hodgson

Using Skills to Understand the Poem

1. Describe the subtle changes in setting and analyze how these shifts reveal Eve's fall from grace.

2. How does the poem's diction contribute to tone and meaning? Consider the use of adjectives, verbs, and participles. Look for patterns, contrasts, and surprising juxtapositions of words.

3. Consider the poet's use of figurative language. How does the choice of comparisons influence tone and meaning?

4. Describe the meter, line length, and pattern of enjambment. What does the rhythm contribute to the mood of the poem?

5. Describe the use of repetition and rhyme. Look for patterns. What does the repetition contribute to the mood of the poem?

Essay Question

Analyze how the sound devices of the poem contribute to its meaning and tone. What irony emerges from the contrast between the poem's age-old theme and the poet's sensuous use of language?

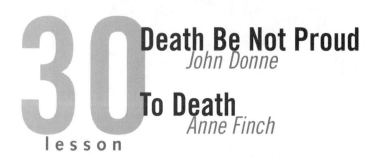

Background and Purpose

John Donne (1572–1631) is best known for his witty love poems rife with metaphysical conceits and his "Holy Sonnets," the tenth of which is presented below. His work is more admired by moderns than it was by his own contemporaries, who tended to prefer the sweetness of perfectly flowing meter and lovely imagery. This sonnet is a bold apostrophe to Death, the mighty and dreadful. Anne Finch, one of the few pre-Romantic women poets whose work has survived, lived nearly a century after Donne (1661–1720). In her poem "To Death," she uses the heroic couplets popular in the neoclassical era.

Death Be Not Proud

Death, be not proud, though some have called thee
Mighty and dreadful, for thou are not so;
For those whom thou think'st thou dost overthrow

Line Die not, poor Death, nor yet canst thou kill me.

5 From rest and sleep, which but thy pictures be,
Much pleasure; then from thee much more must flow,
And soonest our best men with thee do go,
Rest of their bones, and soul's delivery.
Thou'art slave to fate, chance, kings, and desperate men,

10 And dost with poison, war, and sickness dwell,
And poppy, or charms can make us sleep as well
And better than thy stroke; why swell'st thou then?
One short sleep past, we wake eternally,
And death shall be no more; Death, thou shalt die.

—John Donne

---

8 **of:** for

11 **poppy:** opium

12 **swell'st:** puff up with pride

---

1. In what ways does this poem conform to a common sonnet form? What variations are notable, and what is their effect?

2. Describe Donne's use of apostrophe and personification. How do these devices enhance our experience of the poem?

3. Paraphrase each of the sonnet's three quatrains, preserving the clauses but simplifying the syntax. Do the same for the paradoxical couplet. Retain the apostrophe and personification.

To Death

O King of terrors, whose unbounded sway
All that have life must certainly obey;
The King, the Priest, The Prophet, all are thine,
Line Nor would ev'n God (in flesh) thy stroke decline.
5 My name is on thy roll, and sure I must
Increase thy gloomy kingdom in the dust.
My soul at this no apprehension feels,
But trembles at thy swords, thy racks, thy wheels;
Thy scorching fevers, which distract the sense,
10 And snatch us raving, unprepared, from hence;
At thy contagious darts, that wound the heads
Of weeping friends, who wait at dying beds.
Spare these, and let thy time be when it will;
My bus'ness is to die, and thine to kill.
15 Gently thy fatal scepter on me lay,
And take to thy cold arms, insensibly, thy prey.

—Anne Finch

---

4 **Nor would . . . decline:** i.e., Christ (God in his human incarnation) suffered death on the cross.

8 **thy racks, thy wheels:** racks and wheels, used as instruments of torture

Using Skills to Understand the Poem

1. Describe the form and structure of the poem.

2. Which details personify death? What is their effect? With what attitude does the speaker apostrophize death? What does she request of him?

3. Paraphrase each of the three sections of the poem: lines 1–6, 7–12, and 13–16. Use one sentence for each couplet. This time, change all figurative language to literal rather than retaining the apostrophe and personification.

Essay Question

Compare and contrast the tones of these poems, analyzing the means by which the tone is produced.

31
lesson

Bilingual Sestina
Julia Alvarez

Background and Purpose

Julia Alvarez was raised in the Dominican Republic and emigrated to the United States in 1960, where she began her education in literature and writing. She has taught poetry for many years and has published books of poems and well-received novels. "Bilingual Sestina" illustrates this poet's complex feelings about language, culture, and imagination. She says, "English was not my first language. It was, in fact, a colonizing language to my Spanish Caribbean. . . . We are always writing in a form imposed on us. But then I'm Scheherazade in the Sultan's room. I use structures to survive and triumph!" The Spanish words in the poem are not translated for the reader so that the point of the poem can be made.

Bilingual Sestina

Some things I have to say aren't getting said
in this snowy, blonde, blue-eyed, gum chewing English,
dawn's early light sifting through the *persianas* closed
the night before by dark-skinned girls whose words
evoke *cama, aposento, suños* in *nombres*
from that first word I can't translate from Spanish.

Gladys, Rosario, Altagracia—the sounds of Spanish
wash over me like warm island waters as I say
your soothing names: a child again learning the *nombres*
of things you point to in the world before English
turned *sol, tierra, cielo, luna* to vocabulary words—
sun, earth, sky, moon—language closed

like the touch-sensitive *morivivir* whose leaves closed
when we kids poked them, astonished. Even Spanish
failed us then when we realized how frail a word
is when faced with the thing it names. How saying
its name won't always summon up in Spanish or English
the full blown genii from the bottled *nombre.*

Gladys, I summon you back with your given *nombre*
to open up again the house of slatted windows closed
since childhood, where *palabras* left behind for English
stand dusty and awkward in neglected Spanish.
Rosario, muse of *el patio*, sing in me and through me say
that world again, begin first with those first words

20

you put in my mouth as you pointed to the world—
not Adam, not God, but a country girl numbering
the stars, the blades of grass, warming the sun by saying
el sol as the dawn's light fell through the closed
persianas from the gardens where you sang in Spanish,
Estas son las mañanitas, and listening, in bed, no English

25

30

yet in my head to confuse me with translations, no English
doubling the world with synonyms, no dizzying array of words,
—the world was simple and intact in Spanish
awash with *colores, luz, sueños*, as if the *nombres*
were the outer skin of things, as if words were so close
to the world one left a mist of breath on things by saying

35

their names, an intimacy I now yearn for in English—
words so close to what I meant that I almost hear my Spanish
blood beating, beating inside what I say *en inglés*.

—Julia Alvarez

Using Skills to Understand the Poem

1. As the title tells us, this poem is written in a form called a sestina, first used by a French troubadour in the twelfth century. In describing the prosody of Alvarez's poem, you will be describing a sestina. Hint: Instead of looking for a rhyme scheme, look for a pattern in the repetition of the last word of each line. The last three lines of the poem are called the envoy.

2. In the first stanza, what is the effect of personification and allusion? What is the Spanish counterpart to each? Sum up the meaning of the stanza.

3. What mood or feelings are evoked in stanza two? How does language create this mood?

4. What do we learn in stanzas two and three about the difference between names and vocabulary words? How does the example of the plant called the *morivivir* help illustrate this gap? What does the metaphor of the genii in the bottle tell us about the nature of language?

5. In stanzas four and five, why does the speaker invoke Gladys and Rosario from her childhood? How is her childhood sensitivity to words inextricably bound to Spanish, her first language? What is significant about the allusion to Adam, the first man?

Essay Question

Analyze the appropriateness of the six end words chosen for this sestina. How do their many repetitions help articulate the theme of the poem?

32 The Story We Know
Martha Collins

lesson

Background and Purpose

"The Story We Know" was written in 1980 by the American poet Martha Collins. This poem is an example of a villanelle, a medieval French form that has been revived in some fine modern poems. What began as a simple rustic song became, in its modern uses, a form that is unusually important in its contribution to tone and meaning.

The Story We Know

The way to begin is always the same. Hello,
Hello. Your hand, your name. So glad, just fine,
and Good-bye at the end. That's every story we know,

Line   and why pretend? But lunch tomorrow? No?
5   Yes? An omelette, salad, chilled white wine?
The way to begin is simple, sane, Hello,

and then it's Sunday, coffee, the *Times*, a slow
day by the fire, dinner at eight or nine
and Good-bye. In the end, this is a story we know

10   so well we don't turn the page, or look below
the picture, or follow the words to the next line:
The way to begin is always the same Hello.

But one night, through the latticed window, snow
begins to whiten the air, and the tall white pine.
15   Good-bye is the end of every story we know

that night, and when we close the curtains, oh,
we hold each other against the cold white sign
of the way we all begin and end. *Hello,*
Good-bye is the only story. We know, we know.

—Martha Collins

Using Skills to Understand the Poem

1. Describe a villanelle by explicating the stanza pattern and the rhyme scheme of this poem. How many different end rhymes are in the poem? How many times is each sound repeated? Which words are repeated exactly at the ends of lines, in what pattern? How does the last stanza use the rhyming words? Why is this appropriate at the end of the poem?

2. Isolating the *b* rhymes (middle line of each tercet) gives us this list: *fine, wine, nine, line, pine, sign*. What is the significance of each of these words to the whole poem?

3. Incremental repetition tends to augment meaning and accumulate significance. What variations in meaning are present in the following groups of repetitions and what is their effect?

   line 1:   same. Hello,
   line 6:   same, Hello,
   line 12:   same Hello.
   line 18:   end. *Hello,*

   line 3:   Good-bye at the end.
   line 9:   Good-bye. In the end
   line 15:   Good-bye is the end
   line 19:   *Good-bye* is the only

   line 3:   every story we know
   line 9:   this is a story we know
   line 15:   every story we know
   line 19:   We know, we know.

Essay Question

The villanelle form is circular, presenting variations on a theme or subject. Its argument doesn't develop or go forward. Its static form is perfect for establishing a mood, and for conveying the emotional treadmill of a preoccupation or obsession. How does the incremental repetition and circular movement of the form create the tone and meaning of this poem?

33
lesson

Spring and Fall
Gerard Manley Hopkins

The Oven Bird
Robert Frost

Background and Purpose

The English poet Gerard Manley Hopkins (1844–1889) and the American Robert Frost (1874–1963) are both renowned for poetry in which nature gives rise to religious or philosophical rumination. These two poems explore a central motif of poetry, human mortality, through the conventional metaphor comparing the human lifespan to the seasons of the natural year. The two approaches, however, are quite different, as are the tones of the poems. Frost's poem may have been inspired by the distinctive, unmelodious call of the oven bird, which some say sounds like "Teacher, Teacher, Teacher!"

Spring and Fall

Márgarét, áre you gríeving
Over Goldengrove unleaving?
Leáves, líke the things of mán, you
Line   With your fresh thoughts care for, can you?
5   Áh! Ás the heart grows ólder
It will come to such sights colder
By and by, nor spare a sigh
Though worlds of wanwood leafmeal lie;
And yet you *will* weep and know why.
10   Now no matter, child, the name:
Sórrow's spríngs áre the sáme.
Nor mouth had, no nor mind, expressed
What héart heárd of, ghóst guessed:
It ís the blíght mán was bórn for,
15   It is Margaret you mourn for.

—Gerard Manley Hopkins

---

13 **ghost:** soul, spirit

1. Hopkins's short lyric shares some elements with the sonnet, but it is a nonce form, invented for this poem only. Hopkins' idiosyncratic meter, which he dubbed "sprung rhythm," uses accent marks over certain syllables. What is the dominant meter and line length? What is the rhyme scheme? Describe the poem's structure. (Hint: The anomaly in the rhyme scheme is the key).

2. What is the effect of the frequent use of alliteration in the poem? Combined with assonance and consonance, what mood does this device create?

3. Comment on the effect created by such unusual diction as *Goldengrove* and *unleaving* (line 2), *fresh* (line 4), *wanwood* and *leafmeal* (line 8), *springs* (line 11), and *blight* (line 14.) How do the connotations of these words create the poem's mood?

4. Analyze the poet's use of figurative language. How does it suggest the theme of the poem?

The Oven Bird

There is a singer everyone has heard,
Loud, a mid-summer and a mid-wood bird,
Who makes the solid tree trunks sound again.
Line He says that leaves are old and that for flowers
5 Mid-summer is to spring as one to ten.
He says the early petal-fall is past
When pear and cherry bloom went down in showers
On sunny days a moment overcast;
And comes that other fall we name the fall.
10 He says the highway dust is over all.
The bird would cease and be as other birds
But that he knows in singing not to sing.
The question that he frames in all but words
Is what to make of a diminished thing.

—Robert Frost

Using Skills to Understand the Poem

1. Frost's poem, like Hopkins's, borrows from the sonnet form. What is its meter, rhyme scheme, and structure?

2. Paraphrase the three messages of the oven bird, then analyze the meaning of the word *fall* as it encapsulates the theme of the poem.

3. Paraphrase the last four lines of the poem. How does the oven bird symbolize the human condition?

Essay Question

Compare and contrast the approach and attitudes of the two poems to the same subject.

34 Complaint to His Purse
Geoffrey Chaucer

lesson

Background and Purpose

Luckily for us, Geoffrey Chaucer (ca. 1343–1400) wrote in the London speech of his time, which became the dominant dialect as late Middle English evolved into modern English. In applying the resources of his native language to his work, he added greatly to the prestige of English when other writers opted for Latin or French. The inflections of Chaucer's dialect are relatively simple, offering little difficulty to modern readers, though some words in the poem below require a gloss.

We know that "Complaint to His Purse" is Chaucer's last published work because the monarch he petitions in the poem's envoy was crowned in 1399. We also know that the poem was effective: Chaucer received a grant from Henry IV that year. The poem is an early English example of rime royal. Chaucer is credited with introducing into English the five-accent line, which has become the most characteristic line in all English prosody. Though best known for the narratives of his *Canterbury Tales*, Chaucer here employs the lyrical lover's complaint.

Complaint to His Purse

To you, my purs, and to noon other wight
Complaine I, for ye be my lady dere.
I am so sory, now that ye be light,
Line   For certes, but if ye make me hevy cheere,
5   Me were as lief be laid upon my beere;
For which unto youre mercy thus I crye:
Beeth hevy again, or elles moot I die.

Now voucheth sauf this day er it be night
That I of you the blisful soun may heere,
10   Or see youre colour, lik the sonne bright,
That of yelownesse hadde nevere peere.
Ye be my life, ye be myn hertes steere,

---

1 **wight:** person

4 **if:** unless

5 **lief:** I'd just as soon; **beere:** bier

7 **moot:** must

8 **voucheth sauf:** grant; **er:** before

12 **steere:** rudder, guide

Queene of confort and of good compaignye:
Beeth hevy again, or elles moot I die.

15 Ye purs, that been to me my lives light
And saviour, as in this world down here,
Out of this towne helpe me thurgh your might,
Sith that ye wol nat be my tresorere;
For I am shave as neigh as any frere.
20 But yit I praye unto youre courteisye:
Beeth hevy again, or elles moot I die.

Envoy to Henry IV

O conquerour of Brutus Albioun
Which that by line and free eleccioun
Been verray king, this song to you I sende:
25 And ye, that mowen alle oure harmes amende,
Have minde upon my supplicacioun.

Using Skills to Understand the Poem

1. Describe the form called rime royal: meter, rhyme scheme, stanza form.

2. What is the structure of the poem? How do the imagery and argument of each stanza develop and intensify the appeal?

3. In exploring the extended metaphor of the poem, consider how diction accounts for the humor of Chaucer's parody.

4. How does the envoy continue the tone of the poem even as it addresses a specific person?

Essay Question

Account for the humor of the poem by considering the components that make up its tone.

---

18 **tresorere:** treasurer
19 **shave . . . frere:** shaved as close as any friar, an expression of being broke
22 **Albioun:** Britain (Albion) was said to have been founded by Brutus, the grandson of Aeneas, the founder of Rome.
25 **mowen:** may

35 lesson

Auto Wreck
Karl Shapiro

Background and Purpose

Karl Shapiro, a modern American poet, wrote poems that free us from the misconception that only certain pleasant subjects, such as love, nature, and beauty, are suited to poetry. The poem below contains imagery and metaphor which are disturbing to say the least, but lead to some basic philosophical questions.

Auto Wreck

Its quick soft silver bell beating, beating,
And down the dark one ruby flare
Pulsing out red light like an artery,
Line The ambulance at top speed floating down
5   Past beacons and illuminated clocks
Wings in a heavy curve, dips down,
And brakes speed, entering the crowd.
The doors leap open, emptying the light;
Stretchers are laid out, the mangled lifted
10   And stowed into the little hospital.
Then the bell, breaking the hush, tolls once,
And the ambulance with its terrible cargo
Rocking, slightly rocking, moves away,
As the doors, an afterthought, are closed.

15   We are deranged, walking among the cops
Who sweep glass and are large and composed.
One is making notes under the light.
One with a bucket douches ponds of blood
Into the street and gutter.
20   One hangs lanterns on the wrecks that cling,
Empty husks of locusts, to iron poles.

Our throats were tight as tourniquets,
Our feet were bound with splints, but now,
Like convalescents intimate and gauche,
25   We speak through sickly smiles and warn
With the stubborn saw of common sense,
The grim joke and the banal resolution.
The traffic moves around with care,
But we remain, touching a wound
30   That opens to our richest horror.
Already old, the question Who shall die?
Becomes unspoken Who is innocent?

For death in war is done by hands;
Suicide has cause and stillbirth, logic;
35   And cancer, simple as a flower, blooms.
But this invited the occult mind,
Cancels our physics with a sneer,
And spatters all we knew of denouement
Across the expedient and wicked stones.

—Karl Shapiro

Using Skills to Understand the Poem

1. What imagery does Shapiro use in the first three lines to evoke sound and sight? How do these images become increasingly significant in the context of the entire poem?

2. On a literal level, what contextual significance do the following words and phrases have: *mangled* (line 9), "tolls once" (line 11), "terrible cargo" (line 12), "rocking, slightly rocking" (line 13), *deranged* and *composed* (lines 15 and 16)?

3. Analyze the metaphors in lines 3, 18, 22, and 29–30. What pattern do they create and why is it appropriate to the poem?

4. What is added to the theme of the poem by the metaphors in lines 20–21 and the simile in 24–27?

Essay Question

Examine lines 31–39 of the poem, explicating such matters as why the fatal accident causes the witnesses to raise philosophical questions and why death by auto wreck cannot, like other deaths, be explained. How and what does this kind of death "cancel" and "spatter"?

Background and Purpose

The lyrics of Edmund Waller and George Herbert are fine examples of English poetry of the seventeenth century. "Song" and "Virtue" were both written when *carpe diem* was a popular poetic mode. Both the similarities and the differences of the two poems are notable.

Song

Go lovely Rose,
Tell her that wastes her time and me,
That now she knows,
Line　When I resemble her to thee,
　5　　How sweet and fair she seems to be.

Tell her that's young,
And shuns to have her graces spied,
That hadst thou sprung
In deserts where no men abide,
　10　　Thou must have uncommended died.

Small is the worth
Of beauty from the light retir'd:
Bid her come forth,
Suffer herself to be desir'd,
　15　　And not blush so to be admir'd.

Then die, that she
The common fate of all things rare
May read in thee,
How small a part of time they share,
　20　　That are so wondrous sweet and fair.

—Edmund Waller

1. What is the occasion of the poem? What literary device does the poet employ? Describe what you know of the speaker, the listener, and the "she" referred to in the poem.

2. Paraphrase each of the four stanzas.

3. Describe the prosody, including stanza form, rhyme, meter, and notable metrical substitutions (spondees), as well as the structure of the poem. How do these choices help to reinforce the poem's content?

Virtue

Sweet day, so cool, so calm, so bright,
The bridal of the earth and sky,
The dew shall weep thy fall tonight;
      For thou must die.

Line
5   Sweet rose, whose hue angry and brave
Bids the rash gazer wipe his eye,
Thy root is ever in its grave,
      And thou must die.

Sweet spring, full of sweet days and roses,
10 A box where sweets compacted lie,
My music shows ye have your closes,
      And all must die.

Only a sweet and virtuous soul,
Like season'd timber, never gives;
15 But though the whole world turn to coal,
      Then chiefly lives.

          —George Herbert

Using Skills to Understand the Poem

1. Consider first Herbert's use of metaphor and personification. In each case, what two unlike things are being compared, and what do they have in common?

2. How is the poem structured, and how does this structure support its meaning? Consider parallelism, order, and the turn in the poem.

3. How does the prosody reinforce the poem's meaning?

Essay Question

Compare and contrast the two poems, considering such elements as form and structure, content, and theme.

37 lesson Dear March—Come in— Apparently with no surprise
Emily Dickinson

Background and Purpose

These two poems by the revered American poet Emily Dickinson, the first written around 1874 and the second around 1884, exemplify her startling use of diction and personification. Both take as their subject an aspect of nature. However, Dickinson's large range of tone and theme is suggested by the contrast between them. Note that Dickinson lived in chilly New England, where winters are long and summers short.

Dear March—Come in—

Dear March—Come in—
How glad I am—
I hoped for you before—
Line Put down your Hat—
5   You must have walked—
How out of Breath you are—
Dear March, how are you, and the Rest—
Did you leave Nature well—
Oh March, Come right up stairs with me—
10   I have so much to tell—

I got your Letter, and the Birds—
The Maples never knew that you were coming—till I called
I declare—how Red their Faces grew—
But March, forgive me—and
15   All those Hills you left for me to Hue—
There was no Purple suitable—
You took it all with you—

Who knocks? That April.
Lock the Door—
20 I will not be pursued—
He stayed away a Year to call
When I am occupied—
But trifles look so trivial
As soon as you have come

25 That Blame is just as dear as Praise
And Praise as mere as Blame—

—Emily Dickinson

Using Skills to Understand the Poem

1. Describe the prosody of the poem. Dickinson uses her usual "hymn meter" here (the "common meter" that alternates lines of iambic tetrameter and trimeter), but sometimes splits the longer lines into two dimeter lines and does not observe the four-line stanza. Why are these short lines and long stanzas appropriate here? How does the poet handle rhyme? Consider the function of Dickinson's famous dashes in lieu of almost any other punctuation, along with the effect of the capitalized words.

2. Describe the structure of the four stanzas.

3. Unlike many poems that use the convention of apostrophe and so tend toward the lofty and ode-like, this lyric plays with the convention. What is the tone of this address to March, and how is it achieved? Paraphrase as necessary in your explanation.

4. What strikes you as unusual about the speaker's marked preference for the first month of spring rather than the second?

Apparently with no surprise

Apparently with no surprise
To any happy Flower
The Frost beheads it at its play—
Line In accidental power—
5 The blonde Assassin passes on—
The Sun proceeds unmoved
To measure off another Day
For an Approving God.

—Emily Dickinson

Using Skills to Understand the Poem

1. Describe the prosody, structure, and anomalies of the poem.

2. Paraphrase the poem, turning figurative into literal language. Then summarize the plot, referring to the personified characters.

3. Describe the personified characters in the poem, commenting on the effect of Dickinson's use of diction to establish the tone of the poem.

Essay Question

Compare and contrast Dickinson's two poems, considering especially the tone of each and how it is conveyed.

Sonnet 73
William Shakespeare

lesson

Background and Purpose

The structure and prosody of this sonnet by William Shakespeare is a model for the English sonnet form which modified the rhyme scheme and structure of Petrarch's original Italian sonnet. Instead of an octave and sestet, Shakespeare works with three quatrains and a couplet. Like most sonnets, this is a brief, personal lyric about a standard subject, love. This sonnet was written during Shakespeare's thirty-sixth year, a fact that sheds light on the figurative implications of the poem.

Sonnet 73

That time of year thou mayst in me behold
When yellow leaves, or none, or few, do hang
Upon those boughs which shake against the cold,
Line   Bare, ruined choirs where late the sweet birds sang.
5   In me thou seest the twilight of such day
As after sunset fadeth in the west,
Which by and by black night doth take away,
Death's second self that seals up all in rest.
In me thou seest the glowing of such fire
10   That on the ashes of his youth doth lie,
As the deathbed whereon it must expire,
Consumed with that which it was nourished by.
   This thou perceivest, which makes thy love more strong,
   To love that well which thou must leave ere long.

—William Shakespeare

Using Skills to Understand the Poem

1. Describe the meter, line length, and rhyme scheme of the sonnet. Do these match the structure of the poem? What is the contribution of rhetorical devices such as repetition and parallelism?

2. Analyze the figurative language in each of the quatrains. What does the speaker have in common with each of the things to which he compares himself? What progression is implied by each metaphor and its order in the poem?

Essay Question

Analyze the final couplet, considering how it serves to turn the argument of the preceding quatrains.

In Memory of Danny L.
Maxine Kumin

Bells for John Whiteside's Daughter
John Crowe Ransom

Background and Purpose

For centuries, poets have used a form called elegy, which publicly mourns a death while it memorializes and celebrates a life. In these poems, two modern American poets create moving elegies for children by creating a tone that is far from dolorous and by resisting the temptation to overstate the innocence and youth of the dead children. As the best literature does, they show us the person instead of telling us how to feel. Maxine Kumin published "In Memory of Danny L." in 1996. Ransom's poem appeared in 1924.

In Memory of Danny L.

Magnetized
on the refrigerator
prideful in his new glasses

Line   he smiles forth still
5   sounding out the first
parts of words then guessing

the rest and when his
third grade class laughed
at *cowbarn* for *coward*

10   he was pleased to laugh
with them who go forward
this year to junior high

so that after his heart
gave out that day
15   on the playground slide

carrying off the only
Downs child in his
village school this

same passport-size
20 photo went up in
a dozen houses to say

that he who had hugged
every dog, pony, lamb
had come and gone

25 and in some will adhere
as in ours
for years.

—Maxine Kumin

Bells for John Whiteside's Daughter

There was such speed in her little body,
And such lightness in her footfall,
It is no wonder her brown study
Astonishes us all.

Line
5 Her wars were bruited in our high window.
We looked among orchard trees and beyond
Where she took arms against her shadow,
Or harried unto the pond

The lazy geese, like a snow cloud
10 Dripping their snow on the green grass,
Tricking and stopping, sleepy and proud,
Who cried in goose, Alas,

For the tireless heart within the little
Lady with rod that made them rise
15   From their noon apple-dreams and scuttle
Goose-fashion under the skies!

But now go the bells, and we are ready,
In one house we are sternly stopped
To say we are vexed at her brown study,
20   Lying so primly propped.

—John Crowe Ransom

Using Skills to Understand the Poem

1. Sum up the characterization of the living child based on her actions. How do the other images of the child serve as a contrast to the image of her in a "brown study"?

2. What is the form and structure of the poem and how do these elements affect the tone?

3. Analyze the effect of the poem's diction on its tone, considering the repetition and connotation of particular words.

Essay Question

Compare and analyze the tones of these two elegies.

40
lesson

from The Rape of the Lock
Alexander Pope

from The Lady's Dressing Room
Jonathan Swift

Background and Purpose

The two eighteenth-century poets who authored the poems from which these passages are taken both use closed couplets to describe the same scene: a fine lady's dressing table in disorder. Both have a satirical intent, one an example of Horatian and the other of Juvenalian tone. Pope's is part of a long mock epic called "The Rape of the Lock," featuring the cutting of a lock of hair from the head of a young beauty by a fearless gentleman.

The Rape of the Lock
Canto I, lines 121–144

And now, unveiled, the toilet stands displayed,
Each silver vase in mystic order laid.
First, robed in white, the nymph intent adores,
Line With head uncovered, the cosmetic powers.
125 A heavenly image in the glass appears;
To that she bends, to that her eyes she rears.
The inferior priestess, at her altar's side,
Trembling begins the sacred rites of pride.
Unnumbered treasures ope at once, and here
130 The various offerings of the world appear;
From each she nicely culls with curious toil,
And decks the goddess with the glittering spoil.
This casket India's glowing gems unlocks,
And all Arabia breathes from yonder box.
135 The tortoise here and elephant unite,
Transformed to combs, the speckled and the white.
Here files of pins extend their shining rows,
Puffs, powders, patches, Bibles, billet-doux.
Now awful Beauty put on all its arms;
140 The fair each moment rises in her charms,
Repairs her smiles, awakens every grace,
And calls forth all the wonders of her face;
Sees by degrees a purer blush arise,
And keener lightnings quicken in her eyes.

—Alexander Pope

138 **billet-doux:** love notes

1. Describe the prosody and structure of the poem. Consider its setting, characters, and plot, along with rhetorical devices used in the passage. How do all of these contribute to the poem's satiric effect?

2. What role do the diction and imagery of the passage play in producing this overall effect?

The Lady's Dressing Room
lines 1–24

Five hours, (and who can do it less in?)
By haughty Celia spent in dressing;
The goddess from her chamber issues,
Arrayed in lace, brocades and tissues.
5   Strephon, who found the room was void,
And Betty otherwise employed,
Stole in, and took a strict survey,
Of all the litter as it lay;
Whereof, to make the matter clear,
10 An inventory follows here.
   And first a dirty smock appeared,
Beneath the armpits well besmeared.
Strephon, the rogue, displayed it wide,
And turned it round on every side.
15 On such a point few words are best,
And Strephon bids us guess the rest,
But swears how damnably the men lie,
In calling Celia sweet and cleanly.
Now listen while he next produces
20 The various combs for various uses,
Filled up with dirt so closely fixt,
No brush could force a way betwixt.
A paste of composition rare,
Sweat, dandruff, powder, lead and hair. . . .

—Jonathan Swift

---

4 **tissues:** fine, lightweight fabric
24 **lead:** then used to make hair glossy

Using Skills to Understand the Poem

1. Describe the prosody and structure of the poem. Analyze the rhetorical devices of juxtaposition, hyperbole, and catalog, noting the satiric effect of each.

2. Consider the satiric effect of the diction in the passage.

Essay Question

Compare the satiric techniques in these two passages and then account for the difference in tone.

Well, I Have Lost You
Edna St. Vincent Millay

lesson

Background and Purpose

Edna St. Vincent Millay, an American poet who wrote in the first half of the twentieth century, is recognized as one of the great writers of sonnets in English. Her theme, like that of the earliest sonneteers, is love.

Well, I Have Lost You

Well, I have lost you; and I lost you fairly;
In my own way, and with my full consent.
Say what you will, kings in a tumbrel rarely
Line Went to their deaths more proud than this one went.
5   Some nights of apprehension and hot weeping
I will confess; but that's permitted me;
Day dried my eyes; I was not one for keeping
Rubbed in a cage a wing that would be free.
If I had loved you less or played you slyly
10   I might have held you for a summer more,
But at the cost of words I value highly,
And no such summer as the one before.
Should I outlive this anguish—and men do—
I shall have only good to say of you.

—Edna St. Vincent Millay

---

3 **tumbrel:** cart used during the French Revolution to take aristocrats to the guillotine

Using Skills to Understand the Poem

1. Describe the prosody and structure of this sonnet. Note where enjambment is used, as well as where and why initial trochaic substitutions occur.

2. Paraphrase the first quatrain.

3. Paraphrase the second quatrain, explaining the metaphor in line 8.

4. Explain the syntactical structure of the third quatrain, which contains the speaker's proposition, and then provide a paraphrase of the quatrain.

Essay Question

Explain the ways in which the couplet is the culmination of the sonnet. Consider both the poet's manner and her matter, the subject and theme of the work.

42
lesson

Arms and the Boy
Wilfred Owen

Beat! Beat! Drums!
Walt Whitman

Background and Purpose

These paired poems take for their subjects two terrible wars. In "Arms and the Boy," the English poet Wilfred Owen, killed on the front line just before the end of World War I, speaks with authority about the inappropriateness of sending untouched youth to wage war. The poet uses allusion, diction, and figurative language to convey his theme. American Walt Whitman's "Beat! Beat! Drums!" evokes the bloodshed and overheated emotions of the Civil War through the use of apostrophe and sound devices.

Arms and the Boy

Let the boy try along this bayonet-blade
How cold steel is, and keen with hunger of blood;
Blue with all malice, like a madman's flash;
And thinly drawn with famishing for flesh.

Line
5   Lend him to stroke these blind, blunt bullet-heads
Which long to nuzzle in the hearts of lads,
Or give him cartridges of fine zinc teeth,
Sharp with the sharpness of grief and death.

For his teeth seem for laughing round an apple.
10   There lurk no claws behind his fingers supple;
And God will grow no talons on his heels,
Nor antlers through the thickness of his curls.

—Wilfred Owen

Using Skills to Understand the Poem

1. Analyze the prosody and structure of the poem as they contribute to its meaning.

2. What is the effect of diction and imagery in the personifications of the first two stanzas? Consider the effect of the mixture of the literal and the figurative in the descriptions of the weapons.

3. What is the effect of the imagery in the final stanza? In the light of this imagery, comment on the appropriateness of the title's allusion.

Arms and the Boy: The opening words of Virgil's epic poem, *The Aeneid* are, "Arms and the man I sing. . . ."

Beat! Beat! Drums!

Beat! beat! drums!—blow! bugles! blow!
Through the windows—through doors—burst like a ruthless force,
Into the solemn church, and scatter the congregation,
Line Into the school where the scholar is studying;
5 Leave not the bridegroom quiet—no happiness must he have now with his bride,
Nor the peaceful farmer any peace, ploughing his field or gathering his grain,
So fierce you whirr and pound you drums—so shrill you bugles blow.

Beat! beat! drums!—blow! bugles! blow!
Over the traffic of cities—over the rumble of wheels in the streets;
10 Are beds prepared for sleepers at night in the houses? No sleepers must sleep in those beds,
No bargainers' bargain by day—no brokers or speculators—would they continue?
Would the talkers be talking? would the singer attempt to sing?
Would the lawyer rise in the court to state his case before the judge?
Then rattle quicker, heavier drums—you bugles wilder blow.

15 Beat! beat! drums!—blow! Bugles! Blow!
Make no parley—stop for no expostulation,
Mind not the timid—mind not the weeper or prayer,
Mind not the old man beseeching the young man,
Let not the child's voice be heard, nor the mother's entreaties,
20 Make even the trestles to shake the dead where they lie awaiting the hearses,
So strong you thump O terrible drums—so loud you bugles blow.

—Walt Whitman

Using Skills to Understand the Poem

1. What is the occasion of the poem? What does the speaker observe about the occasion? Hint: Consider lines 20–21.

2. Describe the structure, rhetorical devices, and prosody of the poem. What is the effect of the meter, parallelism, anaphora, and other repetition, and sound devices (especially caesura, alliteration, and onomatopoeia) in the first and last lines of each stanza?

3. Consider the order in which people are cataloged in the poem: what is the logic and effect in the three groupings?

4. Whitman's diction suggests force and power. Isolate and list his notable prepositions, verbs, and modifiers, and comment on their effect.

Essay Question

Compare and contrast these two great poems about war.

Independent Analysis

Hanging Fire
Audre Lorde

Fifteen
William Stafford

Background and Purpose

Audre Lorde (1934–1992) was the daughter of immigrants from Grenada. She was still in high school when she published her first poem in *Seventeen* magazine. Her work has been both greatly loved and sharply criticized, holding an important place in modern American poetry. William Stafford (1914–1993) did not publish a collection of poems until he was 48 years old, after teaching poetry for many years. He went on to produce 65 volumes of prose and verse. His poems are deceptively simple.

The poems below are first-person accounts of the miseries of adolescence, one from a girl's point of view, the other from a boy's.

Hanging Fire

I am fourteen
and my skin has betrayed me
the boy I cannot live without
still sucks his thumb
in secret
how come my knees are
always so ashy
what if I die
before morning
and momma's in the bedroom
with the door closed.

Line

5

10

I have to learn how to dance
in time for the next party
my room is too small for me
suppose I die before graduation
15   they will sing sad melodies
but finally
tell the truth about me
There is nothing I want to do
and too much
20   that has to be done
and momma's in the bedroom
with the door closed.

Nobody even stops to think
about my side of it
25   I should have been on Math Team
my marks were better than his
why do I have to be
the one wearing braces
I have nothing to wear tomorrow
30   will I live long enough
to grow up
and momma's in the bedroom
with the door closed.

—Audre Lorde

Fifteen

South of the Bridge on Seventeenth
I found back of the willows one summer
day a motorcycle with the engine running
Line   as it lay on its side, ticking over
5   slowly in the high grass. I was fifteen.

I admired all that pulsing gleam, the
shiny flanks, the demure headlights
fringed where it lay; I led it gently
to the road and stood with that
10   companion, ready and friendly. I was fifteen.

We could find the end of a road, meet
the sky out on Seventeenth. I thought about
hills, and patting the handle got back a
confident opinion. On the bridge we indulged
15   a forward feeling, a tremble. I was fifteen.

Thinking, back farther in the grass I found
the owner, just coming to, where he had flipped
over the rail. He had blood on his hands, was pale—
I helped him walk to his machine. He ran his hand
20   Over it, called me good man, roared away.

I stood there, fifteen.

—William Stafford

Essay Question

Compare and contrast these two poems. Which do you find more compelling, the similarities or the differences? Consider setting, plot, characterization, selection of detail, and such poetic devices as prosody, structure, rhetorical devices, and figurative language.

The Fish
Elizabeth Bishop

Background and Purpose

Elizabeth Bishop (1911–1979) is revered as "the poets' poet." Her technical brilliance and great subtlety in describing the physical world are much admired. Something beyond the imagery and surprising figurative language is waiting to enchant a careful reader.

The Fish

I caught a tremendous fish
and held him beside the boat
half out of water, with my hook
Line   fast in a corner of his mouth.
5   He didn't fight.
He hadn't fought at all.
He hung a grunting weight,
battered and venerable
and homely. Here and there
10   his brown skin hung in strips
like ancient wallpaper,
and its pattern of darker brown
was like wallpaper:
shapes like full-blown roses
15   stained and lost through age.
He was speckled with barnacles,
fine rosettes of lime,
and infested
with tiny white sea-lice,
20   and underneath two or three
rags of green weed hung down.

While his gills were breathing in
the terrible oxygen
—the frightening gills,
25   fresh and crisp with blood,
that can cut so badly—
I thought of the coarse white flesh
packed in like feathers,
the big bones and the little bones,
30   the dramatic reds and blacks
of his shiny entrails,
and the pink swim-bladder
like a big peony.
I looked into his eyes
35   which were far larger than mine
but shallower, and yellowed,
the irises backed and packed
with tarnished tinfoil
seen through the lenses
40   of old scratched isinglass.
They shifted a little, but not
to return my stare.
—It was more like the tipping
of an object toward the light.
45   I admired his sullen face,
the mechanism of his jaw,
and then I saw
that from his lower lip—
grim, wet, and weaponlike,
50   hung five old pieces of fish-line,
or four and a wire leader
with the swivel still attached,
with all their five big hooks
grown firmly in his mouth.
55   A green line, frayed at the end
where he broke it, two heavier lines,
and a fine black thread
still crimped from the strain and snap
when it broke and he got away.

60 Like medals with their ribbons
frayed and wavering,
a five-haired beard of wisdom
trailing from his aching jaw.
I stared and stared
65 and victory filled up
the little rented boat,
from the pool of bilge
where oil had spread a rainbow
around the rusted engine
70 to the bailer rusted orange,
the sun-cracked thwarts,
the oarlocks on their strings,
the gunnels—until everything
was rainbow, rainbow, rainbow!
75 And I let the fish go.

—Elizabeth Bishop

Essay Question

Analyze the diction and descriptive details of the poem in an effort to discover
why the speaker let the fish go.

Nuns Fret Not at Their Convent's Narrow Room
William Wordsworth

Background and Purpose

William Wordsworth (1770–1850) was one of the primary contributors to the Romantic movement in English poetry, which was formed in reaction to the ornate language and formal elements of earlier lyrics. Yet, in this sonnet, Wordsworth praises the seemingly restrictive qualities of the sonnet form.

Nuns Fret Not at Their Convent's Narrow Room

Nuns fret not at their convent's narrow room;
And hermits are contented with their cells;
And students with their pensive citadels;
Line   Maids at the wheel, the weaver at his loom,
5   Sit blithe and happy; bees that soar for bloom,
High as the highest Peak of Furness-fells,
Will murmur by the hour in foxglove bells:
In truth the prison, into which we doom
Ourselves, no prison is: and hence for me,
10   In sundry moods, 'twas pastime to be bound
Within the Sonnet's scanty plot of ground;
Pleased if some Souls (for such there needs must be)
Who have felt the weight of too much liberty,
Should find brief solace there, as I have found.

—William Wordsworth

Essay Question

Analyze the form and prosody of the poem, noting how it diverges at times from the Italian and Elizabethan sonnet forms, and discuss these variations. Consider in your analysis the rhetorical structure of the poem, as well as its theme.

---

6 **Furness-fells:** mountains in the English lake district

If This Be Love
Henry Constable

Mediocrity in Love Rejected
Thomas Carew

Background and Purpose

Henry Constable (1562–1613), author of the first of these poems, "If This Be Love,"
uses many of the witty rhetorical devices more familiar to us from Shakespeare's plays
and sonnets. Thomas Carew (1594/5–1639), author of "Mediocrity in Love Rejected,"
also plays with devices and images that conjure up the pain of romantic attachment.
The following description of Carew by a contemporary applies equally to both writers:
"He is a Person of a pleasant and facetious wit [who] made many poems (especially in
the amorous Way) [with much] Sharpness of Fancy and Elegancy of Language."

If This Be Love

To live in hell, and heaven to behold;
To welcome life, and die a living death;
To sweat with heat, and yet be freezing cold;
Line   To grasp at stars, and lie the earth beneath;
5   To tread a maze that never shall have end;
To burn in sighs, and starve in daily tears;
To climb a hill, and never to descend;
Giants to kill, and quake at childish fears;
To pine for food, and watch the Hesperian tree;
10   To thirst for drink, and nectar still to draw;
To live accurst, whom men hold blest to be;
And weep those wrongs which never creatures saw;
If this be love, if love in these be founded
My heart is love, for these in it are grounded.

—Henry Constable

---

9 **Hesperian:** In Greek mythology, the Daughters of Hesperus watched over a garden where
golden apples grew.

Mediocrity in Love Rejected

Give me more love, or more disdain;
   The Torrid, or the frozen Zone,
Bring equal ease unto my pain;
Line   The temperate affords me none:
5 Either extreme, of love, or hate,
   Is sweeter than a calm estate.

Give me a storm; if it be love,
   Like Danae in that golden shower
I swim in pleasure; if it prove
10   Disdain, that torrent will devour
My Vulture-hopes; and he's possessed
Of heaven, that's but from Hell released:
   Then crown my joys, or cure my pain;
   Give me more love, or more disdain.

—Thomas Carew

Essay Question

Compare and contrast the poems, accounting for the tone of each by analyzing such elements as form, structure, rhetorical devices, and figurative language.

---

8 **golden shower:** In Greek mythology, Zeus appeared to Danae as a shower of gold.

A Fire-Truck
Richard Wilbur

Background and Purpose

Wilbur's poetry has been much admired during his long writing career, which began while he was serving in World War II. He has devoted himself to teaching for most of his life. Wilbur received the Pulitzer Prize in 1956, and was the second U.S. poet laureate in 1987–88.

A Fire-Truck

Right down the shocked street with a siren-blast
That sends all else skittering to the curb,
Redness, brass, ladders and hats hurl past,
    Blurring to sheer verb,

Line

5   Shift at the corner into uproarious gear
And make it around the turn in a squall of traction,
The headlong bell maintaining sure and clear,
    Thought is degraded action!

Beautiful, heavy, unweary, loud, obvious thing!
10 I stand here purged of nuance, my mind a blank.
All I was brooding upon has taken wing,
    And I have you to thank.

As you howl beyond hearing I carry you into my mind,
Ladders and brass and all, there to admire
15 Your phoenix-red simplicity, enshrined
    In that not extinguished fire.

—Richard Wilbur

Essay Question

Discuss how the tone of the poem is created by prosody and other sound devices, diction, imagery, syntax, point of view, and allusion.

Poetry

Analyses
of Skill Questions
and Guidelines for Essays

23 Five O'Clock Shadow

Sir John Betjeman

Analysis of Skill Questions

1. The speaker is a patient in the men's ward of a hospital or nursing home. It is early evening. The title refers to the growth of a man's beard since his morning shave, but also to the lengthening shadows as the sun comes close to setting. The shadow is literal, telling us that it is evening, but also figurative, foreshadowing the deaths of the old men in the nursing home.

2. "Can" refers both to the ability and the right or permission to act. The meaning is thus double. In his exhaustion, the patient physically finds breathing more difficult. When the visitors are gone for the day, doctors are playing golf, and the nurse is taking a break, patients no longer need to behave the way relatives and doctors expect them to behave, striving for more life at any cost. So the second meaning of "can" refers to the patient's right to abandon the fight to stay alive.

3. The visitors start their car engines so they can make their escape back to life. To "rev" is also to excite; the speaker suggests that the contrast between the moribund patients and the healthy visitors makes the latter newly aware of their own vitality. Changing gears is a cliché for any change in activity. In this case, these "loving" people are relieved as they round the bend on their way back to their homes and meals and entertainment, speeding away from the dismal presence of impending death.

4. Lines 4 and 13–14 contain examples of irony and paradox. We might expect that night would bring the worst loneliness and pain, but it is five o'clock P.M., the hour at which the patients' symptoms are exacerbated and the visitors depart, that is the low point of the day. It is paradoxical that the mere weight of bed-clothes, something which the young and healthy have never even noticed, can be more distressing than more blatant physical pain, "a sharp incision of steel." This is perhaps because the bedclothes that cover the patient mark him as one who is not fully alive, whereas the healthy are dressed in street clothing, a badge of their vigor and full engagement with life. The speaker keenly feels that he is at a disadvantage draped in hospital bed linens, passively awaiting the coming of night.

Guidelines for Responding to the Essay Question

The thesis will identify the complex tone of the poem as bitter and anxious. The essay will account for the tone by analyzing the effect of individual words and phrases.

A successful essay might include:

- Identification of words that directly state the attitudes of the speaker;
- Analysis of the effect of phrases that use alliteration and other sound correspondences;
- Analysis of the connotations of particular words;
- Analysis of the effect of double meanings, including literal as well as figurative meanings, of particular words;
- The selection of details.

The conclusion will sum up the effect of the diction in revealing the tone of the poem.

24 The Sound of Night

Maxine Kumin

Analysis of Skill Questions

1. *Chitter* is an intransitive verb, meaning "to twitter or chatter, as a bird." Used as an adjective, the word describes a noise heard as night comes on. It sets the subject of the poem and introduces the first sound from the impending dark. The poem ends as the speaker and her companions wait for the birds to announce the dawn.

The archaic *huggermugger* is normally an adjective meaning "disorderly; jumbled" or "secret." It can also be used as a noun. The poet employs the word as an adverb to create a slightly sinister image of the birds converging to roost in trees at twilight.

"Vespers" is the time for evening prayer, referring also to the service itself. It is also called "evensong." The phrase "vesper cries," in which the word *vesper* functions as an adjective, suggests the speaker's sense of something mysteriously ritual in the song of the birds at evening.

2. The synesthesia here uses the sense of touch—the tactile density of the air—to describe the high volume of sound waves as birds, bats, and frogs make their evening noises.

3. The mysterious cries of the bats are suggested by the alliteration in lines 4 to 6: *snub, seven, skitter, swing, squeak, skim, skates*. The fat frogs described in lines 7 to 9 provide a festival of monosyllables in imitation of their sounds: *wake/prink/wide, ducks/drunk, boozy black, chink-chunk*. In lines 14 to 16, sub-ject-verb pairs alliterate: *night nickers, crickets chorus, paws play* (quietly and quickly). Line 21 is rich with *m* and *n* sounds: *sing, thrum, impinge*, and *rearrange / endlessly*. The poem ends with variations on the *l* sound, soothing as light: *licking light / lost long / lake, locked / lie*.

4. Bat silhouettes are snub because their heads don't show when they are in flight, seven-pointed because there are three joints on each wing and a tail. This shape is also aerodynamically excellent for a kite, which would at first "skitter," then take the wind to "swing out," "dip" as the wind dies, then "skim," riding those smooth "skates of air," thanks to its "wings" and its "tail."

5. Throughout the description, onomatopoeic words create verisimilitude, helping readers tune their ears in order to "hear" what the speaker hears. Word choice also creates a sense of whimsy, as in the case of *prink*, meaning "to primp." The "wide-lipped" frogs are calling attention to their charming selves, though they are neither handsome nor able to sing beautifully. The speaker makes fun of their supposed vanity, comparing their song to that of "noisy" ducks. The frogs are so uninhibited because they are "drunk / on the boozy black"; the speaker suggests that darkness has the intoxicating effect of alcohol on nocturnal creatures. Finally, the melodic quality of the poem is strengthened by rhyme: "prink" is related to the "gloating" sound of the frogs, "chink-chunk."

6. The poet employs a string of verbs that evoke both sound and movement. The bats "skitter," "swing," "squeak," "chirp," "dip," and "skim." They literally squeak and chirp, but their motions are more metaphoric, as though they are moving on solid ground ("skitter") or in water ("dip" and "skim"). The overall impression is one of mystery as the speaker describes this creature of darkness, not quite a bird, fish, or beast, which seems able to navigate with preternatural ease through the elements.

7. Metaphors: Night "nickers," a soft, comforting sound that horses make. Crickets "chorus," or sing in unison. Paws "play" softly on stones, as on a keyboard. All of these metaphors relate to sound.

8. Two relevant meanings are possible: (1) the birds are full of self-importance as they await the dawn so that they can announce the arrival of a new day; and (2) the people awaiting the sun, "lost long ago and sweet," are eager to hear the bird-song that heralds its return.

Guidelines for Responding to the Essay Question

The thesis will address the sense in which humans are "day creatures" by considering the experience and emotions of those who spend the night beside a lake. Successful essays will briefly describe the setting and structure of the poem, and then analyze the connotations of key words to arrive at a sense of what various sounds mean to the humans. Writers will consider such evidence as:

- The descriptions of sounds in the first stanza;
- The verb in line 10;
- The reason for building a fire;
- The descriptions of sounds in the second stanza;
- The descriptions of the voices in lines 19–20;
- The verbs in line 21;
- The three things humans wait for (lines 23–25).

The conclusion will consider the metaphor in the final two lines.

25 Mosquito

John Updike

Analysis of Skill Questions

1. The first two stanzas tell us that the action takes place in a dark bedroom. The speaker is awake in bed, listening to the whine of an invisible mosquito. The conflict is a battle between these "opponents": the mosquito begins to suck the man's blood, the man slaps at the sting, the mosquito dies, and, after a brief feeling of mild remorse, the man sleeps. The speaker's self-congratulatory (and only slightly guilty) feelings are explored in some detail. The purpose of the poem is to produce humor through the hyperbole of the speaker's account of the incident, an example of the very human tendency to exaggerate for effect.

2. The protagonist is the first-person speaker, who reveals his cowardice when he comments, "I lay awake, unconscious of my size," and "We seemed fair-matched opponents." But he boasts of being "cunning and strong" once he has slapped the mosquito, acknowledging that, to the mosquito, he is as huge as "Gargantua."

3. In line 1, the mosquito is compared to a circus performer walking a high wire: the sound he is making, thin and continuous, is imagined as a solid object. The protagonist is sleepless and completely focused on the sound, trying to locate his enemy and fearing the attack. The speaker imagines the insect as a "traitor," giving away his plan of attack through his incessant sound.

    In the double metaphor in line 4, the mosquito's whine is compared to both speech and a spark of light, another physical object: "He talked / A thirsty blue streak" clamoring desperately for blood. The sound is "distinct as a spark" in the silent and darkened bedroom. The protagonist is worried about what that desperation and persistence bode, but is helpless to locate the creature in the dark, no matter how distinct its sound.

    In line 5 the speaker, looking at himself from the mosquito's perspective, sees a large mammal that is a magnificent source of food. The man's body is compared to "a fragrant lake of blood," and the pattern of metaphors continues in line 7 with "reservoir," "a lavish field of food," and, in line 16, "the gross rivers of myself." These metaphorical vehicles offer apt comparisons: the lake with its inviting fragrance, the reservoir of wholesome blood kept just for such emergencies, a huge field ready for harvest, and then the most complex visual image: a system of rivers, similar to a human's veins and arteries. Except for the "lavish field," all of the vehicles depict a large supply of liquid. The protagonist imagines himself as the perfect victim because of the easy access to his large and delectable supply of blood, a hyperbole which has a humorous effect.

In line 5, the mosquito is compared to an anchor, and his "song" to the anchor's chain. The weight and mass of anchor and chain are huge in relation to the tiny insect and his mere "thread" of sound. This underscores how greatly the protagonist overestimates his enemy's power as he hears the sound descend toward him.

The metaphor in line 19 compares the protagonist's feeling of remorse to the small welt of his mosquito bite. Both are uncomfortable feelings but subside quickly. He is revealing that, ironically, the injury to himself was small and temporary, but his reaction to it, turning the insect into "a fleck of fluff," makes him a murderer. In another twist of irony, he cannot sustain a feeling of remorse for his cruel deed for more than a minute or two.

4. The four-line stanzas have a regular scheme of alternating rhymes, *abab cdcd*, etc. Only the first stanza has perfect rhyme. Some of the slant rhymes in the rest of the poem are comically linked by meaning, as in the synonyms *blood / food*; the parallel actions *dropped / slapped*; and the ironically synonymous *flesh / self*.

The meter is regular iambic pentameter, with metrical substitutions that provide emphasis, silliness, or irony. The substitution of a trochaic foot at the beginning of a line is a common trick to provide emphasis, as in line 5, "I was to him," and line 10 Down like an anchor." The spondee that begins line 2, "Unseen," produces an emphatic two- stressed syllables. The four instances of triple meter in lines 11 and 12 produce a silly sound, leading up to the trochee cunning, emphasized for its ironic importance:

His nose sank thankfully in; then I slapped

At the sting on my arm, cunning and strong.

Enjambment occurs only inside of stanzas. The plot advances one stanza at a time, in strictly chronological order, as all serious narratives of combat should. By coming so often at the ends of sentences, the whimsical rhymes are emphasized.

Three caesuras slow down line 15, matching its pace to the feelings of the mosquito: "Lulled by my blood, relaxed, half-sated, stuck . . ." The same effect is created by caesuras in the last line, "By side we, murderer and murdered, sleep." The line is slowed down by commas because the action winds down to sleep.

The frequent alliteration creates a comic effect: in line 1 it is combined with assonance and consonance to produce *fine / wire / whine / walked*. Line 6 adds "drop or die," line 7 "field of food," and lines 11 and 12 contribute, "slapped / At the sting." Consonance enhances alliteration in line 15: *lulled / blood / relaxed* and line 16: *engrossed / gross*. The "fleck of fluff" that the mosquito has become by line 18 is followed by an ending which outdoes itself with alliteration: the admirable remorse of the killer comically "subsides as side / By side we, murderer and murdered, sleep."

The overall effect of the sound devices, including regular meter, a rhyme scheme, and much assonance, is euphonious. This smooth flow of pleasant sound directly contradicts the horrors of the narrative: the speaker's apprehension and fear, the attack, the counter-attack (a mortal blow), and the speaker's brief agony of remorse.

Guidelines for Responding to the Essay Question

A successful essay will show that its writer understands the mocking tone and how it is conveyed. It analyzes the ways in which tone is created by

- Setting and conflict;
- The characteristics, feelings, and motives of the protagonist and antagonist;
- The poem's diction;
- The sound devices in the poem.

The conclusion will summarize how these elements produce a mock heroic poem.

26 Question

May Swenson

Analysis of Skill Questions

1. These short iambic lines have two stresses only. There are five stanzas of irregular lengths. Each line is enjambed except the last, which stops the poem with a question mark. The rhythmic drive of the continuous form, including the triple meter created by trochees, suggests the beating hooves of the horse. Ten of the twenty-one lines begin with a trochaic foot, an interrogative emphatically beginning nine of them: *what, when, where, how, what, where, how, how, how.*

2. The first stanza, addressed to the speaker's own body in an apostrophe, introduces the parallel questions: how will I do without *my house, my horse, my hound* when *you are fallen* (I die, or rather, my body does). The second stanza specifies what actions each supplies with verbs in parallelism: *Where sleep / how ride / what hunt*, and the repetition continues into the next stanza with *where go.* The third stanza voices concerns about similar losses, the loss of "my mount / all eager and quick" and "my good bright dog." The fourth stanza tries to imagine the effects of the loss of the house, invoked as "roof or door." The fifth stanza introduces a new concern: how to hide without any covering but a cloud.

3. A series of metaphors underscores the power and efficacy of the physical body. The speaker's body is her house; without it she will have no eyes (windows) with which to see the world. She will be naked in the sky with nowhere to hide and only wind as a poor substitute for her missing senses. The speaker's body is also a horse, the vehicle of her spirit. The healthy body is eager and quick, a motivating force, and without it she must simply lie down. The body is also compared to a hound, embodying the speaker's good and bright senses and instinct. Without it, she will have no way to intuit the nature of experiences, to differentiate between those that are dangerous and those that are to be treasured.

Guidelines for Responding to the Essay Question

The thesis will assert that form and prosody very strongly embody meaning in this poem. A successful essay will analyze the effects of devices such as:

- Meter and line length;
- Metrical substitutions;
- Structure;
- Figurative language;
- Form.

The conclusion will sum up the economy with which the poem's sounds create meaning.

27

Dolor

Theodore Roethke

Analysis of Skill Questions

1. The speaker is one who has done office work and felt the "inexorable sadness" and other negative emotions evoked by the setting and its tools.

2. The poem's setting is within the "walls of institutions," where modern workers are trapped in the "unalterable" tedium of office work.

3. Roethke's poem is structured in two parts: what "I have known" (lines 1–8), and what "I have seen" (lines 9–13). Each is a complete sentence. The repetition in the first part provides a long catalog of grief and sorrow and their causes. Parallelism intensifies the speaker's complaint by giving evidence of the futility of repetitious days passed in the office. The second part provides a crystallized image of the dust covering the faces of people, a picture that suggests stasis, tedium, and the death of the spirit. This image is the culmination of the speaker's catalog, the point to which his observations have been tending. In line 8, the words "endless duplication of lives and objects" give point and focus to the first part of the poem, showing how emotions and objects are linked: sadness/pencils; dolor/pad, paper-weight; misery/manila folders, mucilage; desolation/places; pathos/basin, pitcher; ritual/multigraph, paper-clip, comma.

4. The concrete nouns represent inanimate objects to be found in an office: pencils, boxes, pad, paper-weight, folders, mucilage, places, room, lavatory, switchboard, basin, pitcher, multigraph, paper-clip, and comma. The adjectives build up the dolorous mood: folders are bland, flat manila in color. The places are "immaculate" and "public." The preternatural cleanliness is coldly formal, and the public domain is the opposite of private human warmth. The oxymoron of "lonely reception rooms" in the office buildings shows that even where human warmth and hospitality are intended, loneliness and isolation result.

5. The list consists almost entirely of unhappy human emotions: inexorable sadness, dolor, misery, desolation, and unalterable pathos. The two exceptions, "ritual" and "duplication," help emphasize, by their very *lack* of emotion, the reasons

underlying the mood of sadness. Each of these abstract nouns is connected to concrete nouns, to the objects and rooms common to offices.

6. The dust, which literally accumulates amidst all the papers, is also figurative, standing for the muffling, depressing, and standardizing effect of human institutions on human beings; ultimately, the dust is also suggestive of death. Unlike flour, it is so fine that it is not easily seen, its effects subtle and cumulative. The dust is alive and dangerous, more so, according to the speaker, than particles of silica that damage fragile lungs. Dust mysteriously sifts, "dropping" from the walls, producing "a fine film" on human nails and eyebrows and "glazing" human hair and faces. The adjectives remind us of human qualities that are covered and dimmed by the "dust" of tedious work: "delicate" eyebrows are filmed, "pale" hair is glazed, as are the "duplicate," "grey," "standard" faces of the victims of dolor.

7. The poem's final line reinforces the meaning of the whole with an unsettling comparison of the office workers to inanimate objects found in the workplace: "duplicate" and "standard" pertain equally to documents, envelopes, carbon copies, all of which are dispensable items. The speaker seems to suggest that the people, like these objects, are also dispensable and interchangeable, becoming insignificant in the repetitious routine of the office. Their faces are grey, suggesting lack of individuality and spirit.

Guidelines for Responding to the Essay Question

A successful essay will consider the effect on meaning of literary elements such as

- Structure;
- Rhetoric;
- Diction and connotation;
- Figurative language.

The conclusion will sum up the meaning of the poem: the effect of stultifying repetition and standardization on the human spirit.

28 Promises Like Pie-Crust

Christina Rossetti

Analysis of Skill Questions

1. Like a simple folk song, the poem has three eight-line stanzas of iambic tetrameter with alternating rhyme. The speaker rejects the idea of exchanging vows with her importunate lover, and provides two compelling reasons for her refusal: they can never know of each other's past, and their future feelings are uncertain. She suggests instead the age-old cliché: we can still be friends.

2. The title and the first two lines use the noun and verb *promises* and *promise* four times. This incremental repetition makes a strong claim for the speaker's point of view. Line 3 begins with an accented syllable, "Keep," and reverses the usual syntax to emphasize that the speaker also has liberty to lose: "Keep we both our liberties." Lines 4 and 6 use both repetition and parallel structure to express a paradox: "Never false and never true," and the manifesto "Free to come as free to go" suggests in its parallel structure that either action is permissible. Lines 7 and 8 play with repetition and syntax, again suggesting that what applies to him also applies to her: "For I cannot know your past, / And of mine what can you know?" The third stanza begins with "If you promised," then continues with "If I promised," the parallel structure emphasizing that either might regret the vow. In another paradox, line 22 claims that the solution offered is "Nothing more and nothing less," showing both the weakness and the strength of the friendship.

3. Line 5 suggests with the figure of "the die uncast" that promises result in unalterable circumstances, and that marriages are subject to all the uncertainties of chance and fate. In lines 9–12, the speaker's earlier romantic experiences are hinted at through the imagery of "Sunlight" and "the sun." This language balances the "warm" . . . "Warmer" imagery with which the speaker refers to her suitor's possibly fickle nature. Line 15 refers to the fading of an image from a mirror to suggest that the past can never be clearly known, and the future is unknowable because its "fortune is not told." This repeats the idea suggested by the casting of dice. Though he "might grieve / For lost liberty" were he to make her a promise, the image of her lost liberty makes this abstraction seem of little account. The picture evoked of the speaker being chained, like a dog or a prisoner, is far more vivid and compelling. The poem that begins with pie-crust comes full circle: the metaphor at the end uses the language of food to speak of love: some relationships "thrive on frugal fare," the affection offered by friendship, which would "perish of excess" in marriage.

Guidelines for Responding to the Essay Question

The thesis will state that the poem effectively uses sophisticated devices along with simple prosody and language to persuade its intended audience. A successful essay will analyze the effect of such devices as:

- The poet's use of simple diction;
- The song-like quality of the prosody;
- Unusual syntax;
- Repetition;
- Parallelism;
- Paradox;
- Imagery;
- Figurative language.

The conclusion will sum up the persuasive power of the poem.

Analysis of Skill Questions

1. The subtle changes in setting reveal Eve's fall by emphasizing the contrast between her original condition of contented innocence and her ultimate disgrace, leading to her exclusion from paradise and the success of Satan's scheme. In the first setting, Eve is alone, picking fruit under the other trees in the wonderful garden. Satan, in the form of a serpent, has been coiled high in a tree, waiting until she is alone. He tumbles down to persuade her to walk with him "Down the dark path to / The Blasphemous Tree," which is the second setting. There, Eve tastes the fruit that God has forbidden her to eat. In the third setting, Eve is in the lane outside the orchard gate, crying and hungry. She has been evicted from the garden by an angry God because she ate the forbidden fruit. In the fourth setting, Satan and his cohorts are having a party under the hill, drinking and making merry as they celebrate the ruin of paradise.

2. Throughout the poem, the language of innocence and corruption are juxtaposed. If we consider the poem's diction by first isolating verbs (*wading*, *picking*, *fell*, *whispered*, *wondering*, *listening*, *whispering*, *tumbling*, *kneeling*, *telling*, *rated*, *hated*, *pitied*, *crying*, and *haunting*), we find a pattern of Eve's innocence (she wades, picks fruit, wonders, kneels, listens, cries, and sadly haunts the garden gate). The pattern of Satan's corruption is found in his actions. His words "fall" just as he fell from heaven, and he "whispers" his corrupting secret twice, "tumbles," and tells in a "low" voice the lie that snares his innocent listener. The birds, not so naïve as Eve, berate Satan, hate him, and pity Eve.

   Adjectives also provide patterns. Eve is associated with the "sweet" berries, her body is the "white" of innocence, she is "supple," "smooth" and "slim" in her beauty, and "simple" in her lack of understanding. The birds remind us that she is "motherless": she is the more easily seduced without a mother's love and care. When Satan is hiding in the tree, biding his time, he is "mute," but when he begins the seduction his voice is "soft," "silvery," and "low" as he weaves his spell. He speaks Eve's name as softly as "a bubble sung / Out of a linnet's lung," as lovely and harmless as a bird song. But the birds cease their singing and make clattering noises of hatred. The path is "dark" and "blasphemous" because it is the way to disobedience and death. Finally, the delight of the devils under the hill is "lewd," as they celebrate the destruction of paradise.

3. The cobra is compared to a mouse because he is mute and apparently harmless, but he will very soon speak all too persuasively, and with fatal consequences. His sibilant syllables fall as lightly as flowers do, creating an illusion of tenderness. Satan is the supreme seducer. Eve is "that orchard sprite"; she seems other-worldly in her innocence. The mood of the seduction scene is all sweetness, though the seducer's intent is evil.

4. The triple falling meter is called dactyllic, with two dactyls to a line. The short lines are nearly all enjambed, with most stanzas comprising only one sentence. The sound of this triple meter suggests a dance, creating a sprightly mood, in ironic contrast to the meaning of the poem. The enjambment causes the dance to continue as though nothing is wrong.

5. Each stanza has many repeating rhymes, often couplets, though there is no regular rhyme scheme. The many times that certain key words appear as end rhymes drive home the key signifiers of the story: *sweet, eat, grass*. Throughout the poem there is repetition of significant words and phrases such as: "bells and grass" three times in the first stanza and again in stanza 6; "Eva!" says the serpent, three times in the third stanza; Eve is left in stanza 4 "Wondering, listening/Listening, wondering." The parallel structure in stanza 7 emphasizes the birds' feelings: "How/How/How" and she is toasted twice at the end of the poem: "Eva!/Eva!"

Guidelines for Responding to the Essay Question

The thesis will describe the tone of "Eve" and state its theme. The essay will analyze how sound devices such as meter, line length, enjambment, rhyme, repetition, alliteration, assonance, consonance, euphony, cacophony, and onomatopoeia contribute to its tone and meaning by creating a marked contrast between the poem's theme and its handling.

The essay may be organized around the following topics:

- How sound devices support characterization;

- How sound devices create mood;

- The effect of the contrast between the mood created by the sounds and the meaning of the poem.

The conclusion will sum up the importance of the sound devices in the poem as they contribute to tone and meaning.

30 Death Be Not Proud   *John Donne*
To Death   *Anne Finch*

Analysis of Skill Questions for "Death Be Not Proud"

1. In structure, Donne's poem is a Shakespearean sonnet: three quatrains and a couplet, each containing one sentence. However, the rhyme scheme does not follow the alternating *abab* scheme, but rather begins with the Italian scheme of *abba*, repeats the *abba*, adds two more rhymes in the third quatrain, (*cddc*), and returns to the *a* rhyme for the couplet. While the Shakespearean sonnet has a total of seven rhymes, the Italian sonnet has four or five rhymes, and Donne uses only four.

2. The drama of apostrophe focuses our attention on humankind's adversary. We overhear a bold statement made to Death himself, and we are heartily gratified that "he" is finally put in "his" place. Instead of being called "Mighty and dreadful," the speaker addresses *poor* Death with something like pity and refers to him as "slave to Fate." Death is subject to personified masters like fate and chance, as well as "kings, and desperate men." He dwells with yet more personifications, unsavory roommates: "poison, war, and sickness."

   Death is reduced to the level of sleeping potions such as "poppy" or "charms," a comparison that envisions mortality as a temporary soporific that merely ushers in our eternal life. He is given the unattractive human quality of being swollen with pride. Finally, the personification makes Death mortal; in the last line, the speaker summarily declares: "Death, thou shalt die."

3. Death, you have no reason to be proud; though some consider you to be powerful and fearsome, you are not. This is because you do not actually kill those whom you think you do, nor can you kill me. We get much pleasure from rest and sleep, which are like you; therefore, we can expect to get even more pleasure from you, as witnessed by the fact that the best people die soonest, achieving rest for their bodies and peace and salvation for their souls. You are forced to do the bidding of such blind forces as fate and chance, powerful persons like kings, and suicides; you keep close company with undesirable companions like poison, war, and sickness, some of the other causes of death. Furthermore, we can use opium or charms to help us sleep at least as well as we would sleep in death—so why are you so proud of your meager powers? The reason you have no power is that our deaths are just a "short sleep," and when we awaken to immortality, you will have lost your power and no longer exist.

Analysis of Skill Questions for "To Death"

1. Finch has written 16 lines of closed heroic couplets. The first three couplets form one unit, followed by a turn in lines 7 and 8 that begins the second unit. The last two couplets, lines 13–16, get to the heart of the speaker's message to Death.

2. Death is personified as a terrifying king who has "unbounded" power that all living things must obey. Death has a list of names, and those it kills go to its "gloomy kingdom." Death is a warrior with a sword, a torturer with racks and wheels, a bringer of fevers and contagious diseases. This king kills with his scepter, a staff that is a symbol of authority. He then takes the dead body in his cold arms, a predator who has killed his prey.

   The speaker acknowledges the absolute power of death over all living things. Yet it is not its finality that frightens her, but its means; she lists the things that make the process of dying so terrifying. She then requests to be spared violent and painful death, and instead be permitted to die peacefully.

3. Death is the most terrifying of all threats to living things because all are subject to it. Even powerful persons such as kings, priests, and prophets must die, as did God incarnate. I have no doubt that I, too, will die.

   I am not afraid to die, but I am very frightened of the agony of some deaths: fevers that kill us when we are unprepared and not in our right minds; contagious diseases that also kill those that surround a deathbed in mourning.

   If I am spared these terrible means of death, then I am not concerned about when I die; I acknowledge that I am mortal, and that I do not know when death will come. What I wish for is to die peacefully.

Guidelines for Responding to the Essay Question

The thesis will describe the tone of each of the poems and preview the ways in which they differ.

Successful essays will compare some or all of the following:

- The structures of the poems' arguments;
- The diction of each poem;
- The uses of apostrophe;
- The uses of personification.

The conclusion will compare of the overall effect produced by these: the tone of each poem.

31 Bilingual Sestina   *Julia Alvarez*

Analysis of Skill Questions

1. A sestina has six stanzas of six lines each, with a 3-line envoy. The six end words of the first stanza are repeated in each of the next five in a strict order:

    Stanza 1: *abcdef*

    Stanza 2: *faebdc*

    Stanza 3: *cfdabe*

    Stanza 4: *ecdfad*

    Stanza 5: *deacfb*

    Stanza 6: *bdfeca*

    In the last three lines, the poem's envoy, all six words are used, the end words being *eca* or *ace*, and the other words found inside the lines.

2. The speaker's conflicted attitude toward English is made clear by her personification of the language as a stereotyped American girl: "snowy, blonde, blue-eyed, gum chewing, " and by the allusion to America's national anthem in line 3: "dawn's early light." This imagery does not evoke for her the embattled American flag but rather the memory of dawn on a Caribbean island and the "dark-skinned girls" who spoke her native tongue, naming with familiarity the bed and dreams of her childhood. The speaker can translate common words from Spanish to English; it is the name of the *persianas* which the servant girls closed each night and opened each morning that she finds she cannot translate. Language has "closed" against her in the act of naming, a symptom of her unease in her adopted culture.

3. Stanza two begins with nostalgia for a lost time and place: childhood on an idyllic island. The musical cadences of "soothing" Spanish evoke "warm island waters." The speaker is again a child learning the names of things as the comforting sounds wash over her. The simplicity of the things she names—*sol, tierra, cielo, luna*—recall the innocence of a child's perception, in which the name of an object is identical to the object. The child did not have to deal with the thorny problem of cultural relativity that troubles her as an adult transplanted to a foreign land.

4. Names are not vocabulary words, which are merely labels for things and tell us nothing about connotation. Mere vocabulary words are closed, like the astonishing plant "whose leaves closed when we kids poked them." Even names, which have connotation and thus wield power, won't always summon the thing, in either language. Because words are frail, pronouncing a word will not always serve to convey the richness of experience that the object itself embodies. At best, language can only approximate "thingness" and our perception of it.

5. The speaker's sensitivity to words cannot be separated from her first language because it was Spanish that originally conjured up the bright and beautiful world for her. Because "words were so close / to the world" in childhood, names had "an intimacy" which they do not have in English, the language of the speaker's adulthood. So she is nostalgic for her first teachers. Although the child was not Adam, the first person to name things, she too participated in the splendor of her world through language.

If Gladys could be summoned back by name, she might open up the house (the childhood) which was closed (ended) when the speaker emigrated, where the shutters and the Spanish word for them alike "stand dusty and awkward" because the speaker has "neglected Spanish" in her new country. Rosario, the gardener, is invoked like a muse of epic poetry to "sing in me" because he taught the little girl her first words as he "pointed to the world." Rosario is given great significance though he is only a simple soul speaking and singing in his native tongue. In "saying" the world again along with Rosario, the speaker would again be not the first to name ("not Adam, not God,") but "what she is nostalgic for: a country girl numbering / the stars." She would recreate a time when there was "no English / yet in my head to confuse me with translations . . . , doubling the world with synonyms. . . ."

Guidelines for Responding to the Essay Question

The thesis will state that the six end words and their patterned repetition constitute an important device in developing the theme of the poem, as follows:

- The end words *words* and *nombres* underscore the difference between mere words and names;

- The end words *English* and *Spanish* underscore the difference between the English and Spanish languages;

- The end word *said*, and its variations *say* and *saying*, provide different ways of articulating the theme;

- The end word *closed* and its variation *close* (near) each provides amplification of the theme in each iteration.

The conclusion will state that the repetition of the six end words, including variations of some, is as effective as rhyme in providing a formal groundwork for a poem based on variations of a theme.

32 The Story We Know

Martha Collins

Analysis of Skill Questions

1. The poem has five tercets rhyming *aba* and a quatrain at the end rhyming *abaa*. The *a* rhyme is used thirteen times, and the *b* rhyme six. Two words serve as a kind of refrain: the word "hello" ends lines 1, 6, and 12 (ending alternate tercets); the word "know" ends line 3, as well as the remaining tercets, lines 9 and 15. Both words are used in the final two lines to sum up the refrains and reiterate the poem's meaning.

2. "Fine" is merely a standard answer to "How are you?" when we first meet someone. In the context of this poem, it also foreshadows that this happy state of enthusiasm will not last. The "chilled white wine" is the perfect complement to

the heady beginning of a relationship. By nine o'clock on a Sunday evening, a sad time at best, the relationship ends. A "line" is part of the story of every relationship, the charming things we say to attract each other, but also a reminder that our actions and feelings are scripted in a certain way—already decided. The story is the same. The "tall white pine" helps set the mood created by the other imagery: "night," "the latticed window," and the snow beginning to "whiten the air." As the emotional coldness resonates with the weather, so the meaning of "pine" is multiplied: it is also a verb for longing and grief. And the "cold white sign" is the final understanding and acknowledgment about the fate of every relationship.

3. The first exchange of hellos is merely the way to begin a first chat. The next step, having lunch together, is another "way to begin" a relationship, rather than a mere acquaintance. This "hello" is labeled simple and sane, but it's not the same as the first hello, ironically neither as simple nor as sane. The rest of the story, including the Good-bye, is told before the "same Hello" is mentioned, and the context this third time is that the story of a relationship is always the same. We know it so well that we don't need to read it through. It always begins with "the same Hello." The fourth repetition comes after the cold statement that all stories begin and end the same way: "*Hello, Good-bye* is the only story."

As we introduce each other by exchanging hellos, we say "Good-bye at the end." But "then it's Sunday," and a relationship that has been established ends with "Good-bye." "In the end" begins the idea that we have lived this story before and know it well. Line 15, "Good-bye is the end of every story we know," reiterates this idea more strongly and sadly; the mood shifts with the feelings of the lovers and the snow on that particular night, a "cold white sign " signaling that all relationships end. The final "Good-bye" once again hammers home that this is the only story.

The idea that every story has the same beginning and ending is introduced in line 3, and line 4 continues, "and why pretend?" introducing the foregone conclusion that the good-bye is contained in the hello. The second repetition adds that this is a story we know so well that we don't bother with its details. The third repetition adds the particulars of one snowy night when we really *know* that every relationship ends with good-bye, even this one. When, at the end of the poem this unwelcome truth is again repeated, "We know, we know" is spoken in sorrow and defeat.

Guidelines for Responding to the Essay Question

The thesis will state the tone and meaning of the poem and assert that its form is vital to conveying that tone and meaning. A successful essay will consider the following:

- Repeated words and phrases may have different connotations in different settings;

- Repeated words and phrases accumulate meaning, becoming richer and more suggestive;

- Repeated words and phrases change subtly with each context and its emphasis;

- The repetition, including the repetition of sound, provides emphasis.

A conclusion will reaffirm the importance of form in creating mood and meaning.

Spring and Fall
The Oven Bird

Gerard Manley Hopkins

Robert Frost

Analysis of Skill Questions for "Spring and Fall"

1. This 15-line poem typically has four accents per line. Most lines have 7 or 8 syllables, forming a loose iambic tetrameter. The perfect rhymes are couplets, except for lines 7, 8, and 9, which all share the same rhyme. With the exception of the extra line, the poem is structured like an Italian sonnet: the first eight lines set out the situation in couplets, and the central line 9 contains both the extra rhyming word and the turn signaled by the words *and yet*. This line is followed by a sestet, three sets of couplets that explain and resolve the situation.

2. In general, the sound correspondences help to create a sorrowful mood, in keeping with the speaker's gentle concern over the child's grief. The first six lines are rich in assonance and consonance. In line 7, "by and by" not only alliterates, but creates an internal rhyme with "spare a sigh." Line 8 also offers two sets of sounds: "worlds of wanwood" and "leafmeal lie." Each set has three repetitions of the consonant and two of assonance, and these sounds slow the line. These and other pairs of words have their meanings linked by sounds such as "grieve"/"gold" (lines 1–2), "sorrow's"/"springs" (line 11), and "heart heard," "ghost guessed" (line 13). In line 9, the initial *w* sound is repeated three times, slowing down the line. Line 11 repeats an initial *s* three times, connecting sound to meaning: "sorrow's springs" = "same." Line 12 contains only two words that do not have the *m* and *n* sounds. Line 14 highlights the key words with alliteration: *blight* and *born*. The alliteration in the last line connects Margaret's name with mourning.

3. "Goldengrove," the perfect name for the setting, is a grove of trees whose leaves have turned golden in the autumn. Hopkins calls this process "unleaving," an original word that leads us to consider this common sight in a "fresh" way, as would the young child. "Wanwood" suggests a pale color, the pallor of death. "Leafmeal" suggests both "piecemeal" and leaf mold, or decay. The "springs" are the deep sources of both ground water and the child's tears. "Blight," associated with disease and death in plants, also presages human mortality.

4. The poem's figurative language illuminates the theme: that the awareness of death that so troubles the innocent child will become fragmented and intellectualized in adulthood. The "heart" in line 5 represents the human capacity for emotion, while in line 12, "mouth," "mind," and "ghost" show the fragmentation of experience: "mouth" and "mind" suppress what "heart," one's emotional core, knew intuitively. These figures build to the final couplet's expressed wisdom, that our awareness of death, the source of all human sorrow, loses its immediacy after childhood. The speaker has lost the capacity for such intense feeling and counsels young Margaret after his own attitudes and experience.

Analysis of Skill Questions for "The Oven Bird"

1. Frost's poem has fourteen iambic pentameter lines with a nonce rhyme scheme: *aabcbdcdeefgfg*. Repetition of "He says" at the beginnings of lines 4, 6, and 10 reveal the structure of the poem, in which the speaker interprets the bird's song to reflect subjectively his own feelings. In the last four lines, the speaker offers his own commentary on this bird that appears only at the height of summer, when the first glories of the season have faded.

2. In midsummer, the bird's song "says" that the leaves are old, and that flowers now number only one-tenth of spring's flowers. The bird's song "says" that the fall of petals from the blossoms of fruit trees on sunny days of late spring, a "shower" that dims the sunlight, is long over, and the other fall, that of the leaves of trees, which "we [humans] name the fall," is coming. The bird's song "says" that the dust of manmade roads covers the beauty of natural things. One fall is of the petals of blossoms in late spring. Another is autumn, when trees lose their leaves. The third is The Fall of man, the loss of innocence and immortality brought about in Eden; it is this "fall" that explicitly suggests the poet's theme.

3. The bird symbolizes the human condition, typified by feelings of loss and nostalgia for perfection. According to the speaker, the bird would not deliver these messages except he knows something that the birds of spring do not know: that the joy of spring doesn't last; its beauty fades into summer and dies in fall. Yet, looking deeper, we see that it is not nature that is imperfect; it is the human being who spoils experience through this pervasive sense of loss, and thus feels "diminished." The bird's call is interpreted subjectively by the poet, who understands its rather grating "song" as the bird's sad question: How are human beings to live in this fallen world?

Guidelines for Responding to the Essay Question

The thesis will identify the subject shared by the two poems and assert that, for all their similarity, they have different themes. In discussing the poems, the writer must compare:

- The attitude and approach of each speaker;

- The tone of each poem;

- The theme and treatment of each poem.

The conclusion will sum up how the approaches and tones of the two poems convey different ideas about the same subject.

34

Complaint to His Purse

Geoffrey Chaucer

Analysis of Skill Questions

1. Rime royal is a seven-line stanza of iambic pentameter with three rhymes in the scheme *ababbcc*. The last two lines serve the unifying purpose of a refrain.

2. The light weight of the speaker's purse necessitates his demand for money. Each stanza develops the argument. In the first, the speaker appeals to his "lady's" mercy to save him from death by starvation. The imagery of the second stanza evokes the cheerful sound of gold coins rattling in a purse. The speaker flatters his lady, calling her the queen of comfort and good company. In the third stanza he begs his lady to help him leave town, calling her the light of his life and earthly savior. The imagery of the shaven *frere* (monk) is a humorous reference that shows how deprived the speaker is of worldly goods. Finally, if the purse will not fill with money, would she at least help him escape his creditors?

3. Chaucer is comparing his purse to his lady love, and employs all the courtesy and flattery of the courtly tradition. The lady is placed on a pedestal and given supreme powers. The speaker "prays" for "mercy" and for aid from his powerful lady: "helpe me thurgh your might." He uses five epithets for her, giving her increasing powers as his argument advances: "my lady dere," "My life," "myn hertes steere," "Queene of confort and of good compaignye," and finally "my lives light / And savior."

4. Henry IV is flatteringly acknowledged to be a conqueror, and his conquest is none other than the glorious land founded by a descendant of the founder of Rome. His royal lineage is proclaimed, and his free election shows that he is no tyrant but the rightful beloved sovereign of his people. The envoy humbly reminds the monarch that he has the power to solve the speaker's problems.

Guidelines for Responding to the Essay Question

The thesis will describe the tone of the poem and assert that it is conveyed through devices such as the following:

- Structure;

- Repetition;

- Imagery, metaphor;

- The hyperbole of parody.

A conclusion will sum up the effect achieved by these devices.

35 Auto Wreck

Karl Shapiro

Analysis of Skill Questions

1. The sound of the bell is described as "quick," "soft," and "silver," the last of these adjectives serving as an example of synasthesia. The ominously repeated "beating, beating," suggests the action of the human heart. The flare's light is ruby, moving "down the dark." The repetition becomes a dire warning as the ambulance approaches to certify that what the bystanders have witnessed is indeed a fatal accident. Both setting and event are red with blood and dark with mortality.

2. The participle *mangled* is used here as a noun, referring almost casually to the bodies of the victims, and thus increasing the horror with understatement. The connotation of the tolling of the ambulance bell is the funereal tolling of church bells. The phrase "terrible cargo" makes the bodies no longer human, underscoring the sickening realization that violent death turns us into mere *things*. The rocking of the ambulance, suggesting the action of comforting a baby, ironically cannot comfort either the "cargo" or the horrified witnesses.

The contrast between the "deranged" witnesses and the "composed" police suggests that even a fatal accident becomes routine to those who deal with such things daily. This routine desensitization is another horror of modern life.

3. In line 3, the ambulance's red light, which turns endlessly, is compared in its "pulsing" to a human artery pumping out lifeblood. In line 18, a policeman uses a bucket of water to rinse the hyperbolic "ponds of blood" into the street and gutter. In line 22, the witnesses cannot speak, their throats "tight as tourniquets," devices used to stop the flow of lifeblood from human arteries. In line 29, the witnesses are unwilling to leave the scene, and in remaining, they touch "a wound / That opens to our richest horror." They cannot escape from their feelings and continue probing them until they again open fully, bleeding "richly" like a wound that cannot heal. The pattern created by these metaphors suggests bleeding to death, an appalling figuration of the action in the poem.

4. The poem explores the way in which pointless and violent death overturns our assumptions about life and its ultimate significance. The "wrecks" of the cars that "cling" to iron poles are compared to "Empty husks of locusts," the shells of grasshopper larvae left behind, stuck to tree trunks, when the insects emerge as adults. This grotesque metaphor suggests that the cars were casings of the victims, who have shucked off these "bodies" in death, such transfiguration being a basic premise of many religions. There being no other evidence of the author's piety, the reader assumes this is an ironic reference to a platitude that sweetens the shocking fact of death.

   In lines 24–27, the witnesses are compared to convalescents: like hospital inmates, their common experiences suddenly make them "intimate." Their behavior is "gauche" as the black humor of the hospital ward can be, with its inappropriate "grim jokes." The conversation is "banal" with warnings and resolutions to drive more safely. Smiles are "sickly." Not only are the witnesses shaken and emotionally traumatized by their experience, they are behaving like accident victims themselves. Their fear of their own mortality leads to the unspoken, unanswerable questions.

Guidelines for Responding to the Essay Question

The thesis will be that a close reading of the last eight lines of the poem raises questions that cannot be answered by arguments based on:

- Morality: Some people are bad and deserve to die;

- Reason: Causation and logic show the reasons for some deaths;

- Physics: The scientific laws of interactions between matter and energy explain some deaths;

- Literature: The denouement, an expected outcome prepared for by the plot and its climax, resolves the situation.

The conclusion will be a statement of the theme of the poem.

Analysis of Skill Questions for "Song"

1. The speaker is an amorous man who is unsuccessfully courting a young woman of shy and retiring disposition. He personifies and addresses the rose, directing it to be his envoy: to go to the woman and plead his case for him.

2. I am sending you, beautiful rose, to the young woman whom I love and who will not decide whether to accept or reject my suit. Your beauty will show her that I think her as sweet and beautiful as you are. Tell this young woman who hides from the sight of men that if you had bloomed in the empty desert, nobody would have appreciated your beauty. Beauty that hides from the light and cannot be seen is not worth much. Therefore, ask her to show herself and allow herself to be desired instead of being embarrassed by my admiration. Then, rose, die, so she will understand that rare things, like a rose and a lovely woman, are wonderfully sweet and fair but do not live long.

3. The rhyme scheme is the same in each five-line stanza: *ababb*. In each, line length alternates dimeter with tetrameter lines, concluding with an extra tetrameter line (2–4–2–4–4). Lines 1 and 3 in each stanza are exactly half the length of the other lines. The short lines share the *a* rhyme, and the long lines share the *b* rhyme. The regular meter and strong rhymes make the poem very much the "song" of the title. The spondees that begin lines 1, 2, 6, 13, and 14 deliver the orders to the envoy: "Go, love" "Tell her," "Tell her," and "Bid her." The spondee in line 16 is the most important direction of all: "Then die."

   The structure of the poem is the perfect vehicle for the message. Each of the stanzas is a complete sentence. The rose is directed to deliver four messages, each more compelling than the last: "Tell her" that I think she is beautiful. "Tell her" that her beauty would have been wasted if nobody had seen it. "Bid her" show herself, and allow herself to be desired and admired. "Then die," shockingly, so that she will understand that all beauty is ephemeral. The death of the rose will deliver the most pointed message: seize the day by plucking the flower.

Analysis of Skill Questions for "Virtue"

1. In the first metaphor, the day is compared to the marriage of the earth and sky because they are brought together by light. The dew is personified as a person weeping for the end of the light and thus the "fall," or death, of day.

   The personified rose is described as so bright that it inspires tears in an observer who rashly gazes at it without shielding his eyes, like one who stares directly at the sun. The season of spring, with its wonderful weather and flowers, is compared to a box of perfumes or scented herbs, but the poem shows that, like the others, the season doesn't last long.

   In the poem's final metaphor, the soul of a virtuous person is compared to seasoned timber, which does not bend with the wind as green wood might, but remains staunch, or virtuous. When "the whole world," all other human souls, are corrupted and become coal, the virtuous soul will be even more gloriously and eternally alive.

2. The speaker first addresses three personified objects, one in each stanza. All three, day, rose, and spring, are called "sweet." In other parallelism, each is further

described with adjectives. The three things are introduced in the order of their length of life: a day is shortest, a rose lasts longer, and spring lasts for three months. Each of these stanzas ends with a short, identical line: "For thou must die," as the thing of beauty is cut off all too soon.

The turn comes at the start of the final stanza: "Only." There is *one* exception to this universal fate. Though the other three are also "sweet," the virtuous soul is sweetened with such moral goodness that when all the world has died, this soul "chiefly lives," a triumphant contrast to the fate of all the rest.

3. The first three of the four-lined stanzas, each a complete sentence, provide three examples of things that "must die," and each of the three contains the *b* rhyme, which repeats the key term: *sky/die, eye/die, lie/die*. In comparison, the new rhyme in the final stanza is *gives/lives*. At the start of each of these stanzas a spondee emphasizes the repetition, "sweet day," sweet rose," sweet spring," to underscore the poignance of the short lives they have, and each ends with a short, nearly identical dimeter line: "For thou/And thou/And all must die."

All of the similarities of the first three stanzas make the contrasts of the last stanza more pronounced. The fourth stanza breaks the pattern by beginning with a trochee, *Only*. With two new rhymes, a new idea is suggested. The last line ends not with *die*, but with *lives*, in a claim that is the point of the poem.

Guidelines for Responding to the Essay Question

The thesis will mention similarities between the two poems, then state their major difference. A successful essay will compare the following elements:

- Prosody;
- Structure;
- Use of Figurative language;
- Content;
- Theme.

The conclusion will comment on Herbert's use of the conventions of the carpe diem poem to overturn its essential argument.

37 Dear March—Come in—
Apparently with no surprise

Emily Dickinson

Analysis of Skill Questions for "Dear March—Come in—"

1. The stanzas have varying numbers of lines, and many are quite short, reflecting the enthusiastic broken nature of the speaker's monologue. There are a few scattered rhymes in the poem rather than a regular rhyme scheme, including the slant rhymes *before/are* (lines 3 and 6) and *come/Blame* (lines 24 and 26). The second stanza has three words that rhyme perfectly: *grew/Hue/you*. Sometimes, dashes serve as semicolons and end stops, or even as question marks. Dashes also indicate

incomplete phrases and pauses. Most of the words capitalized are nouns, but only the important nouns are capitalized. "Stairs" and "trifles" are insignificant. However, the new "Red" of the maples is an important harbinger of spring, and the job of coloring the Hills, which March left for the speaker to "Hue," is another.

2. The setting, characters, and situation are introduced in the first stanza: the first month of spring calls at the home of the speaker, is welcomed at the door, and is invited in. The second stanza continues the one-sided conversation. The speaker reports that she received the letter and the birds sent by March, and confesses that she did not manage to fulfill March's request that she color the hills purple. The plot thickens in stanza three, when the two are interrupted by a knock at the door. April's arrival is not pleasing to the speaker; she does not want to rush through the season but to savor it. Stanza four explains that all is well now that March has come.

3. The playful tone is created by the speaker welcoming March as a dear friend, much missed and looked for. The cozy details, "Put down your Hat," "You must have walked," "How out of breath you are" slyly suggest that March is a bit late this year and puffing windily as usual, rushing in its haste to make up for lost time. In asking after the guest and "the Rest," the hostess suggests that March's family is all of Nature. Full of enthusiasm, the hostess urges her friend to come in and is eager to tell her news. The line "I got your Letter, and the Birds" cleverly uses one verb to suggest that March has written a letter to announce his visit, but also sent the migrating birds ahead to herald his arrival. Lines 12 and 13, about the personified Maples, noticeably break the metrical pattern. The metaphor compares the reddening of the tips of the tree branches in preparation for new leaves with the red face of embarrassment; the trees had not realized that March was about to arrive. The speaker apologizes for having neglected to color the hills purple, her explanation being that March had taken that particular hue with him when he left last year. We are prompted to picture the color of the wooded hills of New England as the hardwood trees begin to swell with buds in March; this color is rare as well as lovely, quickly replaced by April's green. The monologue continues when April knocks at the door. The speaker is annoyed that this next month comes so quickly on the heels of March. He stayed away a year and, just as she is enjoying March's visit, pursues her, crowding in. However, this annoyance is declared only a trifle compared to her joy in March's arrival. Spring is come, and praise and blame are all one.

4. The vernal equinox doesn't come until near the end of March, and in New England winter winds continue to blow for much of the month. Most people look forward impatiently to April, when nature finally begins to green up, and barely notice the change in the color of the hills from winter gray to March's delicate purple. The speaker in this poem is fonder of the subtle signs of spring than of the obvious splash of beauty that arrives in April. She is attentive to the obscure beauty of these small changes, and is sorry that this subdued loveliness lingers for so short a time each year.

Analysis of Skill Questions for "Apparently with no surprise"

1. This eight-line poem is in continuous form rhyming *xaxaxbxb* and employing common meter, doubling the four-line stanza of that form. Dickinson employs her signature dashes and capitalized nouns along with an unexpected use of the adjective.

2. Flowers are killed one night by the first frost. The frost melts when the sun comes up, and the day proceeds. This is in keeping with the natural order of the seasons. The Flowers are not surprised to be killed without warning by the Frost. The Frost has no intention of killing. The Sun is not upset by the deaths, and continues to circle the planet. God approves of all of this.

3. The tone of the poem is casual and removed, mirroring the supreme indifference of nature. The poet's diction first suggests the sentimental view of Nature, then undercuts it with the view that the work of the frost is a necessary part of the natural order. The flowers are "happy," and though they are beheaded while they are "at . . . play," they accept the natural order. It is the tenderhearted human who mourns the ephemeral condition of beauty. Calling Frost a "blonde Assassin" makes him seem more sinister on several fronts: an assassin is a hired killer, and his fatal work is done coldly and dispassionately, his personality matching the nature of his power. Furthermore, his fair coloring is ironic: he doesn't look the part of the villain. The Sun, "unmoved" by the grim murders, continues its routine work of measuring time. The suggestion that the Sun and the Frost work for an "Approving God" is the final argument against the sentimental view: the deity presumably created them as well as the happy flowers.

Guidelines for Responding to the Essay Question

The thesis will describe the contrast in the tones of the two poems. Analysis of the following elements of each poem will include:

- Structure and rhetorical devices;
- Characteristics of the speaker;
- Uses of personification;
- Uses of diction;
- Theme.

The conclusion will sum up these differences and comment on how the same poet can regard nature in these two apparently different ways.

38 Sonnet 73

William Shakespeare

Analysis of Skill Questions

1. The sonnet is written in iambic pentameter, three quatrains followed by a couplet, rhyming *abab, cdcd, efef, gg*. Each pair of rhymes but the last is repeated once; the three quatrains form three sentences; and the end of the poem, a couplet, forms the fourth sentence. Parallelism unites the ideas: the first sentence's "in me behold", the second and third's "In me thou seest", and the final sentence's "This thou perceivest." The presumed response of the person addressed follows, now that his understanding is secured by repetition.

2. In the first three lines, the speaker compares himself to a tree in autumn, as if his lifetime were compressed into a year This seasonal metaphor allows him to play with striking imagery. His aging limbs that feel the cold are like the shaking boughs of the tree. The speaker is balding, and his sparse hair is now grey, just as the tree's remaining leaves have turned yellow. In line four those boughs where

birds once sang are now bare as ruined choirs without singers. The speaker's passion is fading, along with his youthful good looks.

In lines 5–8, the speaker compares himself to the twilight of a day. The fading light may suggest the loss of the speaker's powers, but is equally suggestive of a dwindling passion for the beloved to whom he addresses the sonnet. While night may refer to the speaker's eventual death, it also may suggest an eclipse of love and emotion. Death's "second self" is night: both allow us to rest.

In lines 9–12, the speaker compares his life to a fire in a hearth, further compressing his existence and, possibly, his love, into a few hours. The glowing coals are fueled by a bed of ashes, representing his dead youth and vitality, as well as his fading emotions toward the poem's recipient. This double meaning helps to explain the paradox of the ashes that once nourished but now consume: the speaker's bodily strength and vigor are consumed even as he revels in his powers; passion consumes itself even as it blazes most strongly.

Guidelines for Responding to the Essay Question

The thesis will be that the couplet sums up what went before, then takes a surprising turn. A successful essay will:

- Paraphrase the couplet;

- Comment on the surprising pronouns in the couplet, and how they alter the sonnet's tone;

- Consider the couplet in opposition to what went before.

The conclusion will comment on the several functions of the couplet in creating the complexity in this sonnet.

39 In Memory of Danny L. Bells for John Whiteside's Daughter

Maxine Kumin

John Crowe Ransom

Analysis of Skill Questions for "In Memory of Danny L."

1. The poet characterizes Danny as a loving person who was easy to love. Despite his handicap, or perhaps because of it, he was a friend to everyone in the village. His remembered enthusiasm and innocence form an engaging portrait of the child.

2. The poem is one sentence, a single utterance mirroring an economy of feeling. The nine stanzas each have three short lines. The poem flows without a break, with only the smallest of pauses at most line ends, and none at many.

3. The photo on the refrigerator, Danny's new glasses, the laughter during a reading lesson, the playground slide, the dogs, ponies, and lambs of the rural village, represent the ordinary, everyday stuff of life. There is no suggestion of solemnity, grief, or the funereal. This matter-of-fact tone, with its emphasis on life, rather than death, saves the poem from sentimentality.

4. In what is only a subordinate clause, we are told matter-of-factly that "his heart gave out that day on the playground slide." His "carrying off" is merely a preface

to the simply stated fact that he was "the only / Downs child in his / village school." We know Danny was a third grader, and we are casually told that his classmates "go forward this year to junior high." The passage of three years from the time of his death allows for a measured, affectionate tone of remembrance; the photos that "adhere" to the refrigerators in many homes indirectly reveal that Danny is not forgotten by the villagers.

5. The first word of the poem announces that the photo is "magnetized" to the door of the refrigerator, as Danny himself, still smiling forth, is firmly attached to the memories of the speaker and the village. Feelings about him, especially grief, are subsumed by this correspondence of photo and boy. The photo, like the boy, is small, "passport-size" (line 19), and dispassionately represents a traveler, one who has "come and gone" (line 24). In line 25, we are told only that his photo will "adhere . . . for years," leaving the reader to complete the thought: Danny himself will stay close, not just in houses or on refrigerators, but in the hearts of those who knew him. The poet's restraint leaves the reader to his or her own feelings, without having been emotionally manipulated.

Analysis of Skill Questions for "Bells for John Whiteside's Daughter"

1. In the first stanza, the child's speed, the "lightness in her footfall" (lines 1 and 2) and her "tireless heart" (line 13) present us with an absolute contrast to the "brown study," the gloomy and deep self-absorption of the child's laid out corpse. Her heart was not tireless after all, and "we" are astonished. Her noisy wars with her own shadow, her harrying of the geese, are so typical of the living child that the mourners are "sternly stopped," even "vexed" by the brown study again mentioned in the last stanza. The unbearable contrast is supplied by the description of this most vivacious child "Lying so primly propped."

2. The poem is arranged in five four-line stanzas of loose iambic meter, each stanza rounded off with a short (trimeter) line. The alternating rhymes of each stanza provide more obvious structure than does the meter. The first and last stanzas are each a sentence, set in the present tense, just before the child's funeral. Line 5 introduces the nature of the child's play, and the middle three stanzas form a tireless flow of enjambment mimicking the energy of the little girl. The vivid series of images of a richly lived life ends with a dramatic exclamation point. The start of the final stanza is a slow line beginning with the turn, "But now," and continuing with the contrasting imagery of the funeral bells.

3. In both the title and in line 17, the bells are literally the doleful sound from the church's steeple, announcing the child's funeral. They also suggest, figuratively, the song-like nature of the poem, that it is not just an elegy, but a eulogy to the vitality of the young child. The diction in the middle three stanzas of the poem produces humor. In stanza two we hear of the clamor of the child's "wars," as she "took arms against her shadow" with an imaginary lance and sword, a parody of heroic deeds. The geese that she "harried" with her stick are described and characterized with rich imagery: lavishly compared to a "snow cloud / Dripping their snow on the green grass," the geese do not form a dignified procession to the pond, but are instead being driven by the child with a "rod," "Tricking and stopping, sleepy and proud." Their cries of alarm and protest, translated from the Goose, show how unwilling they are to be awakened from "their noon apple-dreams" and forced to "scuttle" away to escape the energetic goose-girl.

   The image of the child's face, suggesting a deep "brown study," is mentioned in both the first and last stanzas. All who are there awaiting her funeral are "astonished" at such a mood reflected on this, of all faces. They "sternly" pause to go on record that they are "vexed" by it, as though to scold her for being so unlike herself. The picture of the physical state of the body carries a heavy burden of grief with its understatement: "Lying so primly propped."

Guidelines for Responding to the Essay Question

The thesis will state that the tones of these poems are similar in their understated restraint, and that the overall effect in each poem is produced by such devices as:

- Form and structure;
- Vivid imagery;
- Diction with both literal and figurative connotations;
- Understatement.

The conclusion will examine the titles of the two poems, accounting for the effect of their specificity.

40 *from* The Rape of the Lock
from The Lady's Dressing Room

Alexander Pope

Jonathan Swift

Analysis of Skill Questions for "The Rape of the Lock"

1. These heroic couplets are the perfect choice for a mock epic, aptly conveying the humorous incongruity of subject matter and manner; epic poetry uses the same prosody to sing of real goddesses and battles. The setting is equally trifling, a dressing table treated a religious altar where the young lady worships her own image in the mirror and the "inferior priestess" (her maid) assists in the religious rites of beautification. Hyperbole abounds in the catalog of offerings from around the world: all the gems of India enhance her beauty; all the perfumes of Arabia sweeten her flesh; the tortoise's shell and elephant's ivory tusk from which combs are made involve the ultimate sacrifice to the lady's beauty. The details produce the irony of the passage—this beauty is all an illusion, created by artifice and expense.

2. The diction describing the dressing table superficially inspires deep reverence for the lady's beauty: The "toilet" is "unveiled," displaying the holy vessels of cosmetics in "mystic order." The pun on *cosmic* in those "cosmetic powers" adds to the admiration of the "nymph" herself, "robed in white" like a goddess. She worships her own "heavenly image," as does her maid, "the inferior priestess," who "trembling" in awe, begins the "sacred rites of pride!" Though we see the irony of the comparison, the incongruity of this last phrase is surprising.

   In preparation for the battle to come, the pins, like armed warriors, are lined up awaiting their general's orders in "shining rows." As the epic hero ceremoniously puts on his armor, so "awful Beauty puts on all its arms." Her weapons are the alliterative "puffs, powders, patches," but also the incongruous pair, "Bibles" and "billet-doux." If her "smiles" are in need of "repairs," they are hardly genuine.

Equally ironic is that "purer blush," which is created by the artifice of paint rather than maidenly modesty.

Analysis of Skill Questions for "The Lady's Dressing Room"

1. Swift uses closed couplets, but a shorter tetrameter line than the heroic couplet, making the effect of the rhythm less grand. Many of the rhymes are double, setting the satiric tone in the first four lines with *less in / dressing*, and continuing with the disgusting smock which *appeared / besmeared* (lines 11–12). The filthy combs have dirt *closely fixt / betwixt* (lines 21–22). The slant rhyme in lines 17–18 is not true rhyme: *men lie / cleanly*, just as the praise of Celia's cleanliness is based on a falsehood.

   The poem is structured by verse paragraphs. The first explains antecedent action (Celia's spending five hours dressing, then issuing forth). The setting and other characters are seen through the eyes of Strephon, who sneaks into Celia's dressing room and surveys the repulsive "litter." The poem then proceeds in an ironically orderly march of couplets comprising an "inventory" of what this sneering servant finds.

   The two parts of the poem juxtapose the goddess and her filthy dressing room in the best Juvenalian style, exposing the incongruity of means and end. Hyperbole begins the poem with those five hours spent in dressing. The amount of dirt embedded between the teeth of the combs is surely hyperbolic as well; the composition of the "paste" is a catalog of unsavory extrusions: "sweat, dandruff, powder, lead and hair." These devices comprise a most contemptuous way of exposing the ugly truth about the grand lady's personal habits.

2. The first four lines set up Celia for a fall: she is "haughty," a "goddess," "arrayed" in fine and delicate fabrics. Then comes the servant's "strict survey" of the "litter" she left behind, and the promise of an "inventory" for those of us who love gossip, and would like to see the mighty fallen. The first item displayed is the "dirty smock," besmeared by the lady's odiferous armpits. The sound of "besmeared" says it all: this is quite a vicious attack, followed by the reminder that those who do not know the truth call Celia "sweet and cleanly." The filthy "paste" between the teeth of the comb is another secret proof of Celia's true character. What irony that what we see is the opposite of what we expect, and is in itself the product of artifice ("rouge," "powder," and "lead," an ingredient in artificial hair color).

Guidelines for Responding to the Essay Question

The thesis will state that though the two poets use similar techniques, they produce quite different satiric tones, one Horatian and one Juvenalian. A successful essay will analyze the effect of such devices as:

- Prosody;

- Rhetorical devices;

- Diction;

- Imagery.

The conclusion will sum up the results of the analysis, explicating the contrast in the tones of the two passages.

41

Well, I Have Lost You
Edna St. Vincent Millay

Analysis of Skill Questions

1. An Elizabethan sonnet in its structure, Millay's "Well, I Have Lost You" follows the formal pattern made famous by Shakespeare: fourteen lines of iambic pentameter arranged in three quatrains and a couplet, rhyming *abab cdcd efef gg*. Millay's sonnet is grammatically structured to reflect the four divisions of rhyme: the end of each of the quatrains and the couplet is the end of a sentence. Each quatrain is divided into two or more main clauses. The only enjambment in the poem is within the quatrain: lines 3, 5, 7, and 9. Double rhymes appear in lines 1 and 3, 5 and 7, 9 and 11. The couplet has strong single rhymes: "do" and "you." The initial trochaic substitutions that begin lines 1, 3, 4, 6, 7, 8, and 14 reflect the normal patterns of speech and add emphasis to the speaker's words.

2. I make the claim that, though I have lost you, I have lost you (my beloved) "fairly," that I had some control over the ending of the relationship, and that I consented fully. My letting go of you can be compared to kings being ignominiously carted to their deaths: I was proud as they in facing my "death," the grievous loss of your love.

3. I admit that my show of pride did not extend to my private moments. I claim permission to indulge in "apprehension and hot weeping" at night, but I have had the self-restraint to conceal my feelings in public: "Day dried my eyes." The metaphor compares the beloved to a bird who does not want to stay in a cage, and the speaker declares, I am not the sort of person who would keep someone I love against his will, someone who is chafing his wings against the bars.

4. Lines 9 and 10 follow an "if . . . then" syntactical structure, reflecting the speaker's proposition that the end of the love affair was conditional and hinged upon her actions as well as those of the beloved. Lines 11 and 12 begin with *But* and are followed by the speaker's objections to the action she rejected.

    To paraphrase, the speaker says: paradoxically, if I had loved you less or used sly tricks, I might have delayed the end of our relationship and enjoyed another summer. But I would have had to endure the deceptive use of words that I value highly. And I would have had to suffer the painful comparison of a summer of "holding you," like a restless bird in a cage, and the last summer of our genuine mutual love.

Guidelines for Responding to the Essay Question

The thesis will assert that the sonnet's couplet, both in meaning and expression, is a summation as well as an addition to what went before. A successful essay will address:

*   The self-mocking tone of line 13;
*   The possibility of a double meaning in the use of the word "men";
*   The choice of the word "shall" rather than "will."

The conclusion will explain how lines 1–12 lead up to the assertion in line 14.

42

Arms and the Boy
Beat! Beat! Drums!

Wilfred Owen

Walt Whitman

Analysis of Skill Questions for "Arms and the Boy"

1. "Arms and the Boy" has three four-line stanzas of loose iambic pentameter in couplets of slant rhyme. Each stanza except the last is a complete sentence. The poem is in two parts. In the first two stanzas, the speaker instructs us to "Let the boy . . ." (line 1) and "Lend him . . ." (line 5), "Or give him . . ." (line 7). The second part begins with the turn, the first word of stanza 3: "For . . ." The two parts powerfully make the point: Let the boy touch "this bayonet-blade," stroke these "bullet-heads," these "cartridges," all manmade weapons of destruction. For he will need them when he goes to war: his own body is not made for killing—his teeth, fingers, heels, and forehead are innocent of fangs, claws, talons, and antlers. The boy, nature's creation, must find these machine-forged weapons alien. So he should, because war is not nature's creation, but that of madmen.

2. The diction and imagery in the first two stanzas suggest that the weapons are autonomous, having a life outside of those who handle them. The personified bayonet blade is literally "cold," being made of steel and figuratively without warm feelings. It is "keen with hunger of blood," not merely sharp. It is literally "blue," but figuratively "with all malice, like a madman's flash." It is "thin," as though "famishing for flesh." The bullet-heads are literally "blunt," figuratively "blind," unable to discriminate which "hearts of lads" they ironically "nuzzle." The zinc cartridges have fine notches; they are literally sharp and, figuratively, their "teeth," can bite "with the sharpness of grief and death." The juxtaposition of the literal and the figurative make the personification all the more chilling; given the human capacity for volition and evil, the weapons turn into monstrous parodies. They are envisioned as hungry for blood, malicious, madmen, famishing for flesh, longing to nuzzle, wanting to inflict grief and death.

3. The description of the boy is one of beauty and innocence: his teeth are pictured as "laughing round an apple"; his fingers are "supple," not hurtful; his heels have no talons; no weapons protrude from "the thickness of his curls." Virgil's great war epic glorifies *men*: armed warriors and their bloody deeds. Owens's poem makes a crucial distinction, claiming that those who fought in World War I were only boys, beautiful and innocent, having nothing in common with the glorious warriors of old and no idea what awaited them in the trenches.

Analysis of Skill Questions for "Beat! Beat! Drums!"

1. The occasion of the poem is the arrival of a trainload of dead soldiers into a town that is in the midst of a military recruitment day. The speaker observes both the din of the martial music and the silence of the dead who are "awaiting the hearses" that will carry them to the burial grounds.

2. The poem has three stanzas, with seven long lines of loosely iambic meter in each. The first line in each stanza is identical. It has seven syllables, six of which are accented: "BEAT! BEAT! DRUMS!—BLOW! BUgles! BLOW!" There is a caesura after the first three syllables. The last lines are variations of each other, adding

intensity with changes in sound and connotation from *whirr/pound/shrill* to *rattle quicker/heavier/wilder,* to *strong/thump/terrible.* Each of these lines also has a caesura. The lines are long, with far more accented than unaccented syllables: "SO STRONG YOU THUMP O TERrible DRUMS—SO LOUD YOU BUgles BLOW." Other effective sound devices are frequent instances of alliteration and onomatopoeia. The many repetitions of the initial *b* sound and the imitative sounds of words such as *beat, whirr, pound, shrill, rattle,* and *thump* invoke the clangor of war.

3. The poem catalogs people as follows: in the first stanza, a church's congregation, a scholar at school, a bridegroom, and a farmer, categories of people with peaceful occupations. The second stanza lists sleepers (the dead), bargainers, brokers or speculators, talkers, singer, and lawyer, all of whom had been engaged in more vociferous endeavors, but are now silenced by the war drums or by death in battle. The third stanza lists the timid, the weeper, one who prays, the old man beseeching the young man, the child hearing his mother's entreaties, and finally the dead, who cannot be put into hearses until the military celebration concludes. These can be construed in one way or another as victims of military fervor; some are about to become soldiers, some are frightened and unwilling to face war, and some are enthusiastic in the midst of the recruiters' din, though beseeched by loved ones not to enlist. This progression makes the martial spirit increasingly immediate and oppressive, dramatizing the human cost of war as Whitman contrasts the fervent crowd with the silent dead.

4. Prepositions increase the momentum of the action: the repetition of "through" in line 2, "into" in lines 3 and 4, and "over" in line 9 helps to personify the terrible noise of military music as it overwhelms the city, overcoming even the loud noise of traffic, "the rumble of wheels in the streets."

The verbs expressing this martial clangor are uniformly destructive: *beat, blow, burst, scatter, whirr* and *pound, rattle, thump.* Combined with the negatives (*not/no/nor*), the racket overcomes all else: no sleep is possible, no bargaining, no talking, no singing, no parley, no expostulation. This din is commanded to "mind not" the timid, the weeper, the prayer, the words of the old man, the child, the mother. It dares even to shake the dead.

Adjectives and adverbs provide contrast between the sounds of war and those of peace: "ruthless" force destroys solemnity in lines 2 and 3. The "quiet" bridegroom and the "peaceful" farmer have their happiness and peace shattered by the sound. The drums are "fierce" and the bugles "shrill." The rattle of the drums becomes "heavier" and "quicker," and the sound of bugles "wilder." The thump of the "terrible" drums is "strong," and the bugles "loud."

Guidelines for Responding to the Essay Question

The thesis will claim both similarities and differences in the two poems. A successful essay will note and analyze:

- Contrast in the scope of the poems: Whitman's large group of people in an expansive landscape, Owen's single, universal boy;

- Differences in form and style producing different effects.

The conclusion will make the case that the two poems express the same attitude toward war in spite of the many differences in their formal elements.

Norton Editions

The chart below lists the passages or poems in this skillbook that can be found in their entirety in W.W. Norton Critical Editions or Norton Anthologies.

KEY

NCE: Norton Critical Edition

Seagull Lit: *The Seagull Reader: Literature*

Seagull Poems: *The Seagull Reader: Poems*

Seagull Plays: *The Seagull Reader: Plays*

NAEL 7: *The Norton Anthology of English Literature*, 7th Ed.

NAAL 6: *The Norton Anthology of American Literature*, 6th Ed.

NAP 5: *The Norton Anthology of Poetry*, 5th Ed.

NAPF: *A Norton Anthology of Poetic Forms*

NIP 8: *The Norton Introduction to Poetry*, 8th Ed.

NIL 9: *The Norton Introduction to Literature*, 9th Ed.

NISN 3: *The Norton Introduction to the Short Novel*, 3rd Ed.

N Shakespeare: *The Norton Shakespeare, Based on the Oxford Edition*

Fiction

Nathaniel Hawthorne, from *The Scarlet Letter*	NCE; NAAL 6
Charlotte Brontë, from *Jane Eyre*	NCE
Jane Austen, from *Pride and Prejudice*	NCE
Mark Twain, from *The Adventures of Huckleberry Finn*	NCE; NAAL 6
William Faulkner, from *As I Lay Dying*	NAAL 6; NISN 3

Drama

Tennessee Williams, from *The Glass Menagerie*	Seagull Lit; Seagull Plays
George Bernard Shaw, from *Pygmalion*	NCE *George Bernard Shaw's Plays;* NIL 9
Oscar Wilde, from *The Importance of Being Earnest*	Seagull Lit; NAEL 7; Seagull Plays; NIL 9
Richard Brinsley Sheridan, from *The School for Scandal*	NCE *Restoration and 18th-Century Comedy*
William Shakespeare, from *Othello*	N Shakespeare; NCE
William Shakespeare, from *Twelfth Night*	N Shakespeare; NAEL 7
August Wilson, from *Fences*	Seagull Lit; Seagull Plays

Poetry

Christina Rossetti, "Promises Like Pie-Crust"	NAEL 7
John Donne, "Death Be Not Proud"	NCE *John Donne's Poetry;* NIL 9; NAP 5; Seagull Lit; NAEL 7; Seagull Poems
Anne Finch, "To Death"	NAP 5
Gerard Manley Hopkins, "Spring and Fall"	NAP 5; NAEL 7; NIL 9; NIP 8; Seagull Poems
Robert Frost, "The Oven Bird"	NAP 5; NAAL 6
Geoffrey Chaucer, "Complaint to His Purse"	NAP 5; NAEL 7
Edmund Waller, "Song"	NAP 5
George Herbert, "Virtue"	NAP 5; NAEL 7
William Shakespeare, "Sonnet 73"	NAP 5; NAEL 7; N Shakespeare
John Crowe Ransom, "Bells for John Whiteside's Daughter"	NAP 5; NAPF; Seagull Lit; NAAL 6; NIP 8; Seagull Poems
Alexander Pope, from "The Rape of the Lock"	NAP 5; NAEL 7
Jonathan Swift, from "The Lady's Dressing Room"	NAP 5; NAEL 7
Walt Whitman, "Beat! Beat! Drums!"	NAAL 6; NAP 5; NCE *Leaves of Grass and Other Writings*
Audre Lorde, "Hanging Fire"	NIP 8
Elizabeth Bishop, "The Fish"	NAP 5; Seagull Lit; NAAL 6; Seagull Poems
William Wordsworth, "Nuns Fret Not at Their Convent's Narrow Room"	NAP 5; NIL 9
Thomas Carew, "Mediocrity in Love Rejected"	NAP 5

Further Reading

The following list is a broad range of suggestions for further reading and study of literary works. In addition to the titles from which the lessons in this skillbook are taken, the works of fiction and drama represent the best of English literature as well as classics from other languages, providing excellent preparation for the AP English Literature Exam. Many of the passages that have appeared on the examination over the years are the work of writers included here; most of these titles have been listed on the exams as suitable for the "Open Question" essay. Writers' country of origin and/or ethnicity are included.

FICTION

Achebe, Chinua (Nigerian): *Things Fall Apart*

Agee, James (American): *A Death in the Family*

Alexie, Sherman (Native American): *Indian Killer; Reservation Blues*

Alvarez, Julia (Dominican-American): *How the Garcia Girls Lost Their Accents*

Anaya, Rudolfo (Mexican-American): *Bless Me, Ultima*

Arnow, Harriette (American): *The Dollmaker*

Atwood, Margaret (Canadian): *Alias Grace; The Handmaid's Tale*

Austen, Jane (British): *Emma; Mansfield Park; Northanger Abbey; Persuasion; Sense and Sensibility*

Baldwin, James (African-American): *Another Country; Go Tell It on the Mountain*

Brontë, Emily (British): *Wuthering Heights*

Camus, Albert (French-Algerian): *The Plague; The Stranger*

Cao, Lan (Vietnamese-American): *Monkey Bridge*

Cather, Willa (American): *Death Comes for the Archbishop; My Antonia; The Song of the Lark*

Cervantes, Miguel de (Spanish): *Don Quixote*

Chopin, Kate (American): *The Awakening*

Cisneros, Sandra (Mexican-American): *The House on Mango Street*

Connell, Evan (American): *Mr. Bridge; Mrs. Bridge*

Conrad, Joseph (Ukrainian-British): *Heart of Darkness; Lord Jim; Victory*

Crane, Stephen (American): *The Red Badge of Courage*

Danticat, Edwidge (Haitian-American): *Breath, Eyes, Memory; The Farming of Bones*

Davies, Robertson (Canadian): *Fifth Business*

Defoe, Daniel (British): *Moll Flanders*

Dickens, Charles (British): *Bleak House; David Copperfield; Great Expectations; Hard Times; A Tale of Two Cities*

Dostoevsky, Fyodor (Russian): *Crime and Punishment*

Dreiser, Theodore (American): *An American Tragedy; Sister Carrie*

Eliot, George (British): *Middlemarch; The Mill on the Floss*

Ellison, Ralph (African-American): *Invisible Man*

Erdrich, Louise (Native American): *The Beet Queen; Love Medicine*

Faulkner, William (American): *Absalom, Absalom!; Light in August; The Sound and the Fury*

Fielding, Henry (British): *Tom Jones*

Fitzgerald, F. Scott (American): *The Great Gatsby; Tender Is the Night*

Flaubert, Gustave (French): *Madame Bovary*

Ford, Ford Madox (British): *The Good Soldier*

Forster, E. M. (British): *A Passage to India; A Room With a View*

Frazier, Charles (American): *Cold Mountain*

Gaines, Ernest J. (African-American): *The Autobiography of Miss Jane Pittman; A Gathering of Old Men; A Lesson Before Dying*

Garcia, Cristina (Cuban American): *Dreaming in Cuban*

Gaskell, Elizabeth (British): *Mary Barton*

Golding, William (British): *Lord of the Flies*

Goldsmith, Oliver (British): *The Vicar of Wakefield*

Greene, Graham (British): *The Comedians; The Power and the Glory*

Guterson, David (American): *Snow Falling on Cedars*

Hardy, Thomas (British): *Jude the Obscure; The Mayor of Casterbridge; The Return of the Native; Tess of the D'Urbervilles*

Hawthorne, Nathaniel (American): *The House of the Seven Gables*

Head, Bessie (South African): *When Rain Clouds Gather*

Heller, Joseph (American): *Catch-22*

Hemingway, Ernest (American): *A Farewell to Arms; For Whom the Bell Tolls; The Sun Also Rises*

Hurston, Zora Neale (African-American): *Their Eyes Were Watching God*

Huxley, Aldous (British): *Brave New World*

Ishiguro, Kazuo (Japanese-British): *The Remains of the Day*

James, Henry (American-British): *Daisy Miller; The Portrait of a Lady; The Turn of the Screw; Washington Square; The Wings of the Dove*

Jen, Gish (Chinese-American): *Typical American*

Joyce, James (British): *A Portrait of the Artist As a Young Man*

Kafka, Franz (Czechoslovakian): *The Metamorphosis; The Trial*

Kesey, Ken (American): *One Flew Over the Cuckoo's Nest*

Kincaid, Jamaica (Antiguan-American): *Annie John; Lucy; Mr. Potter*

Kingsolver, Barbara (American): *The Bean Trees; The Poisonwood Bible*

Kingston, Maxine Hong (Chinese-American): *The Woman Warrior*

Kogawa, Joy (Japanese-American): *Obasan*

Laurence, Margaret (Canadian): *The Diviners; The Stone Angel*

Lawrence, D. H. (British): *Sons and Lovers*

Lee, Chang-rae (Korean-American): *A Gesture Life; Native Speaker*

Lessing, Doris (Rhodesian-British): *The Golden Notebook; The Summer Before the Dark*

Lewis, Sinclair (American): *Main Street*

Malamud, Bernard (American): *The Fixer*

Márquez, Gabriel Garcia (Colombian): *One Hundred Years of Solitude*

Marshall, Paule (African-American): *Brown Girl, Brownstones; Praisesong for the Widow*

Mason, Bobbie Ann (American): *In Country*

McCarthy, Cormac (American): *All the Pretty Horses*

McCullers, Carson (American): *The Ballad of the Sad Café; The Heart Is a Lonely Hunter; Reflections in a Golden Eye*

Melville, Herman (American): *Billy Budd; Moby-Dick*

Mistry, Rohinton (East Indian-Canadian): *Family Matters; A Fine Balance*

Momaday, N. Scott (Native American): *House Made of Dawn*

Morrison, Toni (African-American): *Beloved; The Bluest Eye; Song of Solomon*

Mukherjee, Bharati (East Indian-Canadian-American): *Jasmine*

Munro, Alice (Canadian): *Lives of Girls and Women*

Nabokov, Vladimir (Russian-American): *Pale Fire; Pnin*

Naipaul, V. S. (Trinidadian-British): *A Bend in the River*

Naslund, Sena Jeter (American): *Ahab's Wife*

Naylor, Gloria (African-American): *Bailey's Cafe; Linden Hills; Mama Day; The Women of Brewster Place*

Ng, Fae Myenne (Chinese-American): *Bone*

O'Brien, Tim (American): *Going After Cacciato; In the Lake of the Woods*

O'Connor, Flannery (American): *Everything That Rises Must Converge; The Violent Bear It Away; Wise Blood*

Okada, John (Japanese-American): *No-No Boy*

Ondaatje, Michael (Sri-Lankan-Canadian): *Coming Through Slaughter*

Orwell, George (British): *Nineteen Eighty-Four*

Patchett, Ann (American): *Bel Canto*

Paton, Alan (South African): *Cry, the Beloved Country*

Percy, Walker (American): *The Moviegoer*

Porter, Katherine Anne (American): *Pale Horse, Pale Rider; Ship of Fools*

Potok, Chaim (American): *My Name Is Asher Lev*

Proulx, Annie (American): *The Shipping News*

Pynchon, Thomas (American): *The Crying of Lot 49; Gravity's Rainbow*

Rhys, Jean (British): *Wide Sargasso Sea*

Salinger, J. D. (American): *The Catcher in the Rye; Franny and Zooey*

Shaara, Michael (Italian-American): *The Killer Angels*

Shelley, Mary (British): *Frankenstein*

Silko, Leslie Marmon (Native American): *Ceremony*

Spark, Muriel (British): *The Prime of Miss Jean Brodie*

Stegner, Wallace (American): *Angle of Repose*

Steinbeck, John (American): *The Grapes of Wrath*

Stowe, Harriet Beecher (American): *Uncle Tom's Cabin*

Styron, William (American): *The Confessions of Nat Turner*

Swift, Jonathan (British): *Gulliver's Travels*

Tan, Amy (Chinese-American): *The Joy Luck Club*

Thackeray, William Makepeace (British): *Vanity Fair*

Tolstoy, Leo (Russian): *Anna Karenina*

Trollope, Anthony (British): *The Warden*

Twain, Mark (American): *Pudd'nhead Wilson*

Tyler, Anne (American): *Dinner at the Homesick Restaurant*

Updike, John (American): *The Centaur; Rabbit, Run*

Valdez, Lius (Mexican-American): *Zoot Suit*

Voltaire (French): *Candide*

Vonnegut, Kurt (American): *Slaughterhouse-Five*

Walker, Alice (African American): *The Color Purple*

Warren, Robert Penn (American): *All the King's Men*

Waugh, Evelyn (British): *Brideshead Revisited; The Loved One*

Welch, James (Native American): *Winter in the Blood*

Welty, Eudora (American): *Delta Wedding; Losing Battles; The Optimist's Daughter*

West, Nathanael (American): *The Day of the Locust; Miss Lonelyhearts*

Wharton, Edith (American): *The Age of Innocence; The House of Mirth*

Wilde, Oscar (British): *The Picture of Dorian Gray*

Wilder, Thornton (American): *The Bridge of San Luis Rey*

Woolf, Virginia (British): *Mrs. Dalloway; Orlando; To the Lighthouse*

Wright, Richard (African-American): *Native Son*

Yezierska, Anzia (Polish-American): *Bread Givers*

DRAMA

Aeschylus (Greek): *The Oresteia*

Albee, Edward (American): *Who's Afraid of Virginia Woolf?; The Zoo Story*

Aristophanes (Greek): *Lysistrata*

Beckett, Samuel (British-French): *Waiting for Godot*

Behn, Aphra (British): *Oroonoko*

Brecht, Bertolt (German): *The Caucasian Chalk Circle; Mother Courage and Her Children; The Threepenny Opera*

Churchill, Caryl (British): *Cloud 9; Top Girls*

Congreve, William (British): *The Way of the World*

Eliot, T. S. (American-British): *Murder in the Cathedral*

Etherege, George (British): *The Man of Mode*

Euripides (Greek): *Medea*

Friel, Brian (British): *Dancing at Lughnasa; Translations*

Fry, Christopher (British): *The Lady's Not for Burning*

Glaspell, Susan (American): *Trifles*

Goldsmith, Oliver (British): *She Stoops to Conquer*

Hansberry, Lorraine (African-American): *A Raisin in the Sun*

Hellman, Lillian (American): *The Little Foxes; Toys in the Attic; Watch on the Rhine*

Hwang, David Henry (Chinese-American): *M. Butterfly*

Ibsen, Henrick (Norwegian): *A Doll's House; An Enemy of the People; Ghosts; Hedda Gabler*

Jonson, Ben (British): *Volpone*

MacLeish, Archibald (American): *J.B.*

Mamet, David (American): *American Buffalo; Glengarry Glen Ross; Oleanna; Speed the Plow*

Marlowe, Christopher (British): *Doctor Faustus*

Miller, Arthur (American): *All My Sons; Death of a Salesman*

Molière (French): *The Misanthrope*

Norman, Marsha (American): *'night, Mother*

O'Neill, Eugene (American): *Desire Under the Elms; Long Day's Journey into Night; Mourning Becomes Electra*

Pielmeier, John (American): *Agnes of God*

Pinter, Harold (British): *The Homecoming*

Shaffer, Peter (British): *Equus*

Shakespeare, William (British): *Antony and Cleopatra; As You Like It; Hamlet; Henry IV, Parts I and II; Henry V; King Lear; Macbeth; The Merchant of Venice; A Midsummer Night's Dream; Much Ado About Nothing; Othello; Richard III; Romeo and Juliet; The Tempest*

Shaw, George Bernard (British): *Major Barbara; Mrs. Warren's Profession; Saint Joan*

Sheridan, Richard Brinsley (British): *The Rivals*

Sophocles (Greek): *Antigone; Oedipus the King*

Soyinka, Wole (Nigerian): *Death and the King's Horseman; The Lion and the Jewel; A Play of Giants; The Swamp Dwellers*

Steele, Richard (British): *The Conscious Lovers*

Stoppard, Tom (British): *Rosencrantz and Guildenstern Are Dead*

Synge, John Millington (British): *The Playboy of the Western World; Riders to the Sea*

Vogel, Paula (American): *The Baltimore Waltz; How I Learned to Drive*

Wilde, Oscar (British): *Lady Windermere's Fan*

Wilder, Thornton (American): *Our Town*

Williams, Tennessee (American): *Cat on a Hot Tin Roof; The Night of the Iguana; A Streetcar Named Desire*

Wilson, August (African-American): *Joe Turner's Come and Gone; Ma Rainey's Black Bottom; The Piano Lesson*

Wycherley, William (British): *The Country Wife*

POETRY

Note: Because poems are too numerous to list individually, this list includes only the names of poets (classic, nineteenth-century, modern, and contemporary) whose work AP students should sample.

Classic Poets

Anonymous, "Sir Gawain and the Green Knight" (trans. W.S. Merwin) (British)

Anonymous, "Beowulf" (trans. Seamus Heaney) (British)

Blake, William (British)

Bradstreet, Anne (American)

Burns, Robert (British)

Campion, Thomas (British)

Carew, Thomas (British)

Chaucer, Geoffrey (British)

Constable, Henry (British)

Donne, John (British)

Dryden, John (British)

Finch, Anne (British)

Herbert, George (British)

Herrick, Robert (British)

Homer (trans. Robert Fagles) (Greek)

Jonson, Ben (British)

Lovelace, Richard (British)

Marlowe, Christopher (British)

Marvell, Andrew (British)

Milton, John (British)

Pope, Alexander (British)

Raleigh, Sir Walter (British)

Sidney, Sir Philip (British)

Shakespeare, William (British)

Skelton, John (British)

Smart, Christopher (British)

Spenser, Edmund (British)

Suckling, John (British)

Swift, Jonathan (British)

Virgil (trans. Robert Fitzgerald) (Roman)

Waller, Edmund (British)

Wyatt, Thomas (British)

Nineteenth-Century Poets

Alfred, Lord Tennyson (British)

Arnold, Matthew (British)

Brontë, Emily (British)

Browning, Elizabeth Barrett (British)

Browning, Robert (British)

Coleridge, Samuel Taylor (British)

Dickinson, Emily (American)

Dunbar, Paul Laurence (African-American)

Gordon, George, Lord Byron (British)

Gray, Thomas (British)

Hopkins, Gerard Manley (British)

Keats, John (British)

Lear, Edward (British)

Longfellow, Henry Wadsworth (American)

Melville, Herman (American)

Meredith, George (British)

Poe, Edgar Allan (American)

Rossetti, Christina (British)

Rossetti, Dante Gabriel (British)

Shelley, Percy Bysshe (British)

Watts, Isaac (British)

Whitman, Walt (American)

Whittier, John Greenleaf (American)

Wordsworth, William (British)

Modern Poets (Active 1900–1980)

Auden, W.H. (British)

Berryman, John (American)

Betjeman, John (British)

Bishop, Elizabeth (American)

Brooks, Gwendolyn (African-American)

Crane, Hart (American)

Cummings, E.E. (American)

Dunbar, Paul Laurence (African-American)

Eberhart, Richard (American)

Eliot, T. S. (American-British)

Ferlinghetti, Lawrence (American)

Frost, Robert (American)

Graves, Robert (British)

H.D. (Hilda Doolittle) (American)

Hardy, Thomas (British)

Hodgson, Ralph (British)

Housman, A.E. (British)

Hughes, Langston (African-American)

Jarrell, Randall (American)

Jeffers, Robinson (American)

Joyce, James (British)

Larkin, Philip (British)

Lowell, Amy (American)

Lowell, Robert (American)

MacLeish, Archibald (American)

Millay, Edna St. Vincent (American)

Moore, Marianne (American)

O'Hara, Frank (American)

Owen, Wilfred (British)

Pound, Ezra (American)

Ransom, John Crowe (American)

Reed, Henry (British)

Robinson, Edwin Arlington (American)

Roethke, Theodore (American)

Sandburg, Carl (American)

Sassoon, Siegfried (British)

Shapiro, Karl (American)

Stafford, William (American)

Stevens, Wallace (American)

Thomas, Dylan (British)

Toomer, Jean (African-American)

Williams, William Carlos (American)

Wright, James (American)

Yeats, William Butler (British)

Contemporary Poets (Active 1950–present)

Alvarez, Julia (Dominican-American)

Ashbery, John (American)

Atwood, Margaret (Canadian)

Bogan, Louise (American)

Boland, Eavan (British)

Brooks, Gwendolyn (African-American)

Bukowski, Charles (American)

Clampitt, Amy (American)

Clifton, Lucille (African-American)

Collins, Billy (American)

Collins, Martha (American)

Dickey, James (American)

Dove, Rita (African-American)

Gilbert, Sandra (American)

Gluck, Louise (American)

Graham, Jorie (American)

Hacker, Marilyn (American)

Hayden, Robert (African-American)

Heaney, Seamus (British)

Justice, Donald (American)

Kinnell, Galway (American)

Kizer, Carolyn (American)

Komunyakaa, Joseph (African-American)

Kumin, Maxine (American)

Lee, Li-Young (Chinese-American)

Levertov, Denise (American)

Lorde, Audre (West Indian-American)

Lynch, Thomas (American)

Merrill, James (American)

Merwin, W.S. (American)

Momaday, N. Scott (Native American)

Muldoon, Paul (American)

Nemerov, Howard (American)

Olds, Sharon (American)

Oliver, Mary (American)

Pastan, Linda (American)

Pinsky, Robert (American)

Plath, Sylvia (American)

Rich, Adrienne (American)

Sexton, Anne (American)

Silko, Leslie Marmon (Native American)

Snyder, Gary (American)

Soyinka, Wole (Nigerian)

Strand, Mark (Canadian-American)

Updike, John (American)

Wilbur, Richard (American)

Wolcott, Derek (West Indian)

Glossary

Abstract language	Diction that describes intangible things like ideas or emotions or denotes general qualities of persons or things. A passage lacking vivid details or specifics may be called abstract. It is the diction of analysis and commentary, the opposite of concrete language.
Alliteration	The repetition of initial consonant sounds.
Allusion	A brief reference to a commonly known historical or literary figure, event, or object. This indirect device works on the knowledge and memory of the reader, tapping associations and emotional resonance.
Ambiguity	In literature, the intentional creation of multiple meanings. In a given context, a word may convey not only a denotation but connotative overtones of great richness and complexity.
Analogy	A device explaining or describing something unfamiliar through a comparison with something more familiar. A simile is an expressed analogy; a metaphor is an implied one. See *Metaphor* and *Simile*.
Analysis	The methodical examination of the parts in order to determine the nature of the whole.
Anaphora	A rhetorical device of repeating the same word or words at the start of two or more lines of poetry.
Antagonist	The character in conflict with the protagonist: rival, opponent, or enemy. See *Protagonist*.
Antecedent action	Events that preceded the starting point of the piece of literature.
Anticlimax	A rhetorical device in which details of lesser importance are placed where something greater is expected, or in which the importance of items in a series is decreased rather than increased.

Antithesis	A rhetorical device contrasting words, clauses, sentences, or ideas, balancing one against the other in strong opposition. The contrast is reinforced by the similar grammatical structure.
Apostrophe	A rhetorical device in which an absent or imaginary person or an abstraction is directly addressed as though present.
Archetype	A recurrent pattern in bodies of literature, such as the loss of paradise.
Argument, literary	The thesis of a poem.
Aside	A convention in drama by which an actor directly addresses the audience, revealing his or her observations or emotions. The aside is not meant to be heard by the other characters in the drama.
Assonance	Repetition of vowel sounds. When it occurs at the end of lines, assonance rhyme does not have the same consonant sounds, so it is not full rhyme.
Atmosphere	The prevailing mood of a literary work, often established by setting or landscape, lending an emotional aura and influencing the reader's expectations and attitudes.
Authorial voice	A discernible authorial presence, distinct from that of the narrator or speaker, revealing a particular perspective. Mood and tone may be conveyed directly by the authorial voice, sometimes directly addressed to the reader. See *Mood, Tone, Point of View, Narrator, Speaker, Persona.*

Ballad	A narrative poem often using common meter and sometimes including a refrain. Popular ballads were originally set to music, whereas modern, literary ballads were written to be read.
Blank verse	Unrhymed iambic pentameter. This meter is well-adapted to dramatic verse in English, such as Shakespeare's plays, as well as to any long poem. In the nineteenth century and modern times it has been used extensively in lyric poetry. Blank verse is marked by freedom from rhyme, a shifting caesura (pause), and frequent enjambment, producing verse paragraphs more often than stanzas.

Cacophony	A combination of harsh, unpleasant sounds, used consciously for effect; the opposite of *Euphony*.
Caesura	A pause in a line of poetry created not by the meter, but by the natural speaking rhythm, sometimes coinciding with punctuation.
Caricature	The exaggeration or even distortion of personal qualities to ridiculous effect, in drawing, but also in literary characterization.
Carpe Diem poetry	From the Latin, the admonition often translated as "seize the day" is more accurately "pluck, as a ripe fruit or flower." It was first used by Horace in classical Rome, and is a common theme in sixteenth- and seventeenth-century English love poetry: yield to love while you are still young and beautiful.
Catalog	A rhetorical device which lists people, things, or attributes, used in epics (heroes, ships, armor), the Bible (genealogy), and Elizabethan sonnets (the physical attributes of the beloved).

Character Dynamic characters, also called round, are three-dimensional and fully realized. These complex people are modified by their actions and experiences. Static characters are called flat or stock, having only two, often predictable, dimensions; they can even be caricatures. They change little if at all, and things happen to them, rather than within them. The action reveals a flat character, but does not change him. A foil functions only as a contrast to a more important character. See *Characterization*.

Characterization Characters can be presented in several ways. Direct characterization employs explicit exposition, illustrated by the action of the story; we are told what the character is like. Indirect characterization requires the reader to infer a character's attributes based only on dialogue and action; we are shown what the character is like. Inner representation reveals only the impact of actions and emotions on the character's inner self, with no authorial comment. See *Character*.

Cliché An expression used so often that it loses its freshness and clarity. What often begins as a striking and colorful metaphor becomes an abstraction, no longer a living image. This quick transition is universally true, as can be seen in how rapidly slang expressions go stale and are discarded by those in the know. In fact, Ralph Waldo Emerson claims that "language is fossil poetry."

Climax The point of highest interest in a story, which elicits the greatest emotional response from the reader, also called the crisis or turning point; a reversal of action from rising to falling.

Comedy In contrast with tragedy, this literary mode involves a less exalted style in which both wit and humor provide amusement. Comic effects are produced by irony and incongruity of speech, action, or character and through verbal devices such as the pun. Comedy may be satirical, mocking human limitations, faults, and animal nature, whereas tragedy presents humans as grand and godlike. A comedy of manners (novel or play) is realistic about weakness and failure. Comedy deflates pretense, mocks excess, and gently leads readers or audience to laugh at the human condition. See *Humor*.

Common meter Alternating lines of iambic tetrameter and iambic trimeter, in four-line stanzas typically rhyming *abab* or *abcb*. Also called hymn meter and ballad meter.

Complaint A lyric poem of lament, regret, and sadness which may explain the speaker's mood, describe its cause, discuss remedies, and appeal for help. The blues is a musical counterpart to the literary form.

Conceit A metaphor of great ingenuity in which a fanciful notion, an elaborate analogy, or a striking parallel between seemingly dissimilar things is spun out at length. A conceit is paradoxical, witty, and startling.

Concrete language The diction of specificity, referring to particular persons or things. Passages that are rich in detail and imagery, creating striking particularity and sensuous detail, are the opposite of abstract language.

Conflict The struggle of two opposing forces providing interest, suspense, and tension in a plot. Conflict may be internal or external. The protagonist may be in conflict with nature, a human antagonist, society, or him/herself.

Connotation Beyond denotation (the literal, basic meaning of a word), connotation is the emotional implications and associations that a word carries. The reader must understand how the word is used in context in order to interpret the emotional coloring. See *Denotation*.

Consonance	Though the final consonants in several stressed syllables agree, the vowel sounds that precede them are different. At the end of a line of poetry, consonance is not full rhyme.
Context	The matter that surrounds the word or text in question, lending it significance, even irony. An accurate analysis of a word or portion of text depends upon a full understanding of the overall context.
Continuous form	Poetry not divided into stanzas.
Couplet	A unit of two consecutive lines of verse with the same rhyme. In an open couplet, the second line depends on the next for completion, and the rhyme is subtle. A closed couplet is a grammatically complete, closed box often characterized by the symmetry created by caesura, parallelism, and antithesis. Couplets are often pentameter lines, sometimes tetrameter; a closed couplet neatly ends an Elizabethan sonnet. See *Sonnet*.
Denotation	The literal, basic meaning of a word, independent of emotional associations. See *Connotation*.
Denouement	From the French for "unknotting," this is the final unraveling of the plot, providing the solution, explanation, or outcome. Also known as "falling action."
Dialect	Speech within the same language with marked social or regional differences.
Dialogue	The conversation of two or more people that presents an interplay of ideas and personalities. In fiction, it provides relief from description and exposition and advances the action. Dialogue should sound natural and be consistent with the character of the speaker.
Diction	The choice of individual words and patterns of words. Diction can help to establish the distinction between the narrative voice and the dialogue or help differentiate between characters. It can indicate social class, educational level, even emotional state. Patterns of diction can be predominantly formal, informal, or neutral; positive or negative in connotation; euphonious or cacophonous in sound; concrete or abstract; specific or general; mono- or polysyllabic.
Direct characterization	See *Characterization*.
Double rhyme	Rhyming stressed syllables followed by identical unstressed syllables. If both syllables are identical, it is sometimes called compound rhyme. This pattern was once called feminine rhyme, an allusion to its being weaker than full or perfect rhyme ("masculine" rhyme). Too much double rhyme in a serious poem can have an inadvertent comic effect.
Dramatic irony	The term comes from ancient Greek drama. The reader or audience understands something that the character does not. See *Irony*.
Dramatic monologue	The speaker is addressing a silent, identifiable listener in a single, sustained utterance. This form is similar to interior monologue.

Elegy	A formal poem meditating on death or another solemn theme, often a lamentation for a particular person.
Elizabethan sonnet	See *Sonnet*.
Emphasis	The weighting and development of particular elements by means of climactic order, placement, repetition, accumulation of detail, or contrast, emphasis indicates the relative importance of such elements to the text.
End-stopped line	A line of poetry that ends when the grammatical unit ends. Its opposite is enjambment.
Enjambment	From the French meaning "a striding over," this term describes a line of poetry in which the sense and grammatical construction continue on to the next line. In an enjambed line, the lack of completion creates pressure to move rapidly to the closure promised in the next line.
Envoy (also Envoi)	A conventionalized stanza at the close of a poem, which is addressed to a prince or a patron, usually having four lines rhyming *abab*, and sometimes repeating the refrain line of the poem. The envoy may provide a summary or simply serve to dispatch the poem.
Epic	A long narrative poem retelling episodes of importance to a nation's history or legend. The epic is characterized by a vast setting, a hero of great valor and superhuman courage, the interest and intervention of supernatural forces, and a sustained, elevated style.
Epigram	A pithy saying, which, in its classical model, is compressed, balanced, and polished. It is often used for satire, and is both witty and memorable.
Epiphany	A realization by a fictional character about the essential nature of being or an event; a sudden perception, an intuitive flash of recognition. James Joyce first used the term in this manner to describe an element of his fiction.
Epithet	An adjective, noun, or noun phrase used to point out a characteristic, often figuratively conveyed. In satire, it can amount to name-calling. Homer's epics use the formula of a compound adjective. Modern poets look for familiar terms, rather than fresh ones.
Euphemism	A term that replaces directness of statement to avoid giving offence. Euphemism is often a result of false delicacy or excessive modesty, but may also be interpreted as ironic.
Euphony	Euphonious sounds are pleasant. Unlike the cacophonous, such sounds are easy to articulate. Though sound cannot be separated from meaning, in general, voiced consonants (b, d, g, v, z) are softer than the abrupt sounds of the unvoiced (p, t, k, f, and s) and simple vowels more pleasant than diphthongs.
Explication	The close analysis of the meanings, relationships, and ambiguities of words, images, and other small units of a literary work.
Exposition	Material that introduces a story or drama by establishing the mood and setting, the characters and their relationship to each other, and antecedent action. The term is also used for a type of essay whose purpose is to explain (for example, analysis).

Figurative language Figures of speech are any intentional departures from the normal order, construction, or meaning of words. They call attention to themselves, either because they are rhetorical figures producing special effects or because they are tropes, loosely called metaphors, involving basic changes in meaning. See *Rhetorical devices*.

Flashback Material presented that occurred prior to the opening scene or chapter. It may take the form of the interior recollection of characters, narration by characters, or dream sequences.

Foil In literature, a character who, through contrast, underscores the distinctive characteristics of another and more important character.

Foreshadowing Preparation for later events in the plot, achieved by establishing mood or atmosphere or revealing a fundamental and decisive character trait. Physical objects or facts may also intimate or suggest later action.

Form The organization or pattern of the elementary parts of a work of literature in relation to the total effect. Verse form refers to the rhythmic units; stanza form refers to groups of lines. Open form refers to free-verse poems that do not follow a conventional pattern, but nonetheless have organic form.

Frame story A narrative that is a framework for another story or stories. The frame usually explains or sets up the interior story; often the narrative returns to the frame situation to provide closure at the end.

Free verse Poetry without a regular pattern of meter and rhyme, relying on other elements for its structure.

Grounds See *Metaphor*.

Heroic couplets Iambic pentameter lines rhymed in pairs. Used in seventeenth-century poetic drama and later by Pope and Dryden, this form is marked by the use of the caesura, symmetry and balance, and antithesis, and is often epigrammatic.

Horatian satire Satire which is indulgent, tolerant, amused, and witty, wryly and gently ridiculing human absurdities and follies, exemplified by the dramatic form known as the comedy of manners.

Humor A mode of comedy that is sympathetic and tolerant toward human nature, exposing the ridiculous, ludicrous, and comical in human affairs. Its cousin, wit, is intellectual, and tends to be satirical and less tolerant. See *Comedy* and *Wit*.

Hyperbole A figure of speech in which one says more than one means, overstating and exaggerating. It may be used for humor or to heighten another effect.

Iamb/iambic	See *Meter*.
Imagery	A literal and concrete representation of a sensory experience or an object that can be known by the senses. Imagery may be visual, of course, but may also be auditory, gustatory, olfactory, or tactile. Imagery may be presented in patterns (e.g., all pleasant or all unpleasant, or all relying on a particular sense). Imagery appeals to sensuous experience or to memory.
Incongruity	The linking of two incompatible things. Such a lack of correspondence may be humorous.
Indirect characterization	See *Characterization*.
Inference	A guess or surmise; in the absence of explicit statement, a reader makes inferences to derive conclusions from the evidence in a text.
Interior monologue	A recording of internal emotional experience on a non-verbalized level, with images representing sensations or emotions. This common form of stream of consciousness is illogical, moving by association. Interior monologue may be presented directly or indirectly with authorial comments. See *Stream of consciousness*.
Irony of situation	See *Irony*.
Italian sonnet	Also called Petrarchan after its most famous practitioner. The fourteen lines are broken into an octave and a sestet, with no more than five rhymes: *abbaabba cdecde*. A variation with four rhymes is *abbaacca cdcdcd*. The sense of the lines falls into groups that are not rhyme groups, thus avoiding couplets (*ab-ba, ac-ca*). There is a marked turn at the end of the octave from question to answer, narrative to comment, or proposition to application. See *Sonnet*.
Irony	A recognition of incongruities in event, situation, or structure in which reality differs from appearance. The operative word is "opposite." Verbal irony uses words that express the opposite of what is meant—praise implies blame and blame, praise. (Irony is not to be confused with sarcasm, which is much more harsh.) Situational irony is a predicament or bit of luck, which is the opposite of what one would expect, given the circumstances. Dramatic irony comes into play when a character's utterance reveals that he or she is unaware of something important that the reader or audience knows. See *Verbal irony* and *Dramatic irony*.

Juvenalian satire	Like its classical Roman progenitor, this mode of satire attacks vice and error with contempt and indignation. It is realistic and harsh in tone.
Juxtaposition	Placing side by side, usually to achieve a particular effect. If two incongruous words are so placed, the effect may be irony.

Line length	The terms for different line lengths use a numerical prefix (one to eight) and "meter," or measure: monometer, dimeter, trimeter, tetrameter, pentameter, hexameter, heptameter, and octameter.

Literal language	The factual sort of discourse that is without embellishment, though not necessarily flat; the opposite of figurative.
Literary present tense	By convention, the present tense is used when writing about imaginative literature, except when discussing antecedent action.
Lyric verse	A short poem expressing an emotional state or a process of thought. It is often melodic and euphonious, and creates a single, unified impression. Sonnets, odes, elegies, and countless nonce forms are lyrics, the most frequently used poetic expression.

Metaphor	An implied comparison in which two unlike things are linked by a surprising similarity. Either thing or both may be unstated. The actual subject may be called the tenor, and the thing with which it is identified may be called the vehicle. The grounds are the aspects of the vehicle that apply to the tenor. See *Analogy*.
Meter	The repeated pattern of stressed and unstressed syllables in a line of poetry. Of the four common meters in English, two are duple (two syllables in a foot) and two are triple (three syllables in a foot). Each kind of foot may be either rising (accented syllable at the end) or falling (accented syllable at the beginning). The Greek names of the meters are iambic for duple rising, trochaic for duple falling, anapestic for triple rising, and dactylic for triple falling. The meter is a predominant pattern, with judicious substitutions for variety and emphasis, variations on a theme.
Metonymy	A figure of speech in which an associated word rather than the literal word is used, as using a part to stand for the whole.
Metrical substitutions	Variations on the basic metrical pattern. The most common involve substituting a trochee for an iamb at the beginning of a line for emphasis (initial inversion); using a spondee (two accented syllables) for emphasis; using pyrrhics (two unaccented syllables) to speed the line; and ending the line with an extra, unaccented syllable to form a double rhyme.
Mock heroic; also Mock epic	A satiric mode that applies the lofty style of the epic to a trivial subject, giving it a dignity which it does not deserve and thus ridiculing it. This mode may also mock epics themselves, and the absurdity of the epic hero's pretentious qualities. Also called burlesque.
Mood	The atmosphere suggested by the setting and diction of the piece, which conjures up an emotional response on the reader's part.
Motif	A dominant idea in a work of literature, which may be expressed through characterization, verbal patterns, or imagery. Such recurrent images, words, objects, or actions help to unify the work.
Motivation	The combination of a character's moral nature and the circumstances he or she is in. The reasons, justifications, or explanations for a character's actions.

Narrator	The teller of the story may be an omniscient narrator who is outside the story and uses the third person. Such a narrator can read minds and be in

several places at once, and is free to comment on the meaning of actions. A narrator who is inside the minds of only one or a few characters has limited omniscience. An objective narrator reports only what s/he can see and hear, without comment. A first-person narrator may be the protagonist or a minor character. Such a narrator may be unreliable, in which case the reader must question or qualify statements of fact or judgment. To a naïve narrator, such as a child, the implications of the narrative are closed, but they are plain to the reader. This choice of this point of view can create great pathos or irony.

Nonce form   See *Stanza forms*.

Occasion   The immediate context of a poetic utterance; the situation which motivated the persona's words.

Octave   Any eight-line stanza, but most frequently applied to the first eight lines of an Italian sonnet, typically rhyming *abbaabba* and ending with a full stop. See *Sonnet*.

Ode   Exalted lyrical verse that is elaborate, solemn, and stately. Having formal divisions in classical poetry, it tends now to have no set form. The ode often uses apostrophe, and is typically a public poem with a lofty subject.

Onomatopoeia   A Greek term for imitative sounds; the sound of the word suggests its meaning. Though sometimes the suggestion is largely associative, the pattern of sound echoes the denotation of the word.

Oxymoron   A Greek word meaning dull/sharp, this rhetorical device is a self-contradictory combination of words.

Paradox   This rhetorical device is a seemingly contradictory or absurd statement that is actually well-founded, often with unexpected meaning, and always pointing to a truth. Epigrams are based on paradoxes.

Parallelism   A rhetorical device that presents coordinate ideas in a coordinate manner. One element of equal importance with another is similarly developed and phrased. In grammar, called parallel structure.

Paraphrase   A restatement of a passage that retains the meaning while changing it to ordinary form and syntax and usually retains the point of view of the passage. When a difficult passage of poetry is paraphrased, it is explained sentence by sentence, with figurative language changed to literal.

Parody   The imitation of a serious piece of literature meant to ridicule the work, its style, or its author. Related to the caricature or cartoon in the visual arts, parody retains the lofty subject but debases the style. Parody is a powerful device for a satirist, and is essentially the creation of a discrepancy between subject and style.

Perfect rhyme   See *Rhyme*.

Persona   Literally, a mask. The "second self" created by the author through whom the story is told; the implied author.

Personification   A figure of speech that endows ideas, abstractions, or inanimate objects with human form.

Plot	The large, controlling frame of a story or play, including the pattern of events and the relationship among events. Aristotle first described an ideal plot as unity of action marked by causality and inevitability. Plots may be simple or complex, single or multiple. A subplot is a separate strand of events related in some way to the main plot.
Poetic justice	Formerly, an ideal judgment that rewards virtue and punishes vice. In modern literature, rewards and punishments are motivated–the logical outcome of situations in conjunction with character.
Point of view	The perspective of the narrator of a story. The perspective may be recent or reminiscent. The story may be told in past or present tense. The point of view may shift in the course of the story. See *Narrator*.
Prosody	Principles of versification, especially meter, line length, rhyme scheme, and stanza form.
Protagonist	The chief character in a story or play.
Pun	A rhetorical device that is a play on words based on the similarity of the sound of two words with different meanings.

Quatrain	See *Stanza forms*.

Refrain	One or more words repeated at intervals in a poem, usually at the end of a stanza. A refrain may have slight variations, sometimes of great significance.
Repetition	A rhetorical device built into rhyme, meter, and stanza form, and also occurring in verbal and grammatical parallelisms and anaphora. Incremental repetition effects successive minor changes or changes in context which enhance and intensify the meaning. These are especially to be found in such fixed forms as the sestina and the villanelle.
Resolution	The events following the climax of a plot; falling action.
Rest	As in music, a pause counted as an element of prosody, for example a short line of poetry followed by a dramatic silence.
Rhetorical accent/Stress	In opposition to metrical accent, a stress on what would normally be an unaccented syllable, which clarifies the meaning or intention of the sentence.
Rhetorical devices	Figures of speech that are not the figurative language of metaphor. These include anaphora, antithesis, apostrophe, parallelism, balance, pun, and the rhetorical question.
Rhetorical question	A question asked for effect, not in order to get a reply. A negative answer is almost always built in. It is chosen over a direct statement for its stronger effect.
Rhyme	Sound correspondence often found at the ends of lines of poetry (end rhyme) or within the line (internal rhyme). Rhyme unifies a stanza, and separates it from the next one or, if enjambment is used, it creates a sense of forward movement. A rhyme scheme is the pattern of rhyming sounds, indicated by a letter of the alphabet for each similar sound. Perfect rhyme, also called true rhyme or full rhyme, has the same vowel, but a different preceding consonant. It is the strongest and most forceful rhyming sound.

Double rhyme has a rhyming stressed syllable followed by an identical unstressed syllable. The effect is weaker than perfect rhyme. Triple rhyme has a rhyming stressed syllable, then two identical unstressed syllables. The effect tends to be humorous. Slant rhyme, also called imperfect, partial, near, and half rhyme, depends on close but not identical sound correspondences. Eye-rhyming words have the same spelling, but different pronunciations. Identical rhyme occurs with words having different spellings but the same pronunciation.

Rhyme scheme   See *Rhyme*.

Rime royal   A stanza with seven lines of iambic pentameter rhyming *ababbcc*.

Rising action   The complication of the conflict on the way to a plot's climax. See *Plot*.

Romance   Fiction with extravagant characters, remote and exotic settings, heroic events, passionate love, and elements of mystery and the supernatural. This mode is free of the restrictions of realism and verisimilitude.

Sarcasm   The caustic or bitter expression of strong disapproval. Sarcasm is personal, jeering, intended to hurt. It is not to be confused with verbal irony.

Satire   A mode of writing, neither comic nor tragic, which blends a critical attitude with witty word play and humor, and is marked by indirection and appeal to the intellect rather than the emotions. It depends largely on irony, and uses distortion and incongruity, hyperbole and understatement, as well as caricature to undercut its subject and make it ridiculous. See *Horatian Satire* and *Juvenalian Satire*.

Scansion   The system for describing conventional rhythms by dividing lines into syllables and laying bare the essential pattern of accented and unaccented syllables in order to discover the predominant rhythm in a poem.

Sentence types   Loose sentences are long and rambling, beginning with subject and predicate followed by many modifiers and subordinate ideas. Nothing in particular is emphasized. Periodic sentences withhold the main clause or its predicate until the end, forcing the reader to pay careful attention while awaiting the ending.

Sentimentalism   Overindulgence in emotion, especially the conscious effort to induce emotion in order to enjoy it; often an excess of romanticism. The reader is asked for an emotional response in excess of what the occasion merits; emotion replaces ethical and intellectual judgment.

Sestina   A fixed poetic form of six, six-lined stanzas and a three-line envoy. It is unrhymed, but has a fixed pattern of end words in a different sequence in each stanza. The envoy uses three of the words at the ends of its three lines, and the other three somewhere within the lines.

Setting   The background of the action, it is of various importance in works of literature. Setting may include the geographical location, the daily manner of living, the epoch or season or time of day, the atmosphere, and the general environment, including religious, mental, moral, social, or emotional conditions and their symbolic meaning.

Shakespearean sonnet	See *Sonnet*.
Sibilance	Hissing sounds represented by *s, z,* and *sh*.
Simile	A similarity between two essentially unlike things that is directly expressed; the tenor is said to be *like* or *as* the vehicle. See *Analogy*.
Slant rhyme	See *Rhyme*.
Soliloquy	A speech delivered when the speaker is alone on stage, meant to inform the audience of what is in the character's mind.
Sonnet	A fixed form that derives from the Italian (Petrarchan) sonnet, 14 lines of iambic pentameter divided into an octave and sestet and rhyming *abbaabba cdecde*. Its Elizabethan (Shakespearean) form preserves this meter and length, but divides into three quatrains and a couplet, rhyming *abab cdcd efef gg*. Modern poets continue to ring changes on this enduringly popular lyric form. See *Italian sonnet*.
Speaker	See *Persona*.
Spondee	Two accented syllables, sometimes substituted for an iambic foot in a line of poetry to provide emphasis.
Stage directions	Added to the text of a play to indicate movement, attitude, manner, style, or quality of speech, character, or action.
Stanza forms	Groups of lines with breaks in between, named for their number of lines: couplet (2), tercet (3), quatrain (4), cinquain (5), sestet (6), septet (7), also called Rime Royal, ottava rima (8), Spenserian (9). Many poets invent a stanza for one poem only, called a nonce form. The form of a poem with no stanza breaks may be called "continuous form."
Stereotype	Derived from a printing term (many exact copies from one plate), a stereotype may be a character who lacks individualizing traits; the word also refers to any oversimplified mental pictures or judgments.
Stream of consciousness	A technique that presents the continuous flow of images, ideas, thoughts, and feelings of a character as they run through his or her mind. See *Interior Monologue*.
Structure	In fiction, the plot itself provides structure; in drama, the plan of acts and scenes structures the action. In poetry, the verse form and other formal arrangements, divisions and internal plans of each part, sequence of images and ideas, and even grammatical patterns comprise structure.
Substitutions	See *Metrical substitutions*.
Subtext	The underlying personality or motivation of a dramatic character implied in the script or text and interpreted by the actor in performance.
Symbol	An image with another level of meaning; something that is itself and also stands for something else. A symbol combines the literal and sensuous qualities of an image with an abstract aspect, suggesting complex, multiple meanings.
Synecdoche	The figurative use of a narrower term for a wider one or vice versa; the part signifies the whole or the whole the part.
Synesthesia	Describing one kind of sensation in terms of another, e.g., sound as color, color as sound, sound as taste, color as temperature.

Syntax The arrangement of words within a sentence. Includes sentence length and complexity; the variety and pattern of sentence form; inversion of natural word order; unusual juxtaposition; repetition; parallelism; use of active or passive voice; level of discourse (see *Usage*); order, including emphatic or subordinate position of elements, etc.

Tenor See *Metaphor*.

Tercet See *Stanza forms*.

Theme A focal idea that controls the piece of writing and provides its central insight. This abstract concept is made concrete in imaginative literature through representation in person, action, and image. Secondary themes are common in longer works.

Thesis An attitude or position on a problem taken by a writer with the intention of proving or supporting it with specific evidence.

Title In a work of literature, a title may function to set expectations, suggest interpretations, name the occasion or the literary type, or address someone directly. The title is a part of the work, and often helps to illuminate its theme.

Tone The author's attitude toward the audience or the subject, implied or related directly through authorial voice. Shifts in tone may be indicated by transitional words (*but, yet, nevertheless, however, although*) that signal a turn; by a sharp contrast in diction; or by a change in sentence length. See *Authorial voice*.

Tragedy According to Aristotle's description of classical Greek tragedy, the tragic mode is the celebration of human courage and dignity in the face of inevitable suffering, defeat, and death; a display of the grandeur of the human spirit as it responds to nature, fate, or ironic circumstance.

Trochee A falling duple foot, sometimes substituted for an iambic foot in a line of poetry for emphasis, often at the beginning of a line.

Turn A rhetorical figure that provides a change in thought signaled by words like *but, however,* and *yet*. In the Italian sonnet, a turn begins the sestet (line 9); in the Elizabethan sonnet, it may occur after the quatrains, as the couplet begins in line 13. See *Sonnet*.

Understatement A figure of speech in which the literal sense is far short of the magnitude of the subject or circumstances.

Unreliable narrator This character may misunderstand or erroneously report the action, motives, or circumstances of a story, leaving the reader with no guide for judgment. A naïve narrator is a subset. See *Narrator*.

Usage In literature, refers to the level of discourse; characteristics of those words that are not standard and require a dictionary label, such as: informal, slang, offensive, cliché, jargon, regional, technical, archaic, obsolete, and chiefly British. Use of such nonstandard words may help create characterization and tone in a work of literature.

Vehicle	See *Metaphor*.
Verbal irony	See *Irony*.
Verse paragraph	Lines of poetry grouped in unequal blocks according to content rather than a stanzaic form. Usually found in blank verse or free verse.
Versification	This term includes all the elements of poetic composition, including accent, rhythm, meter, rhyme, verse form, stanza form, assonance, onomatopoeia, and alliteration. See individual entries.
Villanelle	A fixed form borrowed from early French poetry with nineteen lines (five stanzas of three lines, a last stanza of four lines) of any length or meter and two rhymes only, *aba*, employed in a set pattern. Line 1 is repeated as lines 6, 12, and 18. Line 3 is repeated as lines 9, 15, and 19.
Wit	Like humor, wit produces laughter, but does so with less sympathy and more satiric intent. It requires great originality, imagination, the ability to see similarities in seemingly dissimilar things, and a quick, bright use of language. Wit is intellectual, depending on skillful phrasing, plays on words, surprising contrasts, paradoxes, and epigrams. See *Humor*.

Credits

Cover images: Will & Deni McIntyre/Getty Images, Chris Hackett/Getty Images

p. 3, "The Dentist" from THE THINGS THEY CARRIED by Tim O'Brien. Copyright © 1990 by Tim O'Brien. Reprinted by permission of Houghton Mifflin Company. All rights reserved; p. 5, excerpt from "Sula" by Toni Morrison, Copyright © 1973 by Toni Morrison, Originally published by Alfred A. Knopf, Inc, a division of Random House, Inc.; p. 7, excerpt from "The Curious Incident of the Dog in the Night-Time" by Mark Haddon, Copyright © 2003 by Mark Haddon, published by Vintage Books, a division of Random House, Inc.; p. 9, excerpt from "The Scarlet Letter" by Nathaniel Hawthorne; p. 11, excerpt from "Jane Eyre" by Charlotte Brontë; p. 13, excerpt from "Saint Junior" from THE TOUGHEST INDIAN IN THE WORLD by Sherman Alexie, Copyright © 2000 by Sherman Alexie. Used by permission of Grove/Atlantic, Inc.; p. 16, excerpt from "Pride and Prejudice" by Jane Austen; p. 18, excerpt from "When the Emperor was Divine" from WHEN THE EMPEROR WAS DIVINE: A NOVEL by Julie Otsuka, copyright © 2002 by Julie Otsuka, Inc. Use by permission of Alfred A. Knopf, a division of Random House, Inc.; p. 21, excerpt from "Huckleberry Finn" by Mark Twain; p. 23, excerpt from "As I Lay Dying" by William Faulkner, Copyright © 1930 by William Faulkner, Copyright renewed 1957 by William Faulkner. Notes copyright © 1985 by Literary Classics of the United States, Inc.; p. 26, excerpt from "Somebody's Luggage" by Charles Dickens; p. 28, excerpt from "Eveline" by James Joyce; p. 30, excerpt from "The Witness" from THE LEANING TOWER AND OTHER STORIES, copyright © 1935 and renewed 1965 by Katherine Anne Porter, reprinted by permission of Harcourt, Inc.; p. 32, excerpt from "The Book of Small" by Emily Carr, published 2004 by Douglas & McIntyre Ltd. Reprinted by permission of the publisher; p. 33, excerpt from "Soldier's Home" Reprinted with permission of Scribner, an imprint of Simon & Schuster Adult Publishing Group, from IN OUR TIME by Ernest Hemingway. Copyright 1925 by Charles Scribner's Sons. Copyright renewed 1953 by Ernest Hemingway; p. 35, excerpt from "Joseph Andrews" by Henry Fielding; p. 61, excerpt from "The Glass Menagerie" by Tennessee Williams, Copyright © 1945 by Tennessee Williams and Edwina D. Williams; copyright renewed 1973 by Tennessee Williams. Published by Random House, Inc.; p. 63, excerpt from "Pygmalion" by George Bernard Shaw; p. 66, excerpt from "The Importance of Being Earnest" by Oscar Wilde; p. 68, excerpt from "Master Harold . . . and the boys" from MASTER HAROLD . . . AND THE BOYS by Athol Fugard, copyright © 1982 by Athol Fugard. Used by permission of Alfred A. Knopf, a division of Random House, Inc.; p. 70, excerpt from "The School for Scandal" by Richard Brinsley Sheridan; p. 72, excerpt from "The Crucible" by Arthur Miller, Copyright Arthur Miller, 1952, 1953, 1954, Copyright renewed Arthur Miller, 1980, 1981, 1982, Published by the Penguin Group, Penguin Books USA Inc.; p. 75, excerpt from "Tartuffe" by Molière; p. 78, excerpt from "Othello" by William Shakespeare; p. 81, excerpt from "Twelfth Night" by William Shakespeare; p. 86, excerpt from "Fences" by August Wilson. Copyright © 1986 by August Wilson. Published by Dutton Signet, a division of Penguin Group (USA), Inc.; p. 88, excerpt from "Los Vendidos" from Luis Valdez – Early Works: Actos, Bernabe, Pensamiento Serpentino. Copyright © 1990 by Luis Valdez. Published by Arte Público Press, University of Houston; p. 91, excerpt from "The Rover" by Aphra Behn; p. 113, John Murray Ltd. for "Five O'Clock Shadow" by Sir John Betjeman; p. 115, "The Sound of Night" by Maxine Kumin from *Halfway*. Copyright © 1961 by Maxine Kumin. Published by Curtis Brown Ltd.; p. 117, "Mosquito" from COLLECTED POEMS 1953–1993 by John Updike, copyright © 1993 by John Updike. Used by permission of Alfred A. Knopf, a division of Random House, Inc.; p. 119, "Question" from *New and Selected Things Taking Place* by May Swenson. Copyright © 1954 by May Swenson. Published by Little, Brown and Company and the Atlantic Monthly Press; p. 121, "Dolor" copyright 1948 by Modern Poetry Association, Inc. from THE COLLECTED POEMS OF THEODORE ROETHKE by Theodore Roethke. Used by permission of Doubleday, a division of Random House, Inc.; p. 123, "Promises Like Pie-Crust" by Christina Rossetti; p. 125, "Eve" by Ralph